# TURN AGAIN HOME

# TURN AGAIN HOME

*by*

## Herbert Harker

**RANDALL BOOK CO.**

Library of Congress Cataloging in Publication Data

Harker, Herbert.
Turn again home.
I.   Title.
PZ4.H282Tu3    PR9199.3.H343    813'.5'4    76-53487

Originally published by Random House, Inc., New York
ISBN 0-394-41152-8

Republished by 1984 by Randall Book Co.
Sandy, Utah  84070
ISBN:  0-934126-57-7

To Kenneth Millar

# CARDSTON, ALBERTA
## JULY 7, 1915

**1** Fielding's Corner was a couple of miles west of town, the intersection where Lone Rock traffic turned north across the Indian Reserve. It was marked by a single cottonwood tree, planted, according to local legend, by a man named Fielding— his sole act of husbandry before he abandoned his Alberta homestead and returned to Utah. For all its nearness to town the place seemed remote, lying in a sort of no man's land between foothills and prairie.

At this crossroads Jared sat in his buggy, scanning the right-of-way for some sign of his father. Even in the fading light the road lay visible for miles, and over that distance nothing moved. Far to the south he could see the dark mass of trees that girdled the farmstead of Solomon Hays; on his right the Indian Reserve rose gently to the horizon, broad and mystical by twilight, utterly empty.

The darkening land gathered its shadows; its features slowly blurred to an umber monochrome. Jared watched the sunlight flicker briefly among the top leaves of the cottonwood, and then vanish. Alma wasn't here.

The buggy shifted as his team pressed uneasily against the bits.

Perhaps it had been a mistake to let Alma start out alone. "Act your age," Bessie had told him. "You go with Jared in the buggy."

"I'll ride my horse if I please," Alma replied. "And if I get killed, we'll all be saved the misery of my old age."

"It's too late for that," she huffed.

Jared turned the team and whipped them to a fast trot down the road toward Solomon Hays'. As he swung into the yard, Arthur Hays was at the barn, finishing his chores.

"Have you seen Father?" Jared asked.

"Sure. He stopped in the yard about suppertime to show us his new horse—his birthday present, he called it. A liver-colored gelding."

"How long did he stay?"

"Didn't even get out of the saddle. Said he was s'posed to meet you at the Corner."

3

"He never showed up," Jared said. "He must have gone back to Rachel's." He circled the yard and sped into the road to Tom and Rachel's house.

All day at the birthday party Alma had seemed preoccupied, as if at last he had come face to face with a time of life he felt unwilling to accept. He was little interested in the family dinner on the lawn, and Jared remembered him staring at the birthday candles as they wavered in the breeze, their flames turning in unison like a flock of tiny birds. Suddenly a gust of wind hit the yard, and the candles were out. The cake stood like some preposterous toy flagship, with seventy-seven pale blue banners flying from her masts.

"Now what does that mean?" somebody asked. "Does he get his wish, or doesn't he?"

When Jared got back to Rachel's the family was settled in for a quiet evening. Bessie and the girls, who were staying to visit in Cardston for a few days, sat in the parlor with Rachel and Tom.

"What are you doing back?" Bessie asked when she looked up and saw Jared standing in the door. "Your father will be waiting for you."

"He didn't show up," Jared said. "He stopped at the Hayses', but he never made it to Fielding's Corner."

There was a hushed moment before Rachel said, "Maybe you missed him on the road."

"I don't know how I could have missed him. I went to Fielding's Corner one way, and came back the other."

Bessie sighed. "Twenty-eight years I've been married to that man, and still I can't keep track of him."

"I thought he must have come back here," Jared said. "But I guess he just traveled faster than I expected, and then went on ahead when I wasn't at the Corner. Maybe I can catch him before he gets home." He returned to the buggy and started his journey again.

When he got back to Fielding's Corner it was fully dark, but the leaves of the cottonwood tree glinted dimly in the moonlight. "Father!" he shouted. "Father!" His voice seemed to swoop away from him, swallowed in the limitless hush of the night.

4

The road to Lone Rock was two dirt tracks across twenty miles of buffalo grass. As Jared urged his horses into that long, dim trail, he recalled the day's strange mixture of celebration and misgiving.

In the course of the afternoon's game of hide-and-seek the children had found an old six-gun in a box at the far corner of the attic, and brought it to the picnic table. It was rather a curiosity; somebody had carved a crude figure on one side of the polished walnut grip—a kind of short-necked, feline-looking creature. When they checked the gun they were surprised to find four bullets still in the cylinder.

"Where'd it come from?" Jared asked.

"It's not mine," Tom said.

"I guess I put it there," Alma admitted, "but I'd forgotten all about it."

The inside of the barrel was encrusted with tiny jewels of dust, but Jared cleaned and oiled the gun, and took a wide shot at a tomato can with it. He was about to try again when Tom said, "Better wait. I don't want a herd of cattle stampeding across the lawn today."

It wasn't until then that Jared became aware of a new sound asserting itself above the shouting grandchildren—the bawl and rattle of a moving herd. It was Hickory Jack Haggedorn passing through, taking his cattle to summer pasture in the mountains. As the herd drew abreast of the Roseman place the sound became pervasive, an endless drone of movement underlying the bawl and sniff and crackle. At the gate Hickory Jack dismounted and came through across the lawn, leading a chestnut gelding with honey-colored mane and tail.

He was a large, grizzled man, with worn leather chaps flapping against his legs as he walked toward them. Under his wide hat his face had a slightly swollen appearance, and one of the lines from the corner of one eye curved down and ended in a deep scar, like a nail hole, on the fleshy part of his cheek. He stopped a few feet from the table; his nod was scarcely perceptible. "Al."

"Hick," said Alma.

The grandchildren interrupted their play and gathered to look at the horse.

5

Alma twisted in his chair. "What's this?"

"It's a surprise," Rachel said. "From Tom and me. Happy birthday!"

Slowly Alma rose. "That's a mighty pretty birthday present."

"It wasn't easy to find," Tom said.

"Tom went all over the country looking at horses," Rachel added. "He finally found this one at Hickory Jack's, but he had to pay for half the ranch to get it."

"Fish!" exclaimed Hickory Jack. "I give you a bargain, and you know it."

Alma took the halter rope and patted the chestnut's cheek. "Delivered too, eh?"

Hickory Jack shrugged. "I told Tom I was bringing the cattle today anyway—might as well fetch your new horse. He's one of the prettiest horses ever come off the Arrowhead Ranch. Name's Saratoga." He came two steps closer.

"Care for a piece of cake?" Alma said.

"I'd prefer whiskey."

"Sorry. No whiskey."

Hickory Jack hooted. "You Mormons don't even know how to celebrate a birthday. No wonder you're such a sour-lookin' lot."

"Sober and sour isn't always the same thing, Hick."

"It usually is." Even on the grass, Hickory Jack's spurs rang each time he took a step. "Truth is, I was lookin' at this gun." He took the six-gun which Jared had been holding in his hand. "Colt Paterson," he said. The gun was smooth and curved, as sleek as a walking stick. There was no trigger guard, and the trigger itself was recessed in the handle, but emerged when Hickory Jack thumbed back the hammer. "My Pa had one like this once."

"It's loaded," Alma cautioned.

"I know. I hear shootin', but I don't hear no hittin'." Hickory Jack glanced at the tomato can, raised the gun, and fired. The can jumped straight up, spun against the haystack, and fell to the ground. The gelding lunged, and Jared moved to help his father.

6

"Shoots straight," Hickory Jack said. He handed the gun to Alma.

Alma had shoved it into the front of his belt.

Though he had hoped to overtake his father, Jared crossed the Indian Reserve without seeing anyone. It was late when he rumbled over the river bridge and drove up the hill into Lone Rock. At the Roseman place, there was no horse in the yard, no saddle in the stable. The cow stood at the pasture gate mooing to be milked. Inside the house Alma's room was empty; Lyman's too, the bed still neatly made. Jared lit the lamp and set it on the table in the parlor. Lyman had come home early to do the chores, but the chores weren't done. Alma had left for home, but he hadn't arrived. Jared shook his head; he couldn't think of any explanation for what was happening. Perhaps rest was what he needed, but he realized he couldn't sleep anyway. After he milked the cow he got a fresh horse from the pasture and rode back toward Cardston.

Jared tried to imagine the workings of his father's mind. When Bessie had remonstrated at the foolishness of trying to light seventy-seven candles, Alma told her, "You leave Rachel alone. If she ever gets all of them burning at once, this'll look like the Chicago fire."

As the photographer moved out and in from under his black cloth, Alma muttered, "I'd just as soon have a man come after me with a gun as one of those contraptions."

Sometime during the afternoon a boy brought a telegram from Utah, and the family began to speculate on what it could be, while Alma picked at the flap of the yellow envelope with a stiff forefinger. Finally Bessie cut it open with a table knife.

Alma unfolded the telegram close in front of his face, read it, smiled privately, folded it again, and put it in his shirt pocket.

"It's from Lula Fae," Bessie said confidently. "Birthday greetings from Lula Fae, isn't it?"

Alma didn't look at her, or reply.

When he caught a glimpse of Grace's expression as she

7

watched Norma nuzzle her new bridegroom, Alma said, "There are worse things than living alone, Grace. And some of them are husbands."

Rachel had brought an old carton full of papers she'd found when she was cleaning out one of the closets, and asked Alma whether he wanted it or not.

He opened the carton and looked inside. "Hah! I want it burned."

"We won't read any of it until after you're gone."

"What makes you think I'm going anywhere?" He leaned back and looked at the peak of the old Roseman house where the weathercock veered proudly in the wind. "Why does that old bird look at me that way? Do you suppose a man's soul is like water in a well, that can only be seen from above?" And once, to no one in particular, he muttered, "Can I help it if I have lived too long?"

The confusion of the afternoon slowly subsided—Hickory Jack rode away after his cattle, the ladies cleared the dishes, Tom took Stanley to the barn to show him his new heifer, Lyman started home to Lone Rock to do the chores, and the children, who had been noisily crisscrossing the lawn in an improvised polo match, faded away into some quieter game on the other side of the house. Jared sat at the table, alone with his father.

Alma was not so much like a father as a grandfather, really. He had been fifty-seven when Jared was born. Still, they had planned and worked together, struggling toward some dimly imagined family realm until now here they were, one of them too old and the other still too young for sovereignty, guests in the house where years before Alma had begun his dream.

"Are you tired?" Jared asked him.

"A little."

"Do you want to go home?"

"Is Bessie ready?"

"I think she and the girls have decided to stay with Rachel for a few days."

Alma sighed. "In a while. We'll go home in a while." He looked around him. For years this had been his home. He had built this house, raised his family in it. His expression seemed

8

to ask why he had had to leave it; why he must leave it now. "I can't complain, I guess. The world'll never be so good again." And then he said, "Jared. Put a saddle on Saratoga for me, will you?"

So he had ridden away to show his new horse to Solomon Hays, calling over his shoulder that he would meet Jared at Fielding's Corner. Jared watched them through the gate and down the road, Alma's shoulders seeming to glide above the prancing hooves of Saratoga. The figure darkened and blurred until horse and man were all the same color, then faded against the landscape, not as if they were moving at all, but only growing smaller.

2 When Jared arrived at Rachel's place the sun was up and breakfast was on the table.

Bessie looked up as he walked in. "He wasn't there?"

Jared shook his head. He seemed to feel nothing—neither hunger nor fatigue. While the others ate, he went out on the front porch and sat in the old wicker chair. His eyes traveled down the front walk to the gate and back again over and over, as if, should they do it often enough, they might be able to pick up Alma somewhere and bring him back with them. It was Alma, after all, who had brought Jared for the first time to that front gate, and up that walk, at the end of their long drive from Smithfield, Utah. Jared was seven years old. Almost as soon as Alma had stopped the buggy, the front door opened and children began to come out onto the porch.

"You're home," his father said. "These are your brothers and sisters."

They came down the walk and clustered beside the buggy, looking at Jared.

Alma said, "Jared. This is your family." As he spoke he motioned with his thumb, his hands still holding the lines. "Stanley and Rachel and Norma and Belle and Grace and Lyman and Jane." A smiling woman who had stopped long enough to get herself a cape joined the group around the buggy. "And your Aunt Bessie."

The woman came forward and helped him down.

"Stanley," his father said. "Take care of the horses."

"Yes, sir."

They proceeded up the walk, Jared in front with the woman, her arm around his shoulder. Once inside, she paused and looked around her, as though she too were seeing the house for the first time. "This is your new home, Jared." She walked on, leading him by the hand. "Supper is almost ready, but just today how about a special treat for our new brother?" In the kitchen she took a dish of cookies from the cupboard and held it toward Jared. He took one and began to eat it.

"Thank you."

"Thank you, Aunt Bessie," his father prompted him.

"Thank you, Aunt Bessie."

"How would you like to see your room?" she said. "And then we'll have supper. You have a big brother now to look after you. Show Jared his room, will you, Lyman? And let him take care of his clothes."

Lyman, also eating a cookie, picked up Jared's satchel. "Come on." Jared followed him along the hall and up the stairs. In one of the bedrooms Lyman tossed the satchel onto the bed. "How old are you?"

"Seven."

"I'm ten."

Jared went to the window. There was a wide stretch of lawn behind the house, bordered by several young poplar trees.

"Why did you come here?" Lyman asked.

"I don't know. My mother was sick, I guess."

"Well, she's not your mother now. My mother's your mother now."

"No she isn't."

"You'll see."

Lyman opened the satchel and dumped its contents on the bed. "Where'd you get all the clothes?" Among the things that fell from the satchel he spotted a small stuffed bear, and grabbed it. "Do you play with dolls?"

Jared rushed at him. "You leave that alone!" But Lyman held it beyond his reach, turning so that he couldn't touch it.

"You can't play with dolls in Canada, you know. That's sissy stuff."

"That's not a doll!"

"We don't like sissies in Canada."

"Give that to me," Jared cried, pounding with his fists. He was aware of faces watching from the door.

"You're a sissy," Lyman said. "Well, I ain't going to sleep with a sissy that plays with dolls." He jerked himself free from Jared, and raising the stuffed bear in both hands, impaled it on one of the coat hooks behind the door. Then he pulled it away, twisting; there was a sound of tearing fabric, and white stuffing burst from the bear's belly.

"Don't," Jared cried, reaching for the wounded bear.

Lyman ran around the room with the bear in one hand, while he scooped out the stuffing with the other. The air was full of flying cotton. At last Jared gave up the chase and fell on the bed, crying.

Lyman stopped. "See! What'd I tell you? A sissy! Crying over a stupid bear. Here, sissy. Here's your stupid bear." He threw the limp fabric on top of Jared, and Jared twisted it in his hands, holding it against his body.

"All right," Lyman said. "Clean up this mess and hang up your clothes. And then come down to supper." He stalked out of the room.

The other children stood in the doorway, watching Jared with solemn eyes. As he began to pick up the cotton that lay scattered around the room, the faces disappeared one by one. He noticed, however, that one of the girls remained. Presently she came quietly in and started to help him. Neither of them spoke until the job was finished.

He sat on the bed. "Which one are you?"

"I'm Grace." She came and sat beside him.

"How old are you?"

"Fourteen." She took the limp skin of the bear out of his hand and spread it on her lap. "What's its name?"

Jared shrugged. "It doesn't matter."

11

"I'd like to know."

He looked at her. Reluctantly he said, "Bruno."

She nodded.

"Don't tell Lyman," Jared said.

"I won't." She smoothed the rumpled calico with her hand. "Do you want me to fix it for you?"

"No."

"I will, if you want me to."

"No. He's dead now."

The next morning Jared slipped out of bed early, while Lyman was still sleeping, and went downstairs. Bessie was alone in the kitchen, preparing breakfast.

"Good morning, Jared."

"Good morning, Aunt."

"Did you have a good sleep?"

"Yes, Aunt."

She brushed by him and went to the foot of the stairs to call the others to breakfast. When she returned, Jared asked, "Where's my father?"

"He was up at four o'clock this morning. He's gone to the lease."

"What is the lease?"

She laughed shortly. "I wonder myself sometimes. It's a great stretch of land where they say he runs his sheep, but I've never seen it."

"Will he be back for breakfast?"

"The lease is a long ways away. He won't be back for two or three weeks."

Jared went to the window. The branches of the cottonwood trees and the lawn and the pebbles along the creek were covered with a light skiff of snow. The water of the creek looked almost black.

**3** Jared was stirred from his reverie by the others coming out onto the porch, Tom working at his teeth with a toothpick.

Rachel said, "Maybe Papa took the notion to visit somebody. He doesn't get to Cardston as much as he used to."

"Visiting that late in the day?" Bessie asked. "And all night too?"

"Time means nothing to him any more, haven't you noticed? He acts as if he were living in eternity already."

Tom said, "I suggest we organize a search party. There must be somebody in town who can read sign. All we have to do is follow his tracks."

"Siwash can read sign," Jared said.

"Is he part Indian?"

"When it comes to following tracks, he's got Indian eyes."

"All right. Let's get Siwash."

Siwash lived in an old shack down by the creek, at a point on the boundary between the town and the Indian Reserve. As Jared and Tom rode up, the place appeared deserted.

The outside of the house was a random collection of dry and twisted boards, nailed together as if the whole job had been done in a frenzy between the first roll of thunder and the sudden rush of summer rain. Black, staring windows veined with cracks were half blinded by scraps of cardboard held against the glass with buttons.

Jared swung down from the saddle and walked through the broken gate. The path led to a door which would neither open nor close properly, but half concealed an interior so littered and covered with dust that it was as if he had entered some long-abandoned building. Jared caught the Siwash smell, a faint, fleshly aroma, sweet and sickening. The man himself lay almost indiscernible among the tangle of quilts on the bed. He raised on an elbow. "Roseman!" he said.

"Aren't you up yet?" Jared asked. "I never knew you to sleep past five o'clock in your life."

"I ain't been feelin' too good," Siwash said. He emerged far enough from his nest of blankets to put his feet on the floor.

Through several places in his long underwear his cocoa-colored body showed. "Guess I'm gettin' old."

"You don't look any older than you ever did."

"I ain't felt any older, till the last month or so." Siwash began to pull on some clothes, selecting them at random from the tattered collection within reach of the bed.

"Alma's lost," Jared said.

"Lost?" Siwash exclaimed. "You may be lost, but Al ain't. He could find his way home if the lights went out in Hades."

"He left Tom's place last night, headed for Lone Rock. He never showed up."

"Travelin' how?"

"Riding."

"Hunn!" Siwash said. It was an exclamation which could mean many things, depending on inflection. This time it appeared to mean "Let's go."

Siwash no longer owned a horse. Jared doubled him back to Tom's place, where they saddled another animal, and the three of them started off. The old Indian mounted as easily as a boy, and sat the saddle with the same simple grace that he expressed in every movement. His small slim body appeared unaffected by the pull of gravity or age.

The yard and road around Tom's place were covered with the tracks of horses, but they identified Saratoga's hoofprints by checking a flower bed he had crossed in the front garden.

"How are they?" Jared asked as Siwash studied the prints.

The Indian shrugged. "So-so. He's a big horse. Hooves just been trimmed. If he don't hit hard ground or gravel, we got him."

Siwash led the way into the road, bending slightly from his saddle to look at the tracks. "Whose cattle?"

"Hickory Jack's," Jared replied. "He went through yesterday."

With his hand extended at belt level, Siwash motioned for them to follow him. Jared had forgotten what slight shoulders Siwash had. He gave the impression of a big man because of his enormous head. Fleshy ears protruded through his long hair, as if to hold up the hat which looked as if it would cover him to the waist if it should fall. Jared felt a rush of affection for the old man. He was a good friend to have in time of trouble.

Siwash rode confidently ahead, leaning forward in the saddle and slightly to one side, eyes on the road.

They saw where Alma had stopped at the Hays place and then continued on. Siwash began to ride more slowly, reining his horse in, and finally doubling back a little way. He pointed at the dust. "He passed the cattle," he said, leading them slowly forward again. The horse tracks that Siwash pointed to began to run in among the hoofprints of the cattle, until finally they were obliterated.

"Yes," Jared said. "He left not long after Hickory Jack." It was logical that Alma would overtake and pass the slow-moving herd. "But we'll be all right. We'll pick him up again at the fork in the road."

Where the road forked left and right the cattle tracks continued beside the creek. Siwash looked for Saratoga's tracks leading up over the hill toward Fielding's Corner. "He missed the turn," he said, getting off his horse and studying the gound. "Yup." He pointed to a portion of hoof mark among the myriad prints of cattle. "He stayed with the creek road."

They continued on. Occasionally they saw a clear sign of Saratoga's print exposed in the scrambled dust.

Some distance away, a solitary rider rounded a curve in the road and came toward them. "Father!" Jared was about to cry, but hesitated. The horse was not Saratoga. Nor, when he looked again, could the man be Alma. Too tall, too straight— Alma fifteen years ago, perhaps. As he approached, Jared could see his wide hat brim pulled low against the sun and the fringes of his buckskin jacket dancing from his sleeves. "Hickory Jack," Jared said.

The lone rider drew near and stopped his horse. Jared and his companions rode a little closer. "You see Al last night?" Siwash asked Hickory Jack.

"Yup, I was at the party."

"We mean after the party," Jared said.

"Yeh, I saw him. He passed me on his way home."

"He never went home," Jared said.

"Well, I don't know anythin' about that. He was headed home, looked to me."

"He didn't turn off at the fork. He stayed on this road."

"It was dark before I got to the pasture," Hickory Jack said. "Dark or day, though, I didn't see nothin'." He leaned from his saddle, studying the ground, and reined his horse back and forth. "He wouldn't head this way. They's nothin' up there but a couple of two-bit ranches and ten thousand acres of forest."

"He left tracks goin' in," Siwash said. "And I ain't seen no tracks comin' out."

"Then you don't have to worry," Hickory Jack told them. "He's up there somewheres." He spurred his horse on down the road. A vapor seemed to follow him, and Jared felt a diminishment, as if Hickory Jack's power fattened itself on the will and confidence of other men he passed.

The three continued on. For several miles the road stayed close to the creek. Occasionally they passed a gate, or a trail winding into the hills, but the tracks of the cattle stayed in the main road, and there was no sign that Alma turned to one side or the other. Gradually the road dwindled to a trail, and the trail to a couple of dusty ruts in the grass. Siwash rode more and more slowly. A couple of times he got off his horse and knelt, looking at the ground. "I've lost him," he said.

Jared asked, "So we don't even know if he went this far."

Siwash stood musing. "Let's go on a little further, see if we hit some softer ground." He led his horse forward, and the other two followed. At a place where the road crossed the creek, gravel bars lay on either side of the rocky ford, but beyond the stream and gravel a springtime backwater had left a small curve of soft earth. There the cattle tracks were plain as paint; a single horse had come behind them—Hickory Jack's.

"We've lost him," Siwash said. Still he led them on. A couple of miles beyond the ford they came to the gate that was the entrance to Hickory Jack's summer pasture.

"There's nothing here," Tom said. "Do you think he came up here?"

Siwash looked about him. "He did. He didn't. I can't tell."

The ground everywhere was covered with buffalo grass, tough and wiry, springing back behind each foot that touched it, so that even the passage of the cattle a few hours before scarcely showed.

The three of them crossed the fence and poked around the long-abandoned farmstead—two tiny buildings, a house and a barn, falling down, sinking into the earth; a garden plot deep in thistles. Mice. Blackbirds. The muted sound of water and moving leaves. The air was still, rising slightly, hot and dry.

They found the ashes of Hickory Jack's campfire and the flat place in the grass where he had spread his blankets the night before.

Tom and Siwash roamed into the trees, searching the ground for some break in the sod that might reveal a hoof-print. Jared turned toward the meadow that stood above the creek. It seemed a strange place, now, for a dance hall, but in the days when the old horse trader lived here he had built one and hired an orchestra, and every Friday night for several years the countryside had throbbed with the beat of lonely cowboys stomping to the music at Hickory Jack's.

4 Now the dance hall was gone. Its charred timbers lay almost submerged in the meadow, like black spars floating in a grassy sea. Jared stepped up on one of them and walked the length of it, balancing. He looked around at the wreck of Hickory Jack's dance hall. In retrospect, it seemed that it had been his father's fortunes which were lost that night.

Jared was thirteen and the Roseman family had gathered for supper. Alma took his place at the head of the table, "Where is everybody?"

Bessie replied, "Stanley and Lyman went somewhere. Rachel is getting dressed."

"Is she going out tonight?"

"Tonight, and last night," said Belle, sixteen and no doubt impatient to begin her own social career. "And tomorrow night, and any other night you care to mention. I do not understand—"

She was interrupted by Rachel, sweeping into the room in her party dress, the skirt held high enough to reveal glimpses of her silk-clad ankles. With a flourish, she took her place at the table. "What is it you don't understand, Belle?"

Belle was still busy at the stove, helping her mother serve the dinner. "I don't understand how you can come home from school so exhausted you couldn't possibly help with supper. And the next thing we know you're dressed like a duchess, ready to go again."

Rachel unfolded her napkin. "Well. It's a poor house that can't afford one lady."

Bessie set a large bowl of potatoes on the table. "There. I think we're ready."

The entire family knelt, some beside their chairs, others slightly away from the table, wherever there was room. Alma cleared his throat, and a silence came over the kitchen.

There was a knock at the door. "There he is now!" cried Rachel, jumping to her feet.

"Kneel down, girl," Alma protested. "He can wait a minute."

"But it's not a minute. It's ten minutes, or fifteen. Jane, be a dear and let him in, will you?" Rachel hurried into the hall and up the stairs.

One by one the family rose from their knees; some returned to their chairs, some remained standing. Jane walked primly to the front door.

"Now, what did she go upstairs again for?" Jared wanted to know.

"You don't expect her to greet him in the kitchen, do you?" Belle replied.

"If I went courting, that's just where I'd want to be greeted," Jared said.

"Who is it tonight?" Alma asked.

The kitchen became quiet as they listened to the voices at the front door.

"Good evening," Jane said with exaggerated courtesy. "Won't you come in?"

"Thank you."

The front door closed.

"I suppose you're here for my sister Rachel?"

"Why, yes," the voice said. "Yes, I am. Though maybe I'll change my mind if you happen to be free. You're almost as pretty as she is."

"I mustn't keep company till I'm seventeen," Jane said.

"Perhaps I'll wait."

"Six years!" Jane squealed.

There followed the sound of footsteps on the stairs, slow, even footsteps, accompanied by the rhythmic swish, swish of rustling fabric. "Why, Mr. Baxter!" Rachel cried. "What a pleasure it is to see you."

"And you," Mr. Baxter replied.

"I declare. Do we have an appointment tonight, Mr. Baxter?"

Mr. Baxter paused. "Don't we? I mean, didn't you think we did?"

Rachel laughed. "I'm just teasing you, silly."

Jane returned to the kitchen, and Rachel appeared in the doorway behind her, waving briefly. "Goodnight, everybody."

Alma turned his chair. "Rachel. Come and have prayer with us before you go."

The girl's face colored. "But, Papa, we're late already."

"All the more reason. If you pray first, maybe you'll hurry sensibly."

A strong-looking young man with a mustache came up behind Rachel. "This is Mr. Baxter, Papa," she said.

Mr. Baxter nodded. "Tom Baxter. How do you do, sir?"

Alma looked at him. "I haven't seen you before, Mr. Baxter. What is your line of business?"

"I am an engineer," the young man said.

Alma got up from his chair, and then knelt beside it. "We were just about to have family prayer when you arrived, Mr. Baxter. Would you care to join us?"

The rest of the family knelt. Rachel looked wretchedly up

at Mr. Baxter, then slowly sank, being careful to rest her petticoats and silk stockings on a small rug by the door. Mr. Baxter was the only one still standing. At last Rachel reached and tugged at his sleeve; he reluctantly went down on one knee, like a person about to be knighted, but with eyes wide and head unbowed.

"Don't you believe in God, Mr. Baxter?" Alma said.

"My beliefs are my own affair, sir."

"That is true, but when you call on my daughter, they become my affair too. Don't you agree?"

"No, sir. Most respectfully I do not. Your daughter is a woman of legal age, and free to choose companions on her own."

"What difference does age make? If my daughter was fifty years old, do you suppose I would no longer be interested in her welfare? I have no desire to argue with you, Mr. Baxter, and it is true that Rachel may do as she pleases. But as long as I draw breath, I will use what influence I have with her." Alma paused, and then said to his wife, "I'm sorry. I've become upset. Bess, will you please lead us in prayer tonight?"

At the conclusion of the prayer Mr. Baxter rose from his knee and bowed stiffly to Bessie. Rachel disappeared immediately, and by the time the family started to eat she was back, adjusting her shawl on her shoulders and lifting her long hair over it. "Shall we go, Mr. Baxter?"

Alma looked at her. "Be home early."

"Oh, Papa. I'm always home early." And she was gone, she and her young man. The family heard the front door close behind them.

"Who is this Baxter fellow?" Alma asked.

"It's like he said. He's an engineer," said Bessie, "a university man. He looks so young, but he's in charge of that survey crew working south of town."

"He acts even younger," Alma said. "How did Rachel meet him?"

"At the dance," Belle said.

"What dance?" her father asked. "A church dance?"

Belle hesitated. "At Hickory Jack's. I think."

"Hickory Jack's? What was Rachel doing at Hickory Jack's?"

"Dancing, I guess," Belle said in a very small voice.

"I think Tony Wilson took her there one night," Jane said.

"Ye gods! Hasn't Tony any judgment?"

"It was just for a lark."

"A lark! And look what's happened. Now she's out with another man. Well, it serves Tony right, I guess. But what about Rachel? Tony may not be much, but he's solid gold beside this Baxter."

"This is the first time she's been out with him."

"And the last, if I have anything to say about it." Alma began to eat his pie.

"Don't upset yourself, dear," his wife said. "Rachel can take care of herself."

"Hah! Don't you think the devil is having it easy enough, without us entertaining his angels?"

"Oh, Alma. Mr. Baxter isn't a wicked man."

"No. He's a university man, you said. I don't know what that means to you, but to me it means he's a freethinker. An atheist. Probably believes that men came from monkeys."

"I don't know how he feels about that."

"Where are they going?" Alma asked.

"I don't know," Bessie said. "Maybe a party at the Hayses'."

"Rachel wouldn't take a man like that to a party at the Hayses'." He fell silent, staring straight ahead. As the others left the table, Jared also remained in his chair. Bessie was washing the dishes.

Alma sat very still, his arms resting on the table in front of him. There were lines in his face that Jared had never noticed before; they seemed to divide his features into pieces of a puzzle which, having been put together became a representation of sadness, almost of defeat. For the first time Jared realized that his father was growing older.

Alma rose and put on his hat and coat.

"Where are you going?" Bessie asked.

He looked at her but did not reply. Abruptly he went out into the darkness and closed the kitchen door behind him.

Bessie began to dry her hands. "Jared," she said, "do you know the way to Hickory Jack's?"

Together they went to the window. In a few moments there was the soft thud of hooves in the lane and they got a glimpse of Alma in his rig as his black mare passed swiftly through the gate and into the street.

"Yes, I know the way," Jared replied.

"Will you do something for me? Stanley and Lyman are both gone."

"I can do it."

"I think Rachel and Mr. Baxter are going to Hickory Jack's. I want you to ride out there and tell them he's coming."

Jared slipped on his coat and cap.

Bessie said, "If you cut across the fields, you should be able to get there before your father does."

"Don't worry. It'll be all right."

There was no moon. Once he left the town he couldn't see a light anywhere. He found himself galloping across the dark prairie with nothing to guide him except the stars and his own rather vague sense of direction.

The dance hall, about seven miles from Cardston, was a crude hexagonal building set among the cottonwoods on Lee's Creek. Jared had visited it a few times before when he and his friends had stopped there on their Saturday-afternoon horseback forays. The door was padlocked, but they had climbed through one of the windows and wandered among the dust and squalor and cigarette butts and empty bottles. The air inside was heavy, a composite of odors and imaginings—stale food and drink, stale perfume, music, laughter, memories and dreams, like echoes of past galas still faintly glancing from the old log walls. One time they found a pair of silk stockings under a bench. The stockings were completely ruined, but the circumstances by which they came to be there kept the boys in an agony of sensuous speculation for days afterward. Even empty, and in broad daylight, the place seemed to ooze the smoke of sin.

Jared's direction was true enough so that when he reached the hill above the creek he could hear the music, and following the sound upstream he soon came to a trail which led down the hill to Hickory Jack's. He stopped his horse and listened for the sound of his father's outfit on the road. All he could hear was the music. As he started down he could see the windows far below him, glowing like fireholes in the darkness.

On the flat at the bottom of the hill he tied his horse to a clump of birch and went forward on foot, passing among other saddle horses and teams hitched to buggies. As he came closer to the building he could hear laughter and stomping and sudden shouts above the pounding music. The windows were too high for him to see inside, but their light illuminated a few men standing in a circle by the wall, passing a bottle among them. He was so close now the music seemed to originate within him, as if his throbbing blood created it. He shuddered, disturbed that he should feel the character of such a place so intimately. At the open door he stopped, and almost stepped backward in the rush of color and sound which hit him. Inside the room people were dancing, twisting, swinging, laughing, embracing, while on a low stand at the other end of the room the musicians played—pianist, fiddler and drummer, as wild as the priests of Bacchus.

Jared could not imagine where all the people came from. To ride across this country, you would suppose that it was near desolate, and yet here on a Friday night you could find a crowd like this. He stood outside the door, hoping he could see Rachel, if she was there, and signal to her, but the smoke was thick and the light from the lanterns was dim.

He stepped inside. There were a few faces he recognized. He began to make his way around the outside edge of the room, stepping gingerly between the dancers and the people sitting on the benches. He was so intent on the search for his sister that he inadvertently tripped a lady who danced, or rather staggered, by. The woman turned crossly toward him, but when she saw him she suddenly smiled. "Why, aren't you a darling?" she cried, and flinging both arms around him, pulled him against her. "Let's you and me dance, sweetheart," she said.

Her partner shouted, "Edna!" and swore, then threw up his

arms and walked unsteadily away. The woman whirled Jared toward the center of the floor, her arms crushing him into the soft billows of her body. She must have been almost forty, and smelled of whiskey and cheap perfume—still Jared felt a strange excitement rising in him. With all his strength he pushed his hands against her, twisted from her grasp, and ran to the edge of the floor.

A large body blocked his way. He raised his eyes. Atop the tapering slope of the body he saw an equally large face, solemn as stone in the lantern light—broad nose hooked over his upper lip, nail-hole high in the fleshy part of his face. It was Hickory Jack.

"What you doin' here, kid?"

Jared turned to run, but the big man's hand seized him and spun him around. "What's your name?" Jared squirmed, trying to get free. "I ever see you here again, I'll take you straight home to your pa. You understand?"

"Yes, sir."

"Then git!" The man shoved so hard that Jared went stumbling, ricocheted among the dancers, almost fell, caught himself, and looked around for the way out. But he was too late. His father was standing in the door.

Jared shrank back and quickly moved to the opposite side of the room. Through the shifting screen of dancers he had glimpses of his father, now a couple of steps into the hall, his eyes scanning the faces that dipped and turned in front of him. Jared was trapped; there was only one door to Hickory Jack's.

Alma started across the floor, marching straight as a soldier among the swaying dancers. Following with his eye the line of his father's march, Jared saw Mr. Baxter performing an almost motionless dance, with Rachel's body clasped in his arms. When Mr. Baxter looked up, he found himself face to face with her father.

Alma took Rachel's arm and wrenched her away, so that she staggered uncertainly. "Papa! You hurt me!"

"You're drunk!" Alma cried.

"No I'm not, Papa. Just a little tipsy."

"You're coming with me."

"But the dance isn't over."

"It's over for you. It should never have begun." Still holding her arm, he turned toward the door. Rachel pulled away and shrank back into Mr. Baxter's embrace.

The dancers stopped, one by one, as they saw what was happening. Finally the music stopped, too.

Alma lunged at Mr. Baxter, who spun away, and then faced him with fists raised, dancing. In quick succession he landed several blows to Alma's body and a couple to his face. Still Alma advanced, arms raised against the blows. For all his nimble attack, Mr. Baxter was forced back.

The crowd had gathered in a circle. Except for Alma's breathing and his opponent's shuffling feet and the occasional thud of his fists, the room was quiet. Then Mr. Baxter seemed to get his range. One of his blows stopped Alma, and the next sent him staggering back. The crowd cheered.

Mr. Baxter sensed his advantage, and quickly moved in. Twice Alma tried to grasp him in his arms, but the younger, smaller man evaded him and came back swiftly with fists flashing. Alma's hat had fallen under their feet, and his face was smeared with blood. The cheers of the crowd swelled in rhythm to Mr. Baxter's blows.

Rachel tried to grasp his arm. "No!" she cried. "Don't! Please don't!" Mr. Baxter flung her away.

At last he landed one blow that sent Alma back against the wall; his legs went from under him and he sat heavily on the bench.

Hickory Jack seized Mr. Baxter's arm and held him from his attack. "That's enough," he said.

"Let me finish him."

With a twist of his massive wrist Hickory Jack thrust Mr. Baxter to one side, then stood there, looking down at Alma. "Get out, Al," he said. "Don't come back here again."

Rachel had sunk to her knees, her head bent low beside her father. Alma smoothed her hair with his rough hand.

"You damn Mormons cause me more trouble than bootleggers and Indians combined," Hickory Jack said. "Get out of here, the pack of you."

Alma stood up, glaring at Hickory Jack. "You're the one," he said. "It's your doing. These people can't wait to get to hell,

25

so they go there tonight at Hickory Jack's." He looked down at his weeping daughter. "And take my children with them."

"I'm sorry, Papa," she cried. "I'm sorry."

"I'll have to throw you out, Al."

"No you won't."

Suddenly, before anyone could move, or scarcely realize what was happening, Alma seized a lantern from a nail and dashed it against the floor. The fire rushed across the boards, following the trail of the splattered kerosene. In quick succession he swung another lantern against the wall, and broke a third one on the floor. The flames fanned out. Hickory Jack moved to stop Alma, turned and shouted for "Water!" and then raised his arms in anguished despair. "Get out!" he shouted. "Everybody out!" Women screamed and there was a confused rush toward the door. The musicians grabbed at their music, but some of it was already aflame. With their instruments in their arms, they joined the riotous melee making for the door.

Somehow Hickory Jack had forced his way through the crowd, and now, as the last few people stumbled out, he came back with a pail of water and threw it on the fire. Just before Jared ran, he turned and saw the huge figure standing black against the flames, engulfed in hissing clouds of steam.

**5** It had been six years since Alma burned the dance hall; these blackened timbers made a pretty cold trail, but they were the only sign Jared could find that Alma had even been to this spot. Presently Siwash and Tom came back from their foray. Siwash shook his head.

Riding back to town, they were a silent group. They watched the sides of the road for the place where Alma had turned off, but found nothing. Saratoga's tracks disappeared among those of the cattle, and never showed again.

"Must 'a flew away," Siwash muttered.

Bessie and the girls met them at the gate.

"The tracks gave out on us," Jared told them.

Bessie looked at Rachel. "I told you," she whispered.

"Oh, Mother," Rachel chided. "Don't be silly. He's all right."

"What did you tell her?" Jared asked.

For a moment the women did not reply, but stood looking steadily at each other. Then Rachel said, "Mother has a premonition. She's afraid something has happened."

"Like what?" Jared asked.

Bessie shook her head. "I just have this terrible feeling."

Jared waited for her to go on. "If there's something you know, you have to tell us about it."

"I don't know anything," she protested. "It's all"—she groped for a word—"surmise. For years things have been going from bad to worse."

"Like what, exactly?"

"It started with the outlandish claim from that horrid man."

"Hickory Jack?"

She nodded. "He could have built a dozen dance halls for the damages Alma paid him."

Tom put in, "He bought a ranch instead."

"Hickory Jack was taking him to court," Aunt Bessie went on, "but your father said he wouldn't go to court with any man. He just paid what Hickory Jack asked. It almost broke him. And the next spring he lost his herd. He was an old man by then—over seventy. We could have lived all right. But he was determined to start again."

"So we moved to Lone Rock," Jared said.

"We sold the house in Cardston to Tom and Rachel, and moved to Lone Rock."

Jared said, "Wasn't it what he wanted to do?"

"It finished him. He'd always been healthy—like a young man. At seventy he could work all day. But it had been twenty years since we moved from Utah, and he'd forgotten how hard it is to start again—the hours before daylight and after dark it takes to build a house, and make fence, and break ground. He'd never done any farming, anyway. He was a sheepman."

"Aunt Bessie, why did he leave Utah in the first place?"

"He said he needed more land, and when he heard about a new Mormon settlement in Canada, I guess he pictured empty townships, and that's all it took."

"Also," Jared said, "he had two wives."

"Are you trying to blame me?"

"No, Aunt. I don't think so. There isn't any blame involved."

"That's why many of our men came to Canada, of course— to get away from the sheriffs. I don't know about Alma. I think he would have come, anyway, even if he hadn't married me."

"But you wanted to come."

"We'd only been married a year or so. We had a new little baby. It would have been easier just to stay where we were."

"Still, you were young. You didn't mind moving."

"It was exciting."

"And after that you had him all to yourself, away from my mother."

For a minute or two she didn't say anything. "Jared, you mustn't accuse me. I was your father's wife. I tried to be as good a wife as I could—to help him in whatever he chose to do. It wasn't always easy." She looked away, toward the mountains. "When I was young I always said your father would never die in bed. I thought then it was a joke."

"Then you think he's dead?" Jared asked.

"It's what he would have wanted," she said.

"To die?"

"Some final mystery. I almost feel like he's laughing at us."

"I don't understand you."

"Nobody ever knew your father. His life was a secret."

"And now his death's a secret, too?"

"Something like that."

"I think you're wrong, Aunt. I knew my father."

"Not really."

"And he isn't dead. I'll find out what happened to him."

"Well, put your horses away," Bessie said. "And come and have some lunch."

"I'm not hungry," Jared said.

Grace spoke. "You can't do anything until you get some rest, Jared."

"No. I have to find him. A man can't vanish without a trace."

"What are you going to do?" Bessie asked.

Jared shrugged, and turned his horse.

"You're not being sensible," Tom said. "The thing to do is organize a search, get all the men we can, comb the countryside."

"Yes, if you're looking for a dead man," Jared agreed. "The man I'm looking for is alive."

As he rode away from them the world seemed distant, out of focus, unreal. Even his own body was like a thing apart, its senses telegraphing messages to him across faintly buzzing wires. Perhaps Grace was right. Maybe he ought to rest.

He had no idea where to begin. He turned up over the hill behind the barn. A mile or so across the field he came to a stackyard, empty now—the remains of last year's hay lying like ancient musty pillows on the ground. He tied his horse to the stackyard fence, walked inside, and sat on a hump of the hay. Its dust rose around him, hot and stifling, bringing a tang like ginger to his nostrils.

He thought that here he would be able to think, but his mind seemed encircled by the fence—he could not get beyond it. His thoughts turned back upon themselves.

# 6

The first time he visited this spot had been that November when he was seven, just a couple of months after his father brought him from Utah to Canada, to what had been the family home in Cardston. The cold then had been as dry and palpable as was the heat today.

Alma still had not returned from the lease, and Bessie sent Stanley with the bobsleigh to haul feed for the milk cows. Lyman tied his sled on behind the big sleigh, and this aroused interest in the expedition among some of the other children.

As they left the house, Lyman complained, "Does *he* have to come?"

Bessie looked at Jared. "He is awfully small."

"He's a sissy," Lyman said. "He'll fuss the whole time."

"He'll be all right," Grace said.

"You look after him, Grace," Bessie told her.

"I will."

Stanley was already driving the team out of the farmyard, and they had to run to catch him. Grace dragged Jared by one arm and helped him scramble up before she jumped on the moving rack herself.

Jared and Norma and Grace sat between uprights on the hayrack, their legs swinging over the back. Behind them, Lyman was pulled smoothly over the snow on his coaster sled, the iron runners squeaking fitfully.

"Can I ride?" Norma called.

"Maybe later," Lyman replied.

"I want to now." Norma was a couple of years older than Lyman, and at that time a good deal taller. She suddenly jumped from the moving bobsleigh, and as Lyman came skimming along, shoved him and tipped over his sled. He tried to cling on, but she pushed him with her foot until he let go. Then, while he lay quietly sprawled in the snow, she up-righted the sled and climbed on it.

Jared thought perhaps Lyman was hurt, and was about to cry out, when suddenly he jumped up, laughing, and ran after them. For some distance Norma and Lyman tussled over the sled, alternately riding it and being left behind. They laughed, and Jared and Grace laughed at them. But once when Lyman was running to catch up, Stanley whipped the horses and left him behind, then teased him, allowing him to almost overtake them, then drawing away again. All the while Norma sat on the sled, still laughing.

Finally Lyman made a desperate sprint which climaxed in a sweep with his mittened hand that came within inches of Norma's shoulder. At the last minute Stanley cracked his lines over the edge of the hayrack and the team sprang forward. The sleigh pulled away, and Lyman came to a staggering halt, his face contorted, his body bent as he carefully drew in the air which inhaled too freely could freeze his lungs. As the others sped away he remained standing there looking after them, while his bent, dark figure grew smaller and smaller.

Stanley stopped the bobsleigh. "Come on!" he called.

Lyman didn't move.

"Come on. I won't do it again."

Norma got off the sled and stood up. "You can ride for a while." She backed up to the rack, jumped, and sat beside Jared.

Slowly Lyman walked toward them.

"Hurry up!" Stanley shouted. "It's cold. Let's get going."

Still Lyman didn't hurry. Very deliberately he walked up to the sled and seated himself on it.

Stanley snapped his lines. The outfit moved forward. Lyman sat on his sled, looking at no one, his face dark and sullen.

Presently though, they left the hard-packed road and turned into the open field. Here the snow lay in deep billows just as it had fallen or been rearranged by the wind. The bobsleigh glided smoothly, with a kind of whispering sound, but the coaster sled tossed like a small boat in the ocean. The point of it went sharply up, then down; then the whole sled tipped precariously. Under the weight of the boy, it turned up snow like a plough and spread it back across the legs of its rider. "Yipee!" cried Lyman, twisting his body to try to keep the sled upright, but suddenly it lurched and pitched onto its side. Lyman rolled off, and the outfit went briskly on without him.

"My turn!" Norma cried. She jumped down and scrambled onto the sled.

Lyman ran along behind her. "Bet you can't ride it."

He was right. Within a couple of minutes she was thrust face-first into a drift.

"Now me!" Grace exclaimed. She, too, caught and rode the pitching sled, but was quickly thrown.

When they got to the haystack Stanley began to load the rack, while the others took the coaster sled to the hill above the creek. Lyman's first trip down was not a great success. The sled continually ploughed nose-first into the drifts, then stopped. By the time he reached the bottom his track through

31

the snow was marked by numerous blotches where he had floundered out and started his run again. Still he cheerily made his way back up the hill, dragging the sled behind him, and suggested that Norma try it. Traveling in his old track, she fared better, but frequently had to start the sled again and never built up any speed.

Jared stood watching them, getting colder so slowly that for a while he didn't realize what was happening.

As soon as Norma reached the top of the hill Grace took a turn. She rode clear to the bottom without stopping. As she came back toward them, Lyman jumped on the sled and went swooshing down the slope, his scarf flying behind him. By the time he got back Stanley had finished loading the hay and joined them on the hill. They were coasting faster and faster now, and extending the track further at the end of the run. Each waited anxiously for his turn on the sled.

Jared stood in his tracks in the snow, his head held stiffly back and his arms slightly out from his sides, watching them.

As Stanley scrambled back up the hill one time he said, "It's getting dark. We've got to go."

"Just one more," Lyman said.

"No more," Stanley told him. "If you want a ride home, you'll have to come now."

Jared looked around him. He hadn't noticed that the day was over and darkness was quickly falling.

"Jared hasn't had a ride," Lyman said.

"Would you like a turn, Jared?"

"It's getting awfully late. Maybe another time."

"Ah. It'll only take a minute."

Jared didn't say anything. He was so cold he felt as if an upset would shatter him in a thousand pieces. But he saw that Lyman was determined. In a moment he was seated on the sled, with his numb fingers feebly gripping the hard edges beside him. He assumed that this would be fun—the other children must have enjoyed it, to stay at it for hours on so cold a day.

He had scarcely started to move when a feeling of panic seized him. His impulse was to roll from the sled and end the ride then and there, but already he was going too fast for that.

The hill fell away beneath him; his sled plunged faster and faster. The freezing air burned against his cheeks and forehead.

Each time the sled edged off the track and brushed an untrammeled drift, he was blinded in hurricanes of snow, but nothing could slow his plummeting machine. He felt like a bullet—as fast as a bullet, as hard as a bullet, but as breakable as glass. Suddenly his sled dragged heavily against one edge of the track, plunged against the other side, and began to wobble. He clung, sitting as low as he could, to keep from tipping over. The sled was wild now, plunging erratically into the drift on one side, surfacing, finding the track again, leaping ahead, striking another billow, sliding, tipping . . . He was blind, his face completely buried in snow. Still they hurtled downward. The sled lifted beneath him and he felt as if they left the earth completely. When they landed, the sled pitched head downward into soft snow and stopped, and Jared shot end over end across the drifts.

He lay as he had landed, crumpled on his stomach. The loose snow felt like iron rings around his wrists and ankles, binding him to the earth. To move would only increase the pain. He heard a call, and raised his head. It was dark. He was amazed to think the sun had gone down as fast as his sled. Then he saw that a little daylight still clung above the ground, concentrated at the top of the empty hill. He scrambled to his feet and looked again. There was nobody up there. The hill was a great white dome, grey, really, in the fading light, with the track of the sled like a heavy brush stroke from top to bottom.

Again he heard a call, closer this time. "Jared! Hurry!" It was Grace. He wiped the snow off his face with his spiny mittens. Then he could see her walking down the hill, almost running, sending up crystal sprays of snow with every step. "Don't stand there. Hurry!"

The tone of her voice roused him. He began to flounder through the snow toward her.

"Where's the sled?" she asked. He looked around. It must have been completely buried in the snow. As she came up to him she was breathing heavily. "Where is it? Where's the sled?"

"I fell off it," he said. "I don't know where it is."

She hurried on to where he had fallen, and tramped in a circle around the place. She looked up helplessly. "I can't find it."

"I don't know where it is."

"It must be here some place." She continued to walk around, kicking the snow with every step. Even while they hesitated, the darkness seemed to deepen. "We can't wait," she said at last. "We've got to go." She took Jared by the hand and started up the hill, half dragging him behind her. She had to stop and rest two or three times before they got to the top.

"Have they gone?" Jared asked.

"I don't know." They hurried on. When they reached the stack nobody was around. The team was gone. The trail of the bobsleigh led away through the snow and vanished in the darkness. "Wait!" Grace cried. "Wait!" The night seemed absolutely silent. They could not hear voices or the jingle of the harness. She began to run, dragging him after her.

Jared's lungs were burning. Yet for all the heat inside him, his skin was cold as iron. "I'm cold," he said. "My hands are freezing." The one crushed in her hand felt as if a dart was piercing the ends of the fingers.

Grace stopped. "Let me see." She pulled off her mittens, then his, and rubbed his hand between hers. "Does that feel better?"

"I think so."

She looked at it as closely as she could in the poor light. "I don't think it's frozen."

"It feels frozen. Rub the other one, will you?"

She rubbed the other one for a while. He put his mitts back on. His hands felt better. She took her mitts and pulled them onto his hands, over his own.

"What will you do?" he asked.

"I'll keep my hands in my pockets. But I can't pull you any more. You'll have to run."

"I'll run," he said.

They never did catch the bobsleigh. When they finally got home the rest of the family were eating supper.

"Where have you been?" Bessie said as they stumbled through the door.

"It's below zero," Norma told them. "Didn't you get cold?"

"Where's my sled?" Lyman asked.

Grace could hardly talk. "We couldn't find it."

"You left my coaster sled?"

"It was too dark."

Bessie said, "They waited and waited and called, and finally they had to leave you."

The warmth of the house was almost painful to Jared.

"Didn't you meet Stanley?" Bessie asked.

"Isn't he home?"

"I sent him right back to get you. You must have passed him."

"We cut through the field," Grace explained. "I guess we missed him."

"Well, take off your things," Bessie told them. "And come and have your supper."

Puffing and sniffing, Jared and Grace took off their caps and scarves and coats. The clothes were as stiff as armor and crusted with the rime of winter.

Grace held out her hand. "My fingers are frozen." The ends of two of her fingers were as white as milk.

"What happened to your mitts?" Bessie asked.

"I let Jared use them. His hands were freezing."

Bessie grabbed a saucepan from the cupboard, went to the back door and scooped it full of snow, then came and sat on a chair beside Grace. "Put your hand in here," she said. She began to gently massage the frozen fingers, rubbing them with snow to keep them from thawing too fast. "This is going to hurt," she said.

Bessie and Grace sat on chairs facing each other. Jared was put at the table to wait for his supper to heat. The other children stood or sat around, watching. For a while it seemed that nothing happened; Bessie just continued to gently rub the frozen fingers with snow. But then Jared noticed a tear well quietly out of Grace's eye and slip down over her cheek. "Oh, Auntie."

35

"It's starting to hurt," Bessie said.

Grace gave a quick, shuddering nod, and took her lower lip between her teeth.

"It'll be over soon."

A low keening sound started from somewhere; it seemed to come out of the walls or up from the floor. But then it grew slightly, and Jared realized with horror that it was coming from Grace. It continued to swell louder and took on form and substance, until it became a suppressed wail, broke, and then started again at its beginnings.

Grace lowered her face and covered it with her free hand; her whole body seemed to shake as the wailing began again. This time it was broken by a violent sob that blew away restraint, and Grace collapsed into a sobbing, shuddering heap against Bessie's shoulder.

"There, there, it'll soon be over," Bessie said, still rubbing the fingers in the snow.

Jared was not able to sleep when he went to bed that night. Hours passed while he lay staring at the dim outlines in the room. Beside him Lyman breathed peacefully. At last Jared crept out on the cold floor and hurried down the hall to the girls' bedroom. The house was so cold he could see his breath, like a formless spirit in the dark hallway. The bedroom, with its large windows, was brighter but no warmer. He knew which bed was Grace's and on which side she slept. He knelt there on the freezing boards and whispered, "Grace."

At once she raised her head from the pillow.

"Are you asleep?"

"No," she answered. "Who is it?"

"It's me. Jared."

"Shh." She slipped from under the covers, then led him out of the room, along the hall, down the stairs.

The living room was warmer, and in the fireplace the embers of last night's fire still faintly glowed. They knelt beside the fireplace, facing each other. Grace took his hands in hers. One had some bandages around the fingers. He was afraid to touch it, but as fast as he pulled away, she reached for him.

"Don't they hurt?" he asked.

36

"A little. But they're all right now."

"I'm sorry that I took your mittens."

"I gave them to you. It was my own fault. I wasn't careful enough to keep my hand in my pocket, that's all."

Jared started to cry, and he couldn't understand it. "I feel so bad. I couldn't sleep."

"Don't cry, Jared." She moved closer and put her arms around him. With his own arms he drew her closer.

"Do you think you can sleep now?" she asked him at last.

"I think so."

"We'd better go to bed. If we get too cold we might be sick."

"All right." Still he made no move to draw away from her. "Grace."

"Yes?"

"Why do you call Aunt Bessie 'Auntie'?"

"She is my aunt."

"All the others call her Mama."

"Well, she's their mama."

"What do you mean?"

"I thought you knew." Suddenly she crushed him in her soft arms. "Didn't you know? I'm your sister, Jared. Lula Fae is my mama, too."

**7** A tremor shook Jared's body, and he woke. The sky was dark; it had been a chill that disturbed him. For a moment he forgot what he was about. Then in the darkness beyond the stackyard fence his horse pawed impatiently, and like a stone falling in Jared's stomach, the recollection of his father's disappearance hit him.

He realized that he was lying full length in the hay. The moon had started on its downward course; he could not guess what time it was. Stiffly he rose and stretched himself, and swung his arms to get the blood flowing again. Though the night was mild, a chill seemed to have permeated his body—even his bones.

His mind groped. He didn't want to go back to Rachel's again, after all his big talk. The people there were too emotionally involved anyway. Perhaps Siwash could help him get started again. He mounted his horse and rode back across town to the shack by the creek.

There seemed to be a light in the window, but it was so dim he couldn't tell for sure. He knocked on the half-open door.

A voice inside grunted unintelligibly.

The light came from a coal-oil lamp, its chimney so black with soot that the flame was scarcely discernible. But there was enough illumination to cast vague shadows about the room and reflect from the amber cheeks of Siwash where he sat on the floor in front of the bed.

"Aren't you sleeping?" Jared asked. "What time is it?"

"Don't need a clock," Siwash said. "I know when I'm sleepy."

Jared sat on the only chair in the room. "I can't figure out what happened to him."

"I've been thinkin'," Siwash said. "Al's okay."

"You mean he's not hurt. Just lost, maybe?"

Siwash shook his head. "Al's not hurt, not lost."

"Not home, either," Jared said.

"Hiding."

"Father?"

"Sure."

"You mean Father ran away? He's hiding from us?"

Siwash raised both arms, splaying his fingers as if he were tossing up handfuls of smoke.

"Why do you think so?" Jared asked.

"A man might disappear by himself, maybe so. But a horse is too big. Somebody's got to help him."

"But it doesn't make sense."

The old Indian stared at the charcoal-colored flame. "Maybe so. What if somebody's after Al?"

"My father?"

Siwash shrugged, as if to say he had nothing to do with it. "He ran. Or they got him first."

38

It took Jared a minute to understand. "You mean murder?"
The word echoed in his ears: *Murder* . . . Murder . . . murder . . .

"Kidnapping, maybe. Something."

"Everybody respected my father."

"Yes they did," Siwash agreed.

"Then why should he run?"

"I don't know."

"He was the best friend you ever had."

"Yes he was, Roseman." Siwash rose and lay back on his
bed. "Remember that first time I met your daddy?"

"I remember," Jared said.

Then they fell silent.

It had been during Jared's trip from Utah to Canada with
his father thirteen years before. Late one afternoon they came
over the top of a hill and saw a broad, deep valley beneath
them. In the strange light of evening the stream at the bottom
of the hill showed white against the darkening landscape. As
he looked down it seemed to Jared that a part of the stream
had broken free and was flowing loose across the flat. A
teardrop-shaped patch of white, striated and torn, progressed
point first slowly over the ground.

His father stopped the buggy. "Bless my soul," he said after
a moment. "It's sheep."

The moment of unreality passed for Jared. When he looked
more closely he could see a man walking behind the sheep, and
a moment later he noticed the dog moving back and forth as it
pushed the stragglers ahead.

His father snapped the lines, and they moved swiftly down
the hill. Seen more closely, the water was dark, but as they
forded the stream the legs of the horses sent it up in brief
fountains of silver. Beyond the stream they turned off the
road, and slowly now, bounced over the turf to the place
where the man was settling his herd for the night. A short
distance away Alma stopped the rig, and they climbed down
and walked toward the herder. Already he had a fire going.

He was a small man, and he moved around his camp with
sudden rhythmic gestures. "Set up," he said. "Supper's ready
soon."

The two visitors went near the fire. Jared noticed that though he appeared never to look their way, the herder would catch them with the corner of his eye when he turned.

"Name's Alma Roseman," the boy's father said. "This is my son, Jared."

Without looking up from his work, the little man said, "Where you headed?"

"Canada."

"Is that a fur piece?"

"Not from here. Three more days in a buggy."

The herder snorted. "That's close by, all right. You fellers got plates? I got but one plate."

Jared and his father unhitched the team, took off the harnesses, and turned the horses loose on the creek bottom. They got their plates and cups from the grub box and went back to the campfire. "We have some eggs," Alma said, handing them to the herder. "Didn't know if you might be out." In a few moments the herder dished them up fried potatoes, bacon, beans, scrambled eggs and sourdough bread.

"Black coffee all right?" he said. "I got evaporated milk if you like."

"No coffee," Alma said. "We'll just drink from the creek."

"I might have knowed," the herder said as he hunkered before the fire. "I've heard tell of you Mormons, all right." He began to eat, unmindful of his company. His chin was not far above the edge of his plate, and he had to chew very fast to keep pace with the forkfuls of food that seemed to be always waiting at his mouth for admittance.

"You live around here?" Alma asked him.

"Nope."

"How long you been on the drive?"

"Months. Nigh on a year, I guess."

"A year?"

"Southern Oregon, I started. Got me a hired man and a mule. Figured to bring my herd up here to Montana and sell it to the Army. Somebody stole my mule. Hired man quit and went cowboyin'. Got here and can't find hide nor hair of no Army. Ranchers all talkin' blood if I don't get my sheep off their land. What am I goin' to do?"

"You got about fifteen hundred head?"

"Plus or minus. Bear got a few comin' through the mountains. Coyotes got some. Lost some crossin' rivers. Butchered a couple durin' the winter. But I've got my lamb crop. I reckon I got sixteen, seventeen hundred."

"How much you asking?" Alma said.

"You interested?"

"Maybe. I run sheep in Canada."

The herder studied the fire for a while. "I don't know. Three thousand?"

Alma stroked his mustache with his fingers. "Delivered?"

The herder nodded. "I can bring 'em up there."

"I have about two hundred dollars with me," Alma said.

"I don't need no earnest money."

"You should."

"Earnest money don't do anythin' but raise your expectations. With an honest man you don't need no paper, and with a crook it don't do any good."

"But if I turn out to be a crook?"

"You can't hurt me. When I get to Canada, if you don't have the money, I've still got my sheep. I've just changed locations, is all."

"Don't you care if you never get home?"

The herder pointed at his roll of blankets. "That's my home," he said.

"You never did tell me your name."

"Siwash." He was still hunkered by the fire, his dog leaning against his leg. "You don't have a bottle in that there grub box, do you?"

"I'm afraid not."

"In a small pack you have to choose 'twixt liquor and potaters. Sometimes I wish I'd left out the 'taters."

They went to bed beside the dying fire, and lay looking up into the sky. "Look at that moon," Siwash said. "Bright as a bottle. Glory, how I'd like to get drunk tonight. Everything in the world reminds me of whiskey."

"How far is it to town?" Alma said.

"Must be six, eight miles."

"You go ahead if you want."

"You'll look after my sheep?"

"Just be sure you're back by morning."

"I ain't got a mule no more. Them horses of yours ride?"

"They'll ride if you can ride them."

"Don't worry about that." The herder threw back his blankets, sat up, and began to put on his boots.

"Ride him light," Alma said. "I don't want him all tuckered out come morning." He sighed and rolled over in his bed. "There's some oats in the buggy."

The herder put on his hat and left them. After a few minutes Jared heard him far out in the meadow, talking softly to the horses and shaking the can of oats. Still later there was the drum of hooves on the grass, which became suddenly loud and clipped when Siwash turned his mount onto the hard-packed road to town.

Jared and his father went to sleep.

He became aware of a kind of muffled rumble, and opened his eyes. The sound resolved itself into the clatter of hooves on the road, but this time there were many. He also heard the voices of men, indistinct at first, but becoming more intelligible the nearer they approached. The voices were high-pitched, spirited, and frequently interrupted by loud guffaws or strains of quiet laughter. Jared lay on his back, staring up at the stars, and listened to the gaggle of voices.

"Hey, Sid. What'd you tell that feller, anyway?"

"I just said, 'Mister, you'll just have to shine your belt buckle somewhere's else.'"

"Naugh!"

"That's exactly what I told him."

"Did you see the look on Gunther's face when he sat on that old heifer's lap?"

"What'd it feel like, Gun?"

"How'd I know she was there? I just backed up to the chair, and she was already in it."

"Wa—hoo!"

The noise of the hooves, and the voices, grew louder and louder.

"Hey! Ain't that a fire over there?"

The hoofbeats stopped.

42

"Sure looks like it."

"Now, who's campin' out here tonight? Maybe they got a bottle."

"Yeh. Ours is almost dry."

"It's another passal of them Mormons, I bet. Goin' or comin'."

"*They* got no bottle."

"Not they'll admit to, anyways."

"Did you hear that sheep? That ain't no Mormons. That's old Woolly."

"Sure as thunder!"

One voice raised itself, loud enough to fill the sky. "Hey, Woolly!"

There was a banshee yell and a pistol shot, and the rumble of hooves again, this time on the sod, coming straight for the camp. The dog was barking excitedly. Jared noticed that Siwash had tied her to a tree so she couldn't follow him to town.

Alma was out of bed and pulling on his trousers as fast as he could. "Come on!" He cut the dog's tether as he ran. Jared slipped on his shoes and followed him. It was just as well, he thought, that he hadn't undressed to go to bed.

In the moonlight they could see perhaps half a dozen riders galloping toward them across the flat, shouting, the fire from their pistols like rockets in the sky. The herd was on its feet, and began to mill, bleating. Alma made for the buggy, but before he could reach it the riders hit the herd, running their horses full tilt among the sheep. One horse went down, another reared and began to buck, crazed by the noise and excitement, and the unfamiliar smell. The men lowered their pistols and began to shoot into the herd. One swung his lariat, roped a lamb, and galloped away, dragging it in a wide circle across the open flat. The body of the animal raised a pale skim of dust above the ground.

The dog whirled wildly, barking first at the sheep, then at the cowboys. Sheep ran in every direction, frantic, dividing and rejoining in wheeling clusters. Alma reached the buggy, grabbed his rifle, and fired it. The deep boom of the rifle drowned the scattered pistol shots and echoed sharply from

43

the hillside. "Next time I'll shoot a little lower!" Alma shouted.

A couple of the men seemed to hear his voice above the din. They stopped and turned their horses toward him. "Hey! That ain't Woolly," one of them cried.

"Where's old Woolly?"

Alma fired the rifle again. This time the shot went so close above one of the men that he ducked. "Ain't no cockamamie sheepherder gonna scare me!" he screamed, and galloped his horse straight at the buggy.

Alma stepped back, but the cowboy smashed at him with his pistol and he fell under the horse's hooves. The rifle discharged into the sky.

Jared ran to where his father lay.

The cowboy stopped his horse and wheeled. "Where'd the cub come from?" he cried.

The pistol shots had ceased; the cowboys stopped shouting. They rode toward each other. "What happened? We got the wrong outfit?"

"It's sheep, ain't it? Don't matter what sheep."

They looked toward Jared and the dog, where they bent over Alma. "What happened? He got shot?"

"Naugh! He ain't shot. Just knocked down. He's all right."

"Who's got the bottle? You got the bottle, Simon?"

"We finished mine."

"Let's go get some more."

One cowboy waved his hat. "So long, kid. When your daddy wakes up you tell 'im this here's cattle country." The cowboys laughed, turned their horses, and galloped away.

Jared knelt on the ground and looked at his father. His eyes were closed and there was a dark bruise on the side of his face. It was the face of a stranger—they had only been together for a few days.

"Sir." He cleared his throat. With his hand on his father's breast, he jiggled the body. "Sir." There was no response. "Sir."

Perhaps his father was dead. He had never seen a dead man, so he couldn't be sure. There must be some way to tell, but Jared was uncertain even what death consisted of. He felt frightened, but more than fear, he felt a rising hope. Maybe now he could go back to Utah to his mother.

"Sir." Perhaps something more personal would have better effect. He shook the body again, a little more strongly this time. "Father." He paused, waiting in the moonlight for some response.

"Father." Never in his seven years had he used the word in this way. "Father." All his life he had been without a father, and now it looked as if he had lost him just as they were getting acquainted. At least he could now be able to speak of him with intimacy. When his friends at school talked about their fathers, he would be able to relate how his own father died.

"Father."

The breast beneath his hand moved upward in a heavy sigh. The mouth opened a little wider and sucked quietly at the air. The eyelids raised, so slightly at first that in the darkness Jared didn't notice when it happened. He just became aware at some point that his father was staring at him.

Alma tried to speak, but coughed instead, and his body flinched.

"Are you all right?" Jared asked.

"I'm all right." The voice was low and raspy. "Are they gone?"

"Yes."

Alma tried to raise his head, but shuddered and lay back again. "Where are the sheep?"

"They're still around, I guess."

"They should be all right till morning. We might as well turn in."

Jared silently helped his father back to bed.

The next morning Alma seemed to be feeling better and was able to speak more easily, but each time he tried to raise himself he lay back with a bitter sigh.

"Check the sheep," he told Jared. "Take the dog with you."

The herd had moved some distance during the confusion, but now they lay or stood dumbly, as if stunned by the events of the night. A few had begun to drift away, cropping the grass along the creek bank. Jared found several of them dead. One had a small round hole just above her eye, with a stain of dark blood on the wool beside it. He went back to report to his father.

Alma said, "Looks like Siwash didn't make it home last night. I can't seem to move. I guess you'll have to tend the sheep, Jared."

The boy didn't reply.

"The first thing, though, is breakfast. Did you ever build a fire?"

"No."

It was a long day. Following his father's instructions, Jared got a fire going, and first undercooked and then burned black some bacon and eggs. For lunch he fixed sandwiches, and that was better; at least he didn't burn himself. In between times he and the dog tried to hold the sheep close to camp. His father told him how to use his arms to signal the dog, but she didn't seem to take so small a master very seriously. Still, they managed to keep the herd in view of the camp and get them to the bed-ground just before dark.

"When's old Siwash coming?" Jared asked.

"I don't know," Alma said. "Maybe those cowboys caught him and hung him."

"Really?"

"I'm just joshing you."

The next morning Alma was able to get around a little and help with the cooking. Things went better this time, and they had a first-rate sheepherder's breakfast. As they ate, Jared watched the sheep drifting further and further up the valley.

Alma sat on the tongue of the buggy, eating, and did not even seem aware that there were any sheep. Jared started to speak, but hesitated, then finally said, "Do I have to herd the sheep today?"

His father didn't look at him, just nodded his head and went on eating.

A briny pain rushed up in Jared's eyes; it seemed to require all the muscles of his body to keep the tears in check.

Alma, still sitting on the buggy tongue, reached a hand and raised the bolt that held the doubletrees to it, then let it drop back into place. It fell with a metallic *chunk!* "That little bolt is the kingpin," he said. "That's all that holds the rig together." He looked at Jared. "Right now you're the kingpin of this outfit."

Jared was uncertain how to reply. He looked up and saw that the sheep were almost out of sight. "Yes, sir," he said. "I guess I'd better go."

"Just follow them till about noon," Alma said. "Then turn them around and start back. As long as you stay in the valley, you won't get lost."

**8** When he overtook the last stragglers of sheep, Jared looked back. The bend of the stream had come between him and the camp. He climbed the hill, and at the highest point he could find he turned slowly, looking in every direction. Beneath him the stream flowed through its gentle valley. To the west were the mountains. In every other direction the prairie extended like a buff-colored, uneven ocean from which occasional buttes and ridges protruded. He could not see a tree or post or trail or living creature, except the dog and the sheep and a hawk that hovered above the break of the hill, riding the updraft and crying intermittently. Though it was not yet noon, he decided to turn the sheep back down the valley. He began to hike along the top of the hill, to make his way around the leaders.

But the contour of the valley changed, grew at the same time deeper and more rugged. The sod gave way to exposed rock through which the water had cut a narrow channel, and now gushed, roaring softly. When he reached the lead sheep he found that they had turned outward, away from the rocky stream, and flowed up over the hill onto the open prairie. Clouds came in, bringing cool, damp shadows with them. A chill blew across the land. He began to run.

But the sheep were like waves on the ocean, mysterious and uncontrollable. Before long, as he tried and tried to head them, he found that he was out of sight of the valley. The clouds had covered the sun and the mountains, so he had no idea which way to drive the sheep, even if they would obey him. Slanting curtains of rain fell across the horizon. At least he could no longer see those awesome distances. Now he could only imagine, or remember, that rim at the far edge of the world, the undefined boundary of his lost condition.

As the afternoon passed the air lightened, both in weight and color. He became aware that the sun was shining through a slit in the clouds. By now it was a low sun, without warmth, almost touching the mountains. Its light was ethereal, illusive, not coming from the heavens but rising above the earth like a vapor.

The chill of evening rushed against his skin like a wind out of a cave. If he could find the valley, he still might be able to make his way back to camp. And now that he could see the mountains again, he at least knew the general direction to go. He tried to round up the sheep and drive them in front of him. As he walked back and forth, one old ewe lying peacefully in the grass was reluctant to move. He had to poke her with his toe before she rose and moved away. With his hand he felt the grass where her body had been. It still held a suggestion of heat from the body of the sheep. He lay down with his body curled in the center of the flattened grass, but at once he began to shiver. It would be better to keep moving.

As he hurried on, gathering the sheep before him, the sun went down behind the mountains. The light poured after it, seeming to drain away through that hole in the clouds. There was no twilight. Almost at once the world was dark, the air opaque under a heavy sky.

He could discern the pale oval forms of the sheep that were closest in front of him. He shouted, and walked back and forth, pushing them ahead.

Presently he felt the ground start to fall away beneath his feet. At first he was uncertain—it might have been an illusion created by his numbed senses, but then the slope became more definite. He had found the creek valley. Out of the darkness beneath him, he heard the strange quiet crackle and bleat of sheep disturbed, as the herd slowly flowed backward upon itself, forcing those that were still asleep to rise and travel.

He heard a call. "Jared!" It sounded like his father's voice. "Jared!" The voice came from some distance away. "Halloo!"

For a moment Jared seemed unable to respond. The unreality of his situation had reached a sort of apex. He wondered fleetingly if his father had died and this was a ghost who called him. Or an angel. Half timidly he called, "Halloo!"

The night seemed to grow quiet, with a silence so intense that it was strangely undisturbed by the bleat and shuffle of sheep.

"Jared! Where are you?"

"Father!" he cried out, and started to run down the hill. "Father!" He was running blind; his legs could not keep up with him. He pitched head forward and rolled, landing heavily on his shoulder. Scrambling to his feet, he hurried on, but more carefully now. As he ran he kept calling. His father, too, called out repeatedly, in a strong voice that sounded closer each time he heard it. And slowly the voice took on physical substance. Jared could discern a large dark shadow, darker even than the night, coming toward him. He saw that his father was riding a horse.

As they drew near, his father slid off the horse. The boy ran and collapsed into his father's arms. "How'd you know where I was?"

"The sheep weren't hard to find." Alma's voice was thin now, like the voice of an old woman, and Jared felt his body wince. "And a good herder stays with his sheep." Alma turned to his horse and stood facing it with his hands on its neck. He remained that way for several moments.

"Can you get on?" Jared said at last.

"Sure I can." Alma jumped, trying to land with his stomach over the horse's back. With a heavy sigh he slipped back to the ground and almost fell. He seemed to have difficulty breathing. Presently he straightened, muttering angrily, "I can't jump. It's my gizzard, or something."

"How did you get on in the first place?" Jared asked.

"I climbed on a buggy wheel." As Alma continued to talk, his words came out in bundles, with pauses in between, as though he had to wrap and tie them. "My hired man taught old Nack a trick once." Pause. "That was years ago, though." Pause. "Maybe he can remember." Alma reached across the horse's neck and pulled hard on the far bridle rein, at the same time switching him lightly on the shoulder. "Come on, boy. Down. Down."

Nack's head was turned sharply around by the pull of the rein. He began to side-step toward Alma, forcing him backward. But Alma still maintained the pressure on the bridle rein. "Down. Come on, boy." Nack limped heavily, hesitated, went down on his left front knee, and a moment later his body rolled to the ground. Alma moved backward, out of the way. "That-a-boy."

Still holding the bridle rein tight, he stepped across the horse's back. "Come on, Jared." Jared walked forward uncertainly. Alma patted the horse's back. "Here. In front of me." As soon as they were both settled on Nack, Alma released the bridle rein and the horse turned his head to the front. Alma nudged him with his heels. "Come on, boy." Nack tossed his head. Then, with a sudden snort, he lunged upward, first onto his front feet, then his rear, in an arcing motion so violent and strong that for a moment Jared thought they would be thrown.

"All right?" Alma asked.

Jared nodded. He felt his father's arms around his body. The horse started forward, moving quietly into the darkness.

"What about the sheep?" Jared asked.

"They'll be all right," Alma said. "We'll come back in the morning."

The horse took them through the darkness back to camp. First they built up the fire and warmed themselves. Then Jared went to sleep, snuggled in the curve of his father's body.

9 The next day the sun was shining. The dew-damp prairie gleamed like a crusted jewel. Alma and Jared were up early—they wanted to get back to the herd before it started to move. While Jared rolled up the beds, Alma fixed breakfast.

They had begun to eat when they heard a voice in the distance, growling some strange incantation which sounded half in celebration, half in defiance of the morning sunshine. When the sound came nearer they realized it was intended to be a song.

"Old Siwash," Alma said. "Here he comes at last."

The sorrel gelding came stepping smartly along the road, bridled head high and tail switching. Siwash sat easily on his unsaddled back, legs swinging free, with his face turned up and his hat low to keep the sun out of his eyes. " 'Fare thee well for I must leave thee,' " he sang. " 'Do not let the parting grieve thee . . .' " It was more of a dirge than a hymn.

Alma said, "Sounds like a freight train coming to a stop on a cold track."

"Hallo!" Siwash called when he saw them. "A beautiful good morning! Good morning! Good morning!" His voice dropped down an octave. " 'I can no longer stay with you, stay with you-oo . . .' " He stopped the horse and swung off, but kept hold of its mane with one hand. "I'm just in time for breakfast, ain't I?" He stared at Alma for a moment, then turned to look around the camp. He saw the dead sheep.

"We had visitors," Alma said.

Siwash stood silent, weaving slightly, supported by his hand in the horse's mane. His eyes were focused on some distant place, as though they could not endure the scene close at hand. "Them galldern cowboys?"

"It was cowboys. One of them called Gunther."

"That's the ones."

"They called you old Woolly," Jared added.

Siwash swore. "That's them. Which way did they go? I'll . . ."

"That was night before last," Alma said. "They're long gone."

"They ride for the Turkey Track. I'll find 'em."

"They left a message."

"Yeah, I know their message. 'This is cattle country.' That don't pack no ice with me. This is God's country, and these sheep are God's, as much as any cows you care to mention." Again he looked around. "Where's the sheep?"

"Up the creek a ways," Alma said.

"What are they doin' up the creek? I thought you said you's a sheepman. I could depend on you." The herder spat. "I come back and half my herd's killed dead, t'other half's lost. That's the trouble with runnin' sheep. Ain't nobody you can turn to. Ain't nobody to tend 'em but your own self. Cows? Any pigeon-brain can look after a cow. They ain't no dumber animal on earth than a cowboy, and he can still keep ahead of a cow. But sheep. That's a different proposition. If you was . . ."

"If you was to hurry, you could get there before they moved," Alma said.

"Me?" Siwash cried. "You're comin' too, you know. I ain't goin' on no wild-goose chase. You know where they are, you can show me."

"Jared will show you."

Siwash looked at the boy. "What does he know?"

"He knows where your sheep are."

Siwash tied his horse to the buggy wheel and came over to have some breakfast. While he ate he looked at Jared suspiciously. "How old are you, kid?"

"Seven."

Siwash appeared not to hear. He turned his attention back to his breakfast. "Ain't never goin' to get no sheep again. More trouble'n kids. Eight months I been nursin' these mothers night and day, and the first minute I turn my back they're either dead, lost, et or pizoned, ever' one of 'em. I sell these mothers, I'm through."

"What'll you do?" Alma asked.

Siwash shrugged. "I'll go on an Africa-size drunk. I'll climb Whiskey Mountain till the only thing higher'n me is the sun. And I ain't never goin' to come down." He pushed back his hat and rubbed his palm across his forehead. "How I hate comin' down." He pulled a clump of grass, and with its rough roots and dirt that clung to them, scrubbed the egg off his plate. Then he rinsed it with water from a kettle that steamed over the fire. "Come on, kid," he said sorrowfully. "Where's the sheep?"

"You come right back to camp, Jared," Alma said. "We've got to get started. I want to be home for Sunday."

"You've missed it," Siwash said. "Today's Sunday."

"Today's Tuesday," Alma told him.

For some distance Jared and Siwash walked in silence, side by side, the dog running nearby. "Is that your daddy?" Siwash asked him at last.

"Yes, sir." Jared was uncertain what his attitude toward Siwash ought to be, but as long as they were alone, it seemed wise to be respectful.

Siwash burst out laughing. "They ain't nobody never called me 'sir' before. Ain't nobody never." Then he became serious again. "You tryin' to be smart, kid?"

"No, sir."

"Don't no sir yes sir no sir me sir."

Jared didn't know what to say to that.

"Today ain't Tuesday, is it?"

"I guess so. Father said it was."

"It was Saturday night you guys showed up here. Last night, that was. Saturday night. Today's Sunday."

"That was three nights ago."

"Kid. You tryin' to tell me I don't know what day it is?"

"No, sir. Just that you were gone for two days. I herded your sheep for two days."

"Two days?" Siwash stopped walking and looked at Jared.

"Yes, sir. Last night I got lost, me and the sheep."

"Where was your old man?"

"One of those cowboys ran over him on his horse."

"The divil you say."

"No, sir." Jared wasn't sure whether that was right, "Yes, sir," he added, just in case.

Siwash shook his head. "Life's a boil. We keep waitin' for it to get better." He walked on, more quickly now. For quite a way he didn't say any more. Presently they came around a bend in the valley and saw the sheep, just beginning to graze.

"There they are," Jared said.

"Wait." Siwash reached toward him but didn't touch him. "Wait." Jared looked at the little man. His face seemed to have shrunk, as if the skin were drying, drawing the features into tight little wrinkles of flesh. "Set down a minute, kid. Your daddy won't be ready to start for a while." The watery

53

little eyes of the herder seemed to grow brighter. He placed his hand on Jared's arm. Jared sat on the grass, and Siwash knelt, facing him. "Look, kid. You see what drinkin' does to a man." He rubbed his hand back and forward across the end of his nose. "You tell your daddy . . ." His mind seemed to wander, then cross back over itself. "Tell your daddy I'll fetch the sheep. I'll see you in Canada in a month or so."

"I'll tell him," Jared said.

"I'm sorry, young feller. Sorry I done what I done. Sorry them cowboys done what they done. Sorry . . ."

"It's all right," Jared said and started to rise.

The herder took his arm and pressed him back down again. "You don't know what it's like bein' alone day after day. It ain't no way for a man to live. You take a cowboy, and that's a different breed of animal. They're dumb, but they got company. They go to town, they ain't alone. They play poker with a half a dozen other fellers. They get drunk, and all their pals is drunk beside 'em. But they're cowboys and they have to tend cows, so they lean on each other. But a sheepherder's alone. They ain't nobody'll talk to him. He drinks alone and plays solitary." Siwash snuffled.

"I think I'd better go," Jared said.

Siwash reached toward him again, but checked himself. "That's right, kid. You go. Just remember old Siwash ain't a drunk. Ten months I been, and nary a drop. Ten months and thousands of miles, fightin' bears, blizzards, buzzards and cowboys. Remember that, kid."

Jared backed away from the herder, who still knelt, his dog beside him. "You tell your daddy . . . I'm sorry, what they done to you . . ."

Jared turned and ran.

Now, sitting in the stifling little shack, Jared realized that run as he would, he had never been free of the old Indian again. After he brought the herd to Canada, Siwash was always there, herding, shearing, docking, butchering . . . Even after Alma lost his herd, Siwash had kept in touch, and many times Jared helped his father to carry fresh vegetables or a leg of mutton to the shack on the creek when they made trips to

54

town. For the past three or four years, though, Alma had not been able to travel very well, and their trips had become much less frequent.

The daylight in the room was slowly increasing, neutralizing the pale glimmer of the lamp. Siwash had gone to sleep. Jared rose from his chair and dusted off the seat of his trousers. He looked at the sleeping figure lying among the rags that littered the bed. Then he went out to his horse, mounted, rode toward his sister's place.

# 10

When Jared got to Rachel's house, Bessie was ready to start home. He turned Tom's saddle horse into the pasture and then harnessed the team and hitched them to the rig. He was about to get in and drive around to the gate when he noticed Alma's old carton of papers lying under the seat. Someone had put it in the rig when Jared started home, and then in the concern over Alma, it had been forgotten. Leaning against the side of the rig, Jared opened the carton.

It bulged with paper—pages of all sizes, folded, unfolded; official, personal; handwritten, typed; unsigned, notarized—a dismaying welter of documents. He picked some of them at random to read.

A letter from Bessie:

May 10, 1897.
Dear Alma. I had hoped that you would be home before this. I realize of course that you have things you must do, but it is hard sometimes to feel that you are as concerned about your family as you are the sheep . . . I guess I shouldn't complain. And I don't think I would, but on Friday our little daughter was born, a couple of weeks early. I called her Jane, since we had not been able to agree on any other name than Willard . . .

Other letters from Bessie. Some from Jared's mother, Lula Fae. A bill of sale for cattle. A banknote that had been marked

"Paid." Various business letters from insurance companies and livestock merchants.

One small thick envelope caught his eye. It looked as if it had never been opened. He took it out and turned it over. "Master Jared Roseman, Cardston, Alberta." The postmark was still clear: "Smithfield, Utah. April 4, 1908." It had been mailed a few days before his thirteenth birthday. Dared he open it now, after all these years? It was like reading the mail of someone else—the person he had been seven years ago.

Dear Jared—

Why haven't you answered my letters? Is it because I wasn't a better mother?

He sank to the ground, staring at the letter. He trembled. With what infinite labor and unquenchable hope he had penciled messages to her after his arrival in Canada. How anxiously he had waited for the mail. But the reply never came. The months passed, and in time he had quit writing, had trained himself never to think of letters, not even to think of her.

But how could I be a better mother? What could I do? Do you remember what good times we had when you were a little boy? You're the only child I ever had, really, you know. They took Grace to Canada when she was just a baby. So the happiest time was when you were here. I will always remember having breakfast with you on the blue tablecloth.

You must not be angry with your father. I know that you are disappointed. A boy likes to feel that his father is perfect, but only God is perfect. Remember that.

Your father used to say, "What would my son think of me if he found out?" I think that was why he took you away from me. He pretended it was because I was sick, but the truth is he was afraid I couldn't keep his secret. Well, who'd want to tell a secret like that, anyway? But it doesn't matter—your father is a good man; better than most. That's the way you ought to think of him. He always said his prayers. He told me he was praying all the time that day, even in the very worsed of it. Fancy that.

I shouldn't be telling you all this, I guess. But what difference does it make now? It is all over. All finished. He never pre-

56

tended that he didn't do it. He never put on a show, never tried to be something he wasn't.

The cow kicked Uncle Theodore last night, and now he has a big lump on his leg. He is a good brother; he is the one who always mails my letter. Did you get my letters?

Please write to me when you can.

Mother

Jared crumpled the letter in his hand. Rage came up in him like rising water—rage, shame, dismay, incomprehension. Why had she done it? Bessie must have intercepted all those letters. How many? One, at least. Hundreds, maybe. And he had never received any of them—not one.

He left the team standing and walked up the path to the house, the letter still crumpled in his hand. As he entered the kitchen, Bessie turned. "Are you ready?"

Jared didn't reply. He stood in the open door, wondering what to say.

First Rachel noticed him, and then Grace, and Tom and Jane. They were all looking at him. How could they see the fury—what was there about the look of him alone that made them stare? He wanted to be calm, reasonable, without emotion; surely facts as strong as these needed no special force to carry them. "I found this letter in the cardboard box," he said.

"What letter is it?" Bessie asked.

"A letter from my mother. Never opened."

"It looks opened to me."

"Yes. Now it is. Seven years later."

Bessie straightened from where she had been arranging a lunch basket for the drive home. "I don't understand you, Jared."

He held up the hand with the letter in it. "A letter my mother wrote to me seven years ago. It was never given to me."

"I'm sorry. It must have been misplaced."

"I don't think so. She mentions other letters. I never got any of them."

"Are you suggesting we deliberately kept them from you?"

"Somebody did."

"I did. Is that what you mean?"

"It wasn't enough to take me away from her. You couldn't even let me have her letters."

Bessie sank onto a chair. "Oh, Jared. You don't understand. Your mother wasn't well."

"She was well enough to write."

"That isn't what I mean. She was disturbed in her mind. We could never be sure . . . We didn't want to upset you, that's all."

"Upset me?"

"Maybe it was wrong, I don't know. We thought it was for the best."

"I can't believe it. What kind of person are you, anyway?"

Rachel· said sharply, "Don't speak to Mother that way, Jared."

"She's not my mother." He turned and walked out the door. As he reached the buggy he heard footsteps coming behind him.

It was Grace. "Where are you going?" she asked.

"I don't know."

"Can we go to Lone Rock? Maybe Daddy's there by now."

"What about Aunt Bessie? Doesn't she want to go?"

"She's decided to stay. Tom has fifty men combing the hills this morning. She says she wants to be here."

He climbed in the buggy and took Grace's hand as she scrambled up beside him.

11 An hour later Jared and Grace were side by side in the rig, traveling across the Indian Reserve. Jared glanced at his sister, a plain, freckled woman who by now must have given up any thoughts of marriage. That was too bad, really, because she was a gentle person, and a good cook besides. A man could do a lot worse.

He felt uncertain how to talk to Grace. In some ways she was still a child. "Did Mother ever write to you?" he asked.

"Sometimes. When I was little. Aunt Bessie used to read me the letters."

Jared took the letter from his shirt pocket. "Read it."

Grace turned the letter over in her hands.

"Go ahead and read it." He cracked the front of the rig with his lines; the team trotted smartly along the road. All around them the prairie shimmered in the sun.

When Grace unfolded the letter the paper rustled gently in the breeze. Jared studied her face, as if in that bland countenance he might read some involuntary indicator, pointing the way to Alma's hiding place.

Grace laughed. "She always makes such funny question marks." She read on, with bowed head, but Jared noticed once that she had raised her eyes slightly, looking out toward the prairie. She said, "What's she like?"

"Who—Mother?"

"I've never seen her. They brought me to Canada when I was sixteen months old."

Jared shrugged. "I haven't seen her for a long time."

"But you remember her?"

"Of course."

"I've seen pictures of her. She must be pretty."

"Yes. You look a lot like her."

She looked up sharply. "Don't be silly."

"You do."

Almost reluctantly Grace returned to the letter. After a few moments she said, "What does she mean 'He was praying all the time that day, even in the very worsed of it?' "

"I was hoping you could tell me."

"I don't understand it."

"Haven't you any idea what she's talking about? You were older."

"Father is an unhappy man. But you know that as well as I do."

"Unhappy?"

"He hardly ever speaks."

"Is that all?"

59

"It isn't natural."

"It was natural for Father."

"What do you mean, was? Already you're talking about him in the past."

"I didn't mean that." Jared fell silent.

She folded the letter. "We've got to have faith."

There was scarcely any sound—only a soft jumble of trotting hooves and the hiss of buggy wheels scooping up the dust in the bottom of the wagon tracks.

They came to the river, and as they started down the dugway they could see the houses of Lone Rock strewn across the opposite hill like toys left by some giant's grandchildren.

Five years ago, when that hill had been open prairie, the Mormon church had bought a large ranch at Lone Rock and made parcels available at nominal cost. And one spring day eleven men had come to start the town. Jared and Alma were among them.

There had been no bridge then; there had scarcely been a road. Jared had crossed the river ahead of the wagons, and raced his pony to the place on the hill where the new town would be. On every side survey stakes fluttered their red blooms, half lost in the waving grass.

He stood in one stirrup so he could turn and see the prairie and sky and river, and thirty miles to the southwest, the pale blue mountains, like chips of broken sky lying along the horizon. The wind pushed at him, and along the ground it pressed down runnels of buffalo grass, then let them straighten again, as though a hand had passed over the earth.

He looked back at the tiny caravan coming down the hill opposite. The wagons dipped as they entered the river, bumped across its stony bottom, lurched strongly as the teams scrambled up the bank and for the first time scarred the sod with the iron rim of their wheels. The six-horse teams plunged forward in their collars, heads low, their manes afloat on the wind, their shoulders gleaming in the sunlight as they dragged the heavy wagons up the hill. At the top, each driver turned aside to his particular lot.

The Roseman lot was at the northeast corner of town. Jared and Alma had ridden out from Cardston the week before to pick it out. Now Alma drove the heavy wagon onto the lot and turned it to face east across the river.

He rose from the seat at the front of the wagon, slowly straightening his body as though its joints had grown rusty during the long ride. When he had satisfied himself that the last bend was out of every joint, so that he stood at his full six feet, he squared his shoulders, and leaning slightly backward, turned from his waist to look to the north and south. "The last time, Jared," he said. "I'm never going to move again."

The age-old seal of the prairie was broken by tent pegs, survey stakes, shovels, and on that first day, by the point of a plough, when in a symbolic act of subjugation the bishop himself took the handles.

As Jared watched the bishop plough the ceremonial furrow, the iron point seemed to part him as well as the earth, opening a rich new promise in his own life and covering the matted discontents of the past. Through the soles of his boots he seemed to feel the vigor of the wild land, and silently pledged his life to the work of taming it. There would be houses to build, sod to break, wheat to plant, hay to stack, fences to make, cattle, poultry, gardens to tend, and finally a harvest to be gotten in before the first snowfall, perhaps four months away.

After the animals were tended, the camps made, and supper finished, the citizens of Lone Rock gathered around a bonfire at the brow of the hill. The sun was gone now and the land dark, but above them the sky shone like a pearl in the strange, iridescent glow of the prairie twilight. Abel Wilson played his harmonica while they all sang, "We Thank Thee, O God, for a Prophet . . ." Bishop Frame then stepped out of the circle, one pace closer to the fire. He took his hat from his head and knelt on the ground, holding the wide black brim against his chest with both hands. The wind had lowered with the fading light, and now its trailing currents stirred languidly in the soft hair above the bishop's temples. There was a moment of muted shuffling as the rest of the men made room, then lowered themselves to their knees.

Jared was already kneeling, bareheaded and chin on his chest, when he felt the hard lean fingers of his father's hand grip his shoulder, and then his weight as he lowered himself. He could recognize his father's breathing anywhere; perhaps because of the sworl of hair that plugged his nostrils he seemed to snort rather than breathe, and those exhalations asserted uncommon force and authority. Now the breathing was louder than usual, and Alma cleared his throat lustily.

The bishop said, "Brother Roseman, would you lead us in prayer tonight?"

Jared had expected the bishop himself to offer the prayer this night. Though the Stake President had already dedicated the land for settlement, still, this first prayer in their new home had a special significance and should, it seemed, be in the form of a consecration. But the bishop was a kind and generous man, willing to give recognition to the oldest man in the company.

"Thank you, Bishop," Alma said softly. He cleared his throat a second time. And then he began to pray in a full, vibrant voice.

There were all the familiar things in the prayer: thankfulness for the restoration of the gospel, a prayer for the prophet and the other authorities, and for the missionaries, a prayer for the welfare of their families; an appeal for the gathering of the lost tribes in the Lord's due time, and for the building up of the kingdom in preparation for the coming of the Saviour— words and phrases that Jared had heard his father speak perhaps a thousand times before. He often marveled that a taciturn man could find words so readily when he knelt in prayer.

Jared opened his eyes slightly. Without moving his head, he was able to see several of the men in the circle, the hollows of their faces cast into deep shadow by the light from the fire, the highlights emerging as resolute and solid as bronze masks nailed against the dark. These were the faces of men whom he loved and trusted, men with whom he would spend the rest of his life.

Then a strange thing happened. The sound of his father's voice deepened, and the words coalesced into a solemn pronouncement that forced his attention. He closed his eyes again, and the rising power of the voice, without growing louder, seemed to set a seal on its prophetic words:

". . . Grant us, Father, strength to match this land, to subdue it according to thy commandment, that we may build here a home where our children, and our children's children, may live in peace, and the abundance of the land; that through our labor, and our righteous endeavor, the Zion of which thou hast spoken shall truly be established to the utmost bounds of the everlasting hills . . ."

After the close of the prayer, the men were slow in rising from their knees. Jared glanced at his father, and felt a thrill of pride pass over him. Here was a man of seventy, still able to lead and inspire others—the kind of man this country needed. He almost wished that it were possible for him to die and pass his youth on to Alma, where it would not be squandered on petty weaknesses and discontents like his own.

As Jared and Alma prepared for bed that night, the boy asked his father, "Do you want to go back to Utah?"

"Sometimes I have wanted to. I'd like to see your mother more often than I do."

"Is Mother still your wife?"

"Of course. You think I divorced her?"

"I don't know what to think. You can't have two wives any more, can you? Not since the Manifesto?"

Alma laughed. "I'd better be able to. You were born five years after the Manifesto."

"I don't understand."

"I used to visit your mother every year. The Manifesto ended plural marriage in the church, but it didn't take away the wives a man already had."

"Why didn't we go back to Utah, then, instead of coming to Lone Rock?"

"Never go back, Jared," Alma said. "Going back is a defeat." After a moment he went on. "I was thinking today of Joseph Smith. He didn't ask to be a prophet. Maybe sometimes he would rather have been like anybody else, a simple farmer, raising his family, free from the burden of the kingdom. Did he want to see his people hounded, their homes burned, their children killed? Did he want to die at Carthage?" Alma paused. "Have I ever told you about Carthage?"

"Where the prophet was killed?"

63

"While they were prisoners in Carthage jail—Joseph and Hyrum both."

"That's so long ago. You don't remember?"

"I remember. I was six years old." Alma hesitated. "I remember my mother crying when word came that Joseph and Hyrum had been murdered. The whole city weeping, men and women. People waited in the streets—thousands of people silent, waiting. All morning, standing in the street.

"He had been free, you know—clear of the mobs—on his way west with Hyrum to find a new home for his people. Safe. But some accused him of running away, of abandoning them, and he came back. He knew he would be killed.

"The entire city of Nauvoo standing in the streets, and not a sound. Hour on hour. And then a stir and motion through the crowd, and we knew they were coming, and as they reached us the crowd pushed back to let them through—men on horses, and two wagons, one behind the other, each carrying a box . . .

"One of the men riding behind the wagons was my father. I saw his face as they passed, his eyes straight ahead, dry—almost burning, they were so dry."

After a minute Alma went on. "I am not faced with martyrdom. I am surrounded by friends. My responsibility is not for the whole kingdom, but what small part of it I am called to help in. Tonight I felt a call to this land. And as Joseph proved faithful in his calling, I shall try to be faithful in mine."

They had made their beds outside the tent. The sky was clear. Jared lay on his back with his hands behind his head, looking up at the stars. "And I," he said. He repeated it in his mind, reiterating the pledge to himself, and to God. "And I."

**12** When Grace and Jared arrived at the Roseman home, there was nobody around. The house looked forlorn, abandoned almost, yet Jared realized he must be seeing in it only a reflection of his own feeling. He stopped the rig at the front gate to let Grace out.

As he drove on down to the barn he noticed that a draft team was gone from the pasture. Faintly he heard the sound of a mowing machine. After he had turned out the team he walked to the brow of the hill and saw Lyman cutting hay on the river flat beneath him. At any other time this quiet scene, and the far-off shuttling sound of the mower, might have soothed him. He started down the hill.

When Lyman saw him approach, he stopped the outfit, and turning, dangled one leg from the seat of the mower. "Morning, little brother."

"Where were you last night?" Jared asked.

"Suppose I ask you the same question? I thought you were coming home."

"I was here, Trash. I milked your cow for you."

"Why didn't you stay?"

"I went looking for Father."

"Father?"

Jared realized that Lyman still didn't know what had happened. "He's lost."

"What do you mean, lost?"

"He started home on Saratoga, but he never got here."

"He must have gone back to Rachel's."

"Nobody's seen him. Tom and Stanley have a search party out."

Lyman started to unhitch his team.

Jared moved to help him. "What do you think we'd better do?"

"What can we do?" Lyman asked. "Look for him. I don't know anything else to do." He drove the team up the hill on the trot, and threw off the harnesses. Within a few minutes he had saddled his horse and mounted. "Coming?"

"You go ahead," Jared said. "You'll probably find the search party somewhere along the creek west of Rachel's. That's where the tracks ran out."

"What are you going to do?"

"I've got to stop and think. It seems like I've been traveling too fast—as if there's something I missed."

Lyman turned and spurred his horse down the road toward Cardston. Jared went into the house and sat on the couch in the living room. Grace was arranging and sweeping and dusting. "Where did Lyman go?" she asked.

"He's going to join the search party, I guess." Jared paused, then, "Siwash says he doesn't think it was an accident. He thinks that father wanted to disappear—that he did it deliberately."

She called from one of the bedrooms, "Why would he do that?"

"I have no idea. Have you?"

She came to the door. "What do you mean? What possible reason could there be?"

He shrugged. She went back to her work.

Jared looked around at the little house and through the window that faced the barnyard. How different it was from Rachel's home—the place in Cardston that had once belonged to Alma. It seemed a cruelty to fit a man of Alma's dimensions into such cramped quarters. But he had lived here for five years, building the place around him, like an ant. Maybe it was this house that had caused him to flee.

He called to Grace, "Why did Father come to Lone Rock, anyway? Why did he sell the other place to Tom?"

Again she came to the door. "He had to, I guess, after he lost his sheep."

"It was the storm?"

"That's what I always thought. That and Hickory Jack's dance hall."

"And the petition?"

She paused. "That's right. I'd forgotten about the petition." She went into the kitchen, where she had some laundry soaking. "I don't know what there was about the lease that he loved it so much. I never even saw it. To me it always seemed like the ends of the earth."

Jared could hear the *smack-squish* of the plunger as she punched it up and down in the tub of laundry. He had seen the lease just once, when Alma took him out of school to help with the shearing. The two of them traveled all day in the democrat, his father sitting with the lines in his hand, his elbows on his knees, staring straight ahead across the backs of the horses. They crossed mile after mile of uninhabited prairie, and sometime after dark, came in sight of two lighted windows. Jared could hear the snorts and snuffles and occasional quiet *baas* of the sheep, and as they came nearer he caught the smell of them.

A couple of men came out of the bunkhouse to unload the provisions from the democrat: food, creoline, wool sacks, paper strings for tying the fleeces, and rock salt for the sheep. Jared and his father put away the team in the small, snug stable and then they walked together toward the lighted windows. Alma opened the bunkhouse door and stood back to let Jared enter.

It was a large room, lit by two kerosene lamps that hung on wires from the ceiling. Two tiers of bunk beds lined one wall. In the middle was a large puffin' billy stove and a table. Plain wooden chairs sat at different locations around the room, and on the wall some rustic shelves held stacks of yellow-covered magazines. Three men were playing cards at the table; a couple more sprawled on their bunks, reading. On a chair against the wall a small man sat, whittling something with his pocket knife. Alma stopped beside him. "Remember Jared?"

The little man looked at him. "Well, dog take it. Is this the kid?"

"This is him."

Jared realized the man was Siwash.

"How old are you now?"

"Almost fourteen."

"Have you ever tied fleeces before?"

"No."

"Well, you'd better get your sleep. Tomorrow these fellas'll run your tail off." He nodded toward the other end of the room, where several men had gathered somewhat apart. Some of them were honing their sheep shears.

Siwash started into the little lean-to that served as a kitchen. "I'll fix you a bite."

"If you can cook it, I can eat it," Alma said. And he stretched on one of the lower bunks. "That's yours," he said to Jared, nodding toward the bed above him.

Jared climbed up to try his bed, but soon he heard the crackle of bacon in a hot frying pan and went out to the kitchen to watch the cook.

Siwash, still wearing his hat, as if indoors and outdoors were all the same to him, glanced over his shoulder. "You like 'em sunny-side up?"

"What's that?" Jared asked.

"Your eggs."

Jared wasn't sure what to say. "How do you like them?"

"Why, anybody knows that a fried egg is useless unless it's bleedin' all over your plate."

Jared swallowed. "Yah. I'll have it still bleeding."

"I figured so. Your daddy won't eat 'em no other way."

He was surprised to find how good the soft egg tasted. A couple of the other men came into the kitchen while Jared and Alma ate, and began to talk and laugh. After a while even Alma joined in, telling stories that Jared had never heard. Too soon, though, it ended. When the dishes were done the men started going to bed, and soon the lamps were blown out. Jared lay in the dark bunkhouse, which smelled of tobacco and stale bedclothes, and listened to the men begin to snore, first one and then the other. After a long while he fell asleep himself.

The days that followed were busy ones for everybody. By the time the shearers were ready to start, the men had built a bower over the shearing floor and covered it with green branches gathered from stunted willows that grew beside the slough. The pens had been filled with sheep, the stand for the wool sacks put in place, strings pre-counted for each shearer so that the remainder at the end of the day would give an accurate count of every man's production.

There was no fanfare to mark the start of the work; one shearer reached under the burlap skirt of the pen, seized a leg, and dragged a reluctant ewe onto the boards of the shearing floor. He upended her on her tailbone, leaned her back against his legs, and started the shears in a diagonal down across her belly. The other shearers followed in a moment or two, and the shearing operation was in motion.

It continued for days—weeks, it seemed to Jared—almost without interruption, except for meals and sleep, a half day they lost waiting for the sheep to dry off after a nighttime rainfall, and Sunday, when they shut down completely. Jared's job was to help the tier, and both of them were kept busy gathering each newly sheared fleece between their feet, wrapping it with the string first one way and then the other, tucking in the tag ends, tying it firmly, and then tossing it up to the tromper in the wool sack. It was a monotonous, smelly job, and yet there was a persistent excitement about the situation, of taking his place in a crew of men, that made him feel more exhilarated than anything that had ever happened to him.

As the work progressed, the freshly sheared herds were sent out to summer in the particular patch of prairie allotted to them. Each herd contained about fifteen hundred head, plus their lambs, and was in the care of a herder and his dog. An extra man accompanied each herd, to drive the canvas-topped sheep wagon and help the herder set up his camp.

Meanwhile the near-bursting sacks of wool, seven feet high by three feet wide, piled up like cordwood.

There came a day which was hotter than the others, close and without a breath of wind. Toward midafternoon dark clouds came up in the north, and within a few minutes covered the sun. The men shivered; the sweat nearly froze on their bodies. About four o'clock it started to rain, not in drops, but splatters—huge, shapeless globules of freezing water driven by the wind. One of the shearers cursed, "One day too soon. We'd be finished tomorrow."

"No," Alma said. "Ten days too late. I wish all my sheep had their wool back on."

They corralled all the sheep still at the home ranch, both sheared and unsheared. The rain turned to sleet, and the sleet to snow, and the wind out of the north grew harder.

Jared's father kept an extra set of winter clothes at the lease. He put on a mackinaw coat and fur cap and mitts, and got on a horse.

"Where you going?" Siwash shouted.

"I think I can catch Angus. We might be able to get his herd back to camp."

"You'll never find him out there now. You take my advice, you'll stay home and say your prayers."

"I'll find him."

"Well, hold up a minute. I'm coming with you." And Siwash ran off toward the barn.

Alma stopped his horse beside his son. "You wait here."

Jared nodded. He was wearing only a light coat and summer cap; he was almost frozen.

"Stay inside," Alma told him. "They can't go anywhere. We'll just dig them out when it's over."

Soon Siwash rode up. "Okay, Al. Let's go." They turned their horses and galloped into the storm.

Jared felt imprisoned with the men who were left at camp. They were snug, away from the storm, but they paced uneasily, played cards with solemn desperation, ate without pleasure, and seemed continually to be either bundling up to go outside and look around, or taking off their things when they returned. That respite was denied Jared, since he had no warm clothes, so his forays outside were brief and infrequent. He woke several times during the night, and each time heard the snow as it sifted and howled around the corners of the bunkhouse.

The next morning the first man out crashed back into the bunkhouse, shouting, "The herd's gone!"

There was a rush for the door—a couple of the men went out in their shirt sleeves, but they couldn't have seen much through the dark and the storm. They were back inside in a moment, shivering, and throwing on sweaters and coats.

"Snow drifted over the fence. They walked out, right over the top."

"All of them?"

"Just about. 'Less they're froze or buried."

The men dressed, wrapped, and plunged out the door one

after another. "You stay here, kid. Keep the fire up—we're going to need it."

The door slammed after the last man, and Jared was left alone. Through the window he watched the grey figures move across the yard, growing paler and paler, until they disappeared or blended with the dim smudges of the stable and corral, painted out of existence by the cruel white strokes of the storm.

The inside of the bunkhouse seemed huge, and the old boards groaned and shifted in the wind.

All day Jared sat by the window. He didn't fix any meals, but each time he got hungry, ate a piece of bread and jam. Toward evening the wind seemed to abate, and then, suddenly, like the swirl of snow that rises behind a freight caboose, the last rush of the storm was left to hang in the air. The wind stopped, and tiny bits of crystal slowly sank to the earth through the wintry twilight.

The men had not returned by morning, but it was spring again. The sun came over the horizon warm and silent, smiling, as if to ask forgiveness for its neglect. But the earth could not respond; it lay motionless, staggered by the weight of snow that lay upon it.

The prairie was visible for miles, white and limitless. And as far as Jared could see, nothing moved.

Toward the middle of the morning the men returned with a flock of sheep. Three or four of them walked in front to break trail through the heavier drifts. Jared put on his coat and went out to meet them. The men were sweating from the heat and the effort—they had their coats open, mitts off, earflaps up. One had his shirt sleeves rolled up and was slapping at the sheep with his coat to force them through the snow. The herd looked terribly small.

"Where are the rest?" Jared asked.

"Dead," said one of the men.

Jared noticed that almost all the survivors were unsheared, still protected by their year-long growth of wool. "Froze dead?"

"And smothered dead. They hit a coulee and piled up."

It was like a funeral march back to the corral. There, in

places where the wind had swept the ground almost bare, Jared could see a few dead lambs scattered; their wrinkled bodies glistened with tiny drops of melted snow. But most of the dead sheep were covered with drifts, where they had crowded to avoid the force of the wind. After they'd had some breakfast, the men got out shovels and began to dig. Many of the animals were completely buried; a few of those on top had managed to keep the tips of their noses above the snow and some of these were still alive. But nearly all the freshly sheared sheep were dead, and the lambs, except for a few of the older, hardier ones.

As soon as the men had dug out the sheep that had a chance of living, two of them got on saddle horses, took some food, and went to look for Alma and Siwash. Three others started skinning the unsheared carcasses. The rest continued to clean up. They hitched a team of horses to a stoneboat made from an old steer hide and piled on it the bodies of sheep and lambs. This they hauled across the prairie, the steer hide rippling over the sow, and men walking on either side to hold the slippery, jiggling bodies. At the edge of a coulee about a quarter of a mile east of camp, the man driving the team stopped, and then turned them so sharply that the front of the stoneboat curled upside down, dumping its burden as it slid back over the top of them. On the drive back, the teamster rode standing up on the skid. He invited Jared to join him. The boy tried to step onto the moving steer hide, but it just pulled his foot out from under him and he rolled in the snow. The men laughed, but the teamster held a hand back to him. "Run and jump on with both feet." He ran and jumped, grasping the man's hand, and was slightly surprised to find himself skimming effortlessly over the ground. The roll of the snow beneath him made it difficult to keep his footing, but he took a firm hold on the man's belt and rode without trouble back to camp. They kept on the same track going and coming, so as to smooth the trail for future loads.

All day the men worked, loading the stoneboat, taking turns walking it to the dump, and then riding it back. The track in the snow was soon worn smooth and flat. By early afternoon the drifts were melting swiftly, and seemed to float on a shallow skim of water between the snow and the earth.

The melting snow gradually revealed the mounting horror in the corral—the piles of bodies, frozen or smothered, young and old, sheared and unsheared. The men seemed to move more and more slowly, as if the contagion of the sheep was slowly infecting them. At last darkness intervened, and they unhitched the horses and dragged themselves wearily into the bunkhouse.

"Did anybody count 'em?"

"I figure about three hundred hauled today, and we ain't even made a dint in 'em."

"We ought to leave the sheep and move the buildings. It'd be a sight easier."

The snow melted quickly. The work of hauling the dead sheep continued, and one day followed another with numbing monotony. Angus arrived in camp with the remainder of his sheep, and presently some of the other herds began to come straggling back like defeated armies: silent, wooden, made doubly grotesque by the peaceful meadows through which they moved and the warm spring sun above.

One afternoon several dark figures appeared on the south-east horizon, so far away that it was hard to tell at first what they were.

"Here they come," one of the men said.

Their progress seemed interminable. Eventually they came close enough to see that it was a group of men, some mounted, some walking. They kept moving in front of each other, and overlapping, and then spreading out, until it was difficult to tell how many there were, let alone who they were.

"I don't see Al," someone said.

"He's there," another replied. "Just riding behind the others."

"I never see Al ride behind anybody."

But this troop traveled in listless disregard for order or rank or haste. As they drew near, the men watching them fell silent. Alma was there, all right, leading his horse, which carried one of the herders bent low over the saddle horn. They stopped in front of the corral, and Alma helped the man down. "Take him inside," he instructed. "Put him to bed. He'll be all right."

The men followed Alma and Siwash to the stable, where they tended their horses.

"We even lost the home herd, Al. The first night the snow piled up, and they drifted over the fence."

Alma was currying and brushing his horse's matted coat. He appeared not to have heard.

Presently another said, "How many did we lose, Al?"

"Just one." Alma's voice was distant, weary, numb.

The men looked at each other.

"Fin," Siwash explained. "We couldn't find him."

"Old Fin?"

"We found his herd scattered over three townships. His dog was lookin' for Fin, just like we were. When his dog can't find him, mister, he's lost."

"You found his wagon?"

"His wagon was there, miles from the herd. Only thing missing was Fin."

"What could've happened? It wasn't cold enough to freeze him—not after some of the winters he's put in."

One of the herders said, "I think Fin's on the bottom of the pile in one of those gullies."

"How'd he get there?"

"It could happen, I found that out. When my herd went with the storm, all I could do was stay with 'em. I couldn't see the end of my nose. They must have drifted fifteen miles—them that didn't drop off and die along the way. In the middle of the night they hit a hollow, and the leaders stopped to huddle there in that bit of shelter. The rest just kept comin' right over top of 'em, and stopped on the lea-side, and more piled over them, till there was the goldangdest tangle you ever saw.

"I was tearin' at the pile, tryin' to drag the sheep from underneath, but even when I did it they'd just crowd back up against the pack and get theirselves buried again. Once I slipped and fell under one sheep, and before I could get free, another landed on me, and another—that herd was rollin' just like lava out of a volcano. I scrambled out somehow, and after that I stayed clear. I reckon Fin wasn't as lucky as me, is all."

"Where's Fin's dog?"

"Still out there. She wouldn't leave."

Later, when they sat down to supper, Alma said, "Looks like we lost over half the ewes. Nearly all the lambs. I'm going to have to let some of you go."

"We know that already, Al," one of the men said.

"You can ride back to town with Jared. I'll give you your summer's pay."

"It hit you harder'n anybody, Al—'cept Fin. We'll make out."

"No. I want to pay you. Herder jobs'll be scarcer than hen's teeth after this."

"I don't want no other job, anyway," Angus said. "Is it all right if I just stay still here at the lease with Siwash? Odd-job for my board?"

Alma looked at Siwash. The old man shrugged. "I don't mind. I don't need no help, but if you want to feed 'im, I don't mind sweepin' around 'im."

The next morning, though, Angus filled a sack with food and slung a roll of blankets from his shoulder. "I keep thinkin' about old Fin," he said. "I ain't got nothin' else to do all summer long—I guess I'll see if I can find him."

He took a small shovel from behind the bunkhouse door, and started off, his roll of blankets bumping on his hip, the spade over his shoulder like a flag. His dog trotted beside him.

After they finished shearing, Alma and Siwash were gone for three or four days, checking on the shrunken herds. Other men brought in sheep wagons that had been deserted after the consolidation of the herds. The air of solemnity at the camp was unrelieved. The same night that Alma and Siwash came back, Angus also returned. He had two dogs with him.

"You find him?"

Angus nodded. "His dog did. I found her sittin' there waitin' for him to move. But he was just like Charlie said, half covered over in a pyramid of dead sheep."

**13** Jared drove home in the democrat loaded with out-of-work herders. Alma stayed behind, and didn't follow until mid-August. When he finally did return from the lease he seemed a stranger on two counts: one, that he had been away so long; and two, that he had changed—grown old in a single season. After supper he went out to sit in his rocking chair on the porch.

Jared and some of the other children joined in a game on the lawn, dodging out and in among the aspen trees. Even at that distance they could hear the creek, its voice among the stones seeming louder at low water than it had during the full rush of spring. For several moments one stretch of water was the color of flame, the same color as the sky.

Into this mystic, twilight land of children marched Rachel, the big sister, who stridently ordered everyone inside the house. Gradually the children detached themselves, almost as though haste would be fatal and they must spend time preparing their spirits to reenter the adult world. As she came along behind the stragglers Rachel paused on the porch, where Alma still gently rocked.

"Can you come in for a few minutes, Papa?" she said.

"Just as soon as I get the sun down."

"We'll be in the parlor."

The parlor was almost square, with one wall open to the dining room. On the other side a brick fireplace rose like a throne. The furnishings consisted of an old leather couch, two armchairs, a day bed, a rug and a large fern stand in front of the window. At that time of evening the room appeared to be colored completely in different tones of brown. Only the fern, catching the last light of day that fell through the window, seemed to have any color of its own.

"Everybody in the parlor!" Rachel called.

Still, people assembled themselves slowly.

"What's it all about?" Jane asked. She was twelve then. She sat curled on the floor beside the cold fireplace, running ribbons of her hair between the fingers of one hand.

"Haven't you heard?" asked Stanley, a man now, tall and

slim-faced, with his nose hanging like a blob of candle wax ready to drop from the bridge of his spectacles. He stood behind the couch, leaning his back against the wall. "Rachel has a plan to take over the world."

"Oh, be quiet, Stanley," Rachel said crossly. "Lyman, would you bring some chairs from the kitchen?"

Lyman had just come into the room. He looked about him. He was a handsome young man, strongly built, with his father's heavy brows and lashes. "It's not going to take that long, is it?"

In reply, Rachel went herself and brought a couple of chairs from the kitchen. Bessie immediately sat on one of them, but Rachel chided her and moved her to one of the armchairs, and during the evening the straight, hard kitchen chairs sat on the fringes of the family circle, empty and neglected.

Belle, dark and beautiful, though still only a girl, stretched out on the sofa in a Cleopatra pose, slowly undulating her body with the quiet movement of some imaginary Nile.

"Belle!" her mother said. "Please try to be a lady."

Rachel brought a match and lit the coal-oil lamp that stood on the table. The soft light infused the room slowly, gradually, as if it were made from tiny bright particles that turned and dipped like grains of sand suspended in quiet water.

The glow seemed to concentrate itself upon the faces around the room, eight of them now: Bessie in the armchair, Jane on the floor by the fireplace, Lyman on the couch beside Belle, Grace and Jared sitting on the day bed, and Stanley leaning against the wall. Rachel had taken her place at the end of the fireplace opposite Jane, and stood there waiting.

There was a hush, one final twist and mutter from Lyman and Belle on the couch, then silence.

The door opened and Alma Roseman started through, then stopped. "Well," he said. "What have we here?"

"Come in, Papa," Rachel said. "We're waiting for you."

He closed the door behind him. "This looks ominous."

"It isn't, really."

He touched the empty armchair. "Is this for me?"

"We're saving it for you."

He sat down rather stiffly.

Rachel cleared her throat, in the tone she probably used in the classroom every morning. Her graduation from normal school had established her as a sort of oracle in the town, and particularly among her own family. She took out her wire-rimmed spectacles and placed them delicately on her nose. "Now, all of you children listen. We want you to sign this." She opened the sheet of paper in her hand and began to read:

"Petition Cardston, Alberta, August seventh, nineteen hundred and eight.
"Regarding Alma Roseman, our beloved husband and father."

"Sounds like a gravestone," Alma said.
Rachel tossed her head nervously and glanced at him, but did not reply.

"To whom each of us owes his life, his home, his habiliment, and the very bread he eats."

"What is habili—whatever it is?" Jane asked.
"Hush," Bessie said.
"It's your clothes," Rachel explained. She returned to her reading. ". . . the very bread he eats."
"Then why don't you say clothes?" Jane wanted to know.
Rachel sighed. "This is a formal petition. You don't use the same kinds of words as you would in a letter. If you were to meet the Queen, you wouldn't talk like you do every day, would you?" Rachel studied her paper for a moment, then continued:

"We respectfully address this humble adjuration. To wit:
"Whereas Alma Roseman, the revered master of our house, has now been absent from us for more than two months, and
"Whereas we have good reason to suppose that during this time he has escaped the diverse perils that beset him only by the merciful grace of the one great Father who rules us all (and we declare our thanks for this deliverance) and
"Whereas this house is desolate without him; this house and this wife and these children feel keenly each day that absence, as if it were a wound, and
"Whereas the calamities of past months, whether or not they be of God, have still inflicted upon one Alma Roseman a devastating toll . . .

"Now, therefore, we beseech and implore and supplicate our revered and honored husband and father that he quit his lease, sell his remaining sheep, and enter a new line of business which will permit him to be home with us each evening.

"Respectfully submitted,

"Signed."

Rachel took a pen from the table, dipped it in the inkwell, and handed it with the paper to her mother. Solemnly Bessie took the document and signed. Then Rachel bent over the table and signed beneath her mother's name. She turned. "Stanley, and then the rest of you, oldest by oldest."

Stanley, Grace, Lyman, Belle, all came forward and signed in order.

"Jared," Rachel said.

Jared still sat on the day bed, all alone now. "I don't understand it."

"Of course you understand it. It's perfectly simple."

"I think it says that he has to sell his sheep."

"He doesn't have to. This is only a suggestion."

Bessie added, "Then he can stay home. You know how anxious you've been for him to come home. You almost wore the road out staring down it."

"I won't sign it," Jared said.

"You want him to be gone all winter, like he was gone all summer? Is that what you want?"

"I won't sign it."

"He doesn't have to sign it," Stanley said. "That doesn't make any difference."

Rachel hesitated. "Very well. Come then, Jane. You're the last one." Jane rose, walked to the table, and signed her name at the bottom of the list.

Rachel put the lid back on the inkwell, raised the document, and blew on the ink to be sure it was dry. "There you are, Papa." She handed it to him. "A petition from your family."

Alma took the paper, but let it fall to his lap without looking at it. He coughed. "Yes, well, thank you." He looked around at the room, his eyes hovering, not touching the faces he saw.

Rachel, still standing at one end of the fireplace, began to fidget. "Aren't you going to say anything, Papa?"

"What is there to say?"

"Do you like the idea?"

"I don't know. I would have to think about it."

"Arn Cooper wants to go back to Utah," Bessie said. "Maybe you could buy his dry-goods store."

"That is quiet, dignified work," Rachel said. "You would have your hours to work each day, and on Wednesday afternoon you could go fishing."

"The children could help you," Bessie went on. "It would be a good chance to teach them responsibility."

"And you'd be home every night. Doesn't that mean anything to you?"

Alma did not reply, or look at them.

Lyman said, "I was wondering about the freight line to Lethbridge. Everybody complains about it. If we got some good wagons and mules, and gave people dependable service . . ."

"Your father wouldn't set out to ruin Bernard," Bessie said.

"Buy him out," Lyman replied.

"That won't do," Rachel said. "Papa would still be out in the weather all day and night, and always away from home."

"Besides, the railroad's coming," Stanley said. "Then you'd have nothing."

Lyman said, "From what I hear, that railroad is a long way down the track."

"How about a grocery store?" Belle suggested. "Or a butcher shop?"

"We don't want a little corner store." Rachel sniffed.

"We could buy some land," Lyman said. "They're talking about new land at Belly River—new towns. We could start farming."

"That would give the boys something to do," Bessie said.

"I don't want to be a farmer's daughter," Belle protested.

"You're an intelligent man," Rachel told her father. "You can be anything you want to be."

Alma rose from his chair, the petition in his hand. "Can I? Even a sheepman?" He turned and walked wearily to the door. They heard his footsteps mounting the stairs to his bedroom.

**14** Whether Alma had acted on the urgings of the petition, or out of necessity, Jared didn't know. Anyway, he had come to Lone Rock to start farming, and built this humble cottage.

Grace came in from the kitchen. "You're a quiet one."

He roused himself. "Just thinking."

"Remember this?" Grace held a photograph toward him—a sepia-tone print of Lula Fae. "I found it in Daddy's drawer when I was putting away his clothes."

The photograph showed a middle-aged woman sitting stiffly for the camera, a startled expression in her eyes.

"I never saw it before," Jared said.

"I remember seeing it when I was a child."

As Jared held it up, Grace noticed something written on the back. She took it from him and read, "Your loving wife, Lula Fae." Grace thoughtfully touched her finger to her lips. "That's the answer, don't you see. Daddy's gone to Utah." She said it wisely, as if she had special knowledge.

"He couldn't start out for Utah. No money, no clothes."

"That wouldn't stop him. Not if he made up his mind."

"Maybe not."

"He hadn't seen Mother for years. You remember the birthday telegram—it must have been from her. Maybe he thought with a new horse he could really do it. He'd never have another chance."

Jared nodded. "Maybe. That would explain why he'd try to throw our trail. He knew we wouldn't let him go." He rose from the couch. "Will you fix me a lunch?"

"Where you going?"

"I think I'll check the road to Utah."

"You're as silly as Daddy," she said. "You can't start out on a trip like that without clothes or money, either."

"I'll take some clothes, and I can get money." He got a horse from the pasture, tied his grub bag and bedroll to the saddle, waved good-bye to Grace, and left the Roseman gate.

As he rode up to Rachel's house in Cardston, Bessie and

Rachel and Jane came out on the porch. "Any word?" Bessie called.

Jared shook his head. "Did Lyman come?"

Rachel answered, "He was here just long enough to get a bite. Then he went to see if he could find Tom and the others."

"Are you going, too?" Bessie asked.

"They're probably on their way home. It'll be dark soon." Jared rode on to the barn and tended the horse. Back in the kitchen, he found the ladies had dished his supper. He took his chair and began to eat.

"Something terrible has happened," said Bessie. "I know it."

"Siwash doesn't think so," Jared told her.

"What does that old savage know?"

"He says father disappeared deliberately. Otherwise, we could have tracked him."

"That's ridiculous. Why would your father want to disappear?"

"I don't know. But right now it's about the only idea that makes any sense."

"How does it make sense?" Rachel asked.

Jared replied, "Just suppose, for example, that he decided to go to Utah."

"Utah?" Bessie asked.

"Then he'd have to go on the sly," Jared continued. "He'd know we wouldn't let him."

"If he wanted to go to Utah, he'd go on the train," said Bessie in a voice that sounded as if it were meant to close the matter.

But Jane said, "He wanted to go on the train last year. Remember?"

"He mentioned it, that's all."

"You said he was too old."

"If he'd wanted to go, he would have gone."

It was late when they heard the sound of horses approaching. "There they are," Bessie said, and led the way onto the porch and down the front walk.

In the darkness they could see them—twenty or thirty mounted men, riding down the creek road out of the mountains. Horses plodded with drooping heads; men sat deep in the saddle, shoulders bent. Lyman drew up in front of the gate, and the others rode close behind him and stopped. One horse lowered his head with a weary snort and rattled his bit.

"Nothing," said Lyman to his mother.

"I knew it," she whispered.

"We combed those hills. If there'd been a nickel lying in the grass, we'd have found it."

Tom nudged his horse to the inner circle, close beside Lyman's. "He just disappeared."

There was silence, except for the incessant shift and jangle of horses, bridles, spurs. A voice said, "You want to go again tomorrow, Tom?"

Tom looked at Lyman. "What do you think?"

"I guess you better come if you can," Lyman told the group.

The horsemen moved on, Tom and Lyman toward the barn and the others into town. The figures quickly faded into the darkness, but their quiet, voiceless sound remained, diminishing slowly.

A few minutes later, when Rachel served Tom and Lyman a warmed-over supper, they began to eat carefully, as if the scrape of a fork was taboo. The kitchen took on a solemn, midnight air. From its place on the wall the clock ticked steadily; it alone seemed left to carry the weight of the hour.

**15** The next morning Jared made final preparations for his trip, waved good-bye, and rode to the bank. The teller was Hugh Coffee, an old friend of Alma's.

"I'd like to draw out my money," Jared said.

"Just one moment." Hugh checked in a large book he had on the counter. "Yes. You have a hundred and fifty-seven dollars and thirty cents. How much would you like?"

"All of it."

Hugh smiled. "I guess this means you have your mission call?" He began to prepare a withdrawal slip, forming each letter with elaborate care. "I remember when I got my call. To the German Mission, it was. I guess I was even younger than you. I looked at that letter signed by John Taylor himself— the President of the Church, the Prophet of God. Makes you think, doesn't it?"

Jared didn't reply.

"Those were the greatest two years of my life, as they say—teaching the gospel every day."

Jared remembered a day years before when his father led him into a field in late summer. As they walked among the waving grain it stood level with his eyes. Alma plucked a head of wheat, rolled it between his palms, poured it from hand to hand and back as he blew away the chaff, and then ate what remained, his teeth crackling against the hard kernels. "It's about ready to cut."

Jared tried to imitate his father, but his hands were too small and soft to roll the wheat very well, and he could not seem to get rid of the chaff.

"This is young country, Jared. You go together, you and the country. You belong here." Alma plucked another stem from the field and held it for Jared to see. "Can you make a head of wheat?"

"What do you mean?" the boy asked.

"Can you take some starch and sugar and paste from the grocery store and make a head of wheat?"

"No."

"Can any man?"

"I don't think so."

"Of course he can't." He turned the stem of wheat so it twirled in his fingers. "This is the hand of God. Now, how did the wheat come to be here in the field?"

"You planted it."

"That's right. It was planted by the hand of man." Alma held up Jared's palm, small but having almost lost its boyish plumpness. "This is the hand of man. Without the hand of God, there would be no seed, and without the hand of man, there would be no harvest. Do you understand?"

"I think so."

"It means that even God needs men to accomplish his work.

He needs you, Jared. You've been baptized. In a few years you'll receive the priesthood. When you're old enough, I want you to go on a mission."

"I will," Jared said.

Hugh Coffee, still working on the deposit slip, asked, "Where are you going on your mission?"

"I'm not."

The teller looked up at him. "I don't understand."

"I don't have a mission call."

"But that's what you've been saving your money for—to go on a mission."

"I need the money now," Jared said.

Hugh quit writing, a little reluctantly it seemed, like an artist being torn away from his easel. "Have they found your father?"

"No."

Hugh held the pen poised. "I don't know. I really should have your father's signature."

"It's not his money."

"Are you twenty-one yet, Jared?"

"Not until next spring."

"If you are going on a mission, I certainly wouldn't hesitate, but ... What are you planning to do with the money?"

"I'm going to look for Father."

"Oh? Where, that you need all this money?"

"I think he may have gone to Utah."

"Ah." Hugh nodded. He released his hand, and the pen continued its interrupted course across the paper, lingering over ornamental scrolls and flourishes. "It's really very strange. I only heard about it yesterday." He passed the slip to Jared. "Now I need your signature."

Jared wrote his name on the bottom line of the slip. Placed so close to Hugh's penmanship, his own looked crude and even childish.

Hugh counted the money into his hand. "I hope you'll be successful."

With his money in his pocket and his bedroll tied to the saddle, Jared started out of town on the road south.

*       *       *

85

By suppertime he was well into Montana. He should have stopped—he had a long trip ahead of him—but still he went on. The sun set. Darkness rose from the earth like smoke, obliterating any features of the land, and soon he rode through unremitting night.

Perhaps he should have said good-bye to Paula before he left Lone Rock. But he no longer knew what his relationship with Paula was, whether she liked him, or even if he liked her—ever since that day in the blacksmith shop.

A gentle rain had been falling all week. It was as if the sky had overflowed, flooding the hollows of the earth with its color—the streets of the village, the ditches, the pastures at the edge of town, all matte-white, like molten mother-of-pearl. Frosted silhouettes of houses and young trees floated eerily in this pale sea. Riding his horse along the grassy roadside, Jared hadn't minded the cold rain soaking through his coat.

At Gibson's blacksmith shop he bent low over the saddle horn and rode in through the wide doors. His horse's hooves rang hollowly against the plank floor. Jared got down, took off his hat, and shook the rain from its brim. He could feel the warmth of the forge.

There were several men inside the blacksmith shop, driven there by the weather. On good days most of them would have been busy in the field. Now they stood with hands outstretched to the forge, or leaned against the bench and watched the rain.

Thor Gibson moved back and forth between the forge and the anvil. He turned quickly, like a bear, with a sort of twist, as though his hips were set too far apart. In one hand he carried the tongs which plucked the iron from the fire, with the other, he turned the forge and swung the hammer.

"Crazy rain," a man said. "Why couldn't it come in June, when it would do some good?"

"You'll be happy enough for it, come spring."

"The Kaiser done it," another replied. "He's turned the whole world upside down."

"We'll take care of the Kaiser. I only wish gettin' a decent crop was half as easy."

Jared reached down and tapped his horse's right front foot

and raised it to check the shoe. "You got time to tighten a loose shoe?" he asked Thor.

"If you ain't in a hurry."

Jared dropped the horse's foot and straightened. "I can wait." He moved closer to the forge.

The talk inside the shop continued, listless, intermittent, inconsequential, having to do with crops and weather, neighbors and the war, with occasional efforts at homespun humor.

". . . him and his wife opened a restaurant in Macleod, but within six months she'd folded."

"Ha, ha. She 'foalded' once a year, restaurant or not."

Jared's horse stood with head down, its wet body steaming in the warmth of the shop. Presently Thor came over and began to take off the loose shoe. "This horse is ready for new shoes," he said, holding up the slender iron crescent.

"Can you just put it back on for today?" Jared said. "It'll be okay as long as the ground is soft."

Thor picked up his hammer and nails, and began to replace the shoe. The hammer clicked firmly on the horseshoe nail.

The men watched Thor file the horse's hoof, fitting it to the shoe. It was as if he needed all their concentration to do the job properly. When he finished, he lifted each of the horse's other feet, checking the shoes. "Well," he said to Jared. "That should last you till you get to the post office. You stay in really soft mud, you might even get home."

"Thanks," Jared said.

Somebody asked, "Thor, you goin' to let Jared marry your daughter?"

"Haven't you heard?" another said. "Lyman took her away from him."

"Big brother?"

"Them London duds just dazzled her."

"I didn't know that."

The words fell on Jared like blows. What a fool he'd been not to see it, or seeing it, not to admit it. He felt both feverish and stupid. He would have left the shop then, but he didn't want the men to think their joshing had driven him away.

"Never mind, Jared," another said. "You're better off. Can you imagine old Thor for a daddy-in-law?"

"What you talkin' about? Thor's got a heart of gold."

"Hard as gold, maybe. It's made of old ball bearings."

"You was settin' pretty till Lyman came home," another told Jared. "You had the farm and the gal. Now what you got?"

The men laughed.

"I guess I'll go to war," a voice said. It was the Taylor boy, over by the window, drawing designs with his finger on the steaming glass. His words floated down, neglected.

Jared should have known she was only playing with him. But he couldn't face the thought of it then, and even now, two years later, he teased himself with the idea that maybe she loved him. It was just as well he was going to Utah.

At last he stopped in some remote Montana meadow and made his camp.

It was a long journey. In the days that followed, his progress forward was also a journey backward into the past. He remembered the last time he had traveled this road, coming north with his father.

One evening after supper he had sat across the fire from his father, waiting for the word to unroll his blankets and go to sleep.

They heard voices out of the darkness to the north, the creak of a wagon and the soft thud of hooves on the road. For several moments they listened to the sounds growing louder; then his father rose and walked toward them. "Hallo!" he called.

"Whoa!" The wagon stopped abruptly. "Who's there?" a voice asked.

"It's beddin' time," his father said. "Come on. The fire's waiting."

The wagon moved forward. Jared ran and stood beside his father, watching the outfit slowly take form as it moved out of the darkness toward them. It was a four-horse team and a covered wagon. "I'm glad to hear a voice," the man said as he stopped his team again, this time close beside them. "I was feeling as if we were the only mortals left." He climbed over the wheel and walked toward Jared and his father. "Mister,

I've been following your fire for an hour, hoping that was the creek."

Jared's father said, "Henry, is that you?"

The man stepped closer. "How'd you know my name?"

"I know your voice. I know everything about you, Henry Cross."

"Who's that?" He looked still closer. "Why, sure it is. Al Roseman, I'll be go to hill."

The two men embraced.

"Cora!" Henry called. "Look who's here. It's Alma."

A woman came forward out of the back of the wagon. "Al," she cried and tumbled down into his arms.

"You know Cora!" Henry exclaimed. "Always scared we'll meet bandits, or Indians, or something worse."

"And sure 'nough you did," Alma said.

"Sure 'nough we did."

There were some children who also got out of the wagon. Alma greeted them all by name.

"Come on," Alma said. "Let's get this team unhitched and put some supper on. You must be starved."

"Cora wanted to stop," Henry said. "But I kept telling her the creek was just another mile or so."

Cora laughed. "That started ten miles up the road."

Henry put his hand on Jared's shoulder. "So this is the young 'un."

"This is Jared," Alma said.

"He looks all right."

As soon as the horses were tended they all gathered around the fire. Alma and Cora prepared the meal while they talked.

"I don't understand," Alma said. "Where you folks headed, anyway?"

For the first time the warmth of their meeting chilled. Jared sensed a hesitation.

"Back to Utah," Henry said.

"Back to Utah? To stay?"

"To stay. I've learned my lesson. I'm never going to leave again."

For a long time Alma looked into the fire. "I don't know what to say. I sure didn't expect it."

"We didn't expect it," Henry said. "Just one day it had been raining for a week. You couldn't step outside the house without sinking to your knees in mud. When the sun finally came out the wind started blowing a hurricane. The baby was sick again. Cora was complaining that the kids were driving her crazy—they couldn't go outside to play. I told her that the ground would be dry in a day or two. 'A day or two!' she says. 'I can't wait a day or two. In a day or two it'll start to snow. Don't you know this is the summer? This is supposed to be the good season, and it's almost over!' You know, Al, I suddenly realized what was happening. We came to Canada to get rich, you and I. Remember? We were going to be land barons, or something. We'd have something to leave our kids. And what have we got? Drowned out in the spring, dried out in the summer, or froze out in the fall. And I said to Cora, 'Remember the springtime in Utah—the orchards all in blossom? And those beautiful still, hot summer days?' "

Cora went on, "So suddenly I said, without even thinking, 'What are we doing here, anyway?' "

"And I said, 'I don't know. Let's go back to Utah.' "

"But your ranch," Alma said. "Your cattle. What did you do with it all?"

"Sold everything. Land, cattle, machinery, furniture. Almost sold the clothes off our backs."

"I can't believe this, Henry."

"You've no idea what happens. It's like a fever. It's like getting religion. All at once you see there's only one thing to do, and you do it, and hang what it costs you."

"You should have waited for the fever to pass. You might have thought better of it."

"No, Al. I'm satisfied."

Supper was ready. The Cross family came forward with their plates, and then sat quietly around the fire to eat.

"You'll see," Henry said between bites. "One of these times it'll hit you, too."

Alma shook his head. "No. I'll never leave Canada."

"I felt the same way."

"You didn't feel like I do, Henry, or you'd still be there."

He sighed. "I hate to see you go."

"It wasn't easy, to think of leaving our friends."

"I hope things work out for you in Utah."

"We'll be all right. I never sold my land there, you know."

"That's right. I'd forgotten." Alma asked, "Did you see Bessie?"

"She waved us good-bye."

"I think we almost broke her heart," Cora said.

Alma nodded. "You haven't made it any easier for me, you know."

"I hope not," Henry said with a smile. "I hope Bessie puts a burr under your blanket till you come back, too."

"I'll just have to scratch it," Alma said. "I sold my land in Utah."

Now, riding that same long trail, Jared wondered if Alma had decided to follow the Crosses back to Utah, after all.

# SMITHFIELD, UTAH
# EARLY AUGUST, 1915

# 1

Crossing Idaho it seemed to Jared that for hours at a time he scarcely moved; that his horse was like a trapped beetle, working his legs but moving only the sand beneath him, never himself. It took more than two weeks to reach Smithfield. As he approached, the silhouette of the town seemed vaguely familiar, like a long-forgotten postcard one finds in a bottom drawer. Closer, it was like a mist around him, in which he sensed echoes from his childhood.

He was able to find the Roseman house, but when he stopped his horse at the gate he did not feel the sense of recognition that he had expected. The house was right as to his recollection of it; nothing had changed, really. The trees were bigger, perhaps. The rope swing hanging from one of the high branches seemed familiar, and even more so, the dusty hollow in the grass beneath it. But it was the home of a stranger.

He got down from the saddle and entered the gate. Backing between the weathered grey ropes of the swing, he took one in each hand and lowered himself onto the board. Idly he pushed at the ground. The ropes were so long that the board scarcely seemed to arc at all, only moved straight back and forth, like a shuttle. He had been sitting here, gently moving back and forth in just this way, that time when he was seven years old and looked up to see the tall man standing by the fence with a valise in his hand.

The huge yellow leaves drifted down into the yard from the cottonwood trees. His father's eyes looked grey, colorless, almost transparent, yet deep, like clear water where sunlight never reaches the bottom. "Seven years old," he said. "You're getting to be a big boy."

His mother had not been feeling well, and during the several days of his father's visit she remained in her room most of the time.

One morning when he, came downstairs dressed for school he found his mother in her kimono, preparing breakfast. He took his place at the kitchen table with his father. Though they spoke back and forth at intervals, the meal was strangely silent. Presently his mother said, "It's a beautiful day, any-way."

And his father replied, "Yes, it is."

Jared pushed back his chair. "I'd better go to school."

"No," his mother said quickly, reaching for his arm. She paused. "Not today," she added. "I want you to stay home today."

After the meal was over, and without even clearing up the dishes, his mother went upstairs, and a few moments later his father followed her. Jared was left alone in the kitchen. He could hear his parents moving around above him. He began to play with the salt and pepper shakers. He had seen his father balance the salt shaker on the rim of a drinking glass, but when he tried it the shaker always fell down into the glass.

At length he heard their footsteps on the stairs. From where he sat he could look down the dark hallway and see them arrive in the vestibule, two haloed shadows against the light which streamed through the curtained glass of the front door. His father was carrying his suitcase.

"Come here, Jared," his mother said. He walked toward them. She took him upstairs and gave him some new clothes to put on. It seemed strange—one never wore new clothes until Sunday. But today was not like other days, and he did as he was asked. While he dressed she packed his things in a valise, then took his hand and walked with him down the stairs. It had always pleased him to live in a big house, though it was puzzling why only two people should need so many rooms.

His mother put the valise in his hand. "There you are, just like Papa." The little grey grip was heavy, but he tried to pretend he could carry it easily. He didn't want his parents to think there was anything wrong.

Some of his uncles and aunts and cousins began to gather at the house. The occasion began to take on the look of a funeral, but he had not heard of any deaths in the family. Besides, the atmosphere was not really sad—Uncle Clyde was laughing as if it were a party. "Well, well, Jared." He always rubbed Jared's head with his hand as if he were trying to scrape the hair off. "So you're leaving us . . ."

Jared went out in the yard and sat on the swing, dragging

his toe in the dust. The tree grew close enough to the edge of the yard so that by climbing on the fence he could reach the lowest branches. He had done it many times before, and he did it now. The soles of the new shoes were slippery, but he managed to thrust the edges into the rough bark of the tree and raise himself to the first branch. Above that the branches were frequent enough so he could scramble from one to the other quite easily. He tried to be careful not to snag his new trousers. Before long he realized that he was higher than he had ever climbed before; still he kept on. He noticed the trunk of the tree becoming smaller, and the branches more and more slender, but he did not pause.

Suddenly he felt a vague dizziness. He became aware that the top of the tree was moving, swaying gently, either from his weight or from the wind. For the first time he glanced down, and quickly slid onto a branch, with his legs and arms wrapped around the tree trunk. The ground was like a distant country, far below him.

"HeavenlyFatherblessmehelpmetobeagoodboy." That clot of words was a touchstone, to which he turned in any situation of difficulty or alarm.

As his fright passed, he began to look about him with interest. He could see down on the roof of the house, and was amazed at the expanse of that massive shelter, which all his life had kept him from the storms without his even being aware of it. The leaves were gone from the cottonwoods now. He could see them far beneath him, scattered on the lawn like pirate treasure. The dooryard was like a toy, and his mother, when she came out on the front porch, was a doll who played there.

"Jared!" she called. She looked around the yard. "Now where could he have gone?" she said and returned into the house.

He saw his uncle's rig drive smartly down the road and stop in front of the gate. His uncle hurried up the path. "Time to go!" he called.

His father and mother and some of the others hurried out onto the porch, and stopped, looking this way and that, and then continued down into the yard. From the top of the tree they looked like round little toys floating about as if the grass were water. From inside the house there were the sounds of footsteps hurrying up and down the stairs, and voices calling, "Jared!"

"What can have happened to him?" his mother said.

"I'll check the shed," said one of the aunts.

"You're sure he isn't in the house somewhere?" his father said.

"I checked everywhere," his mother replied.

"Jared!" his father shouted toward the south, and then, facing north, he called again, "Jared!"

They all floated together like a cluster of toy ducks, and then apart again, turning their heads this way and that.

Other friends began to gather, and disperse, calling and looking, which sent an ever-widening ripple of concern through the neighborhood. From the top of the tree, the yard and street appeared to be alive with men and women and even children hurrying back and forth, talking loudly to each other or simply calling, "Jared!"

Jared began to feel important, and perhaps a little bit bold. When the treetop swayed again, he leaned with it, causing it to sway further, then back again, further still. It was frightening, but it seemed appropriate for him to contribute something to the atmosphere of anxiety and motion. The world beneath him tipped and floated, and he wondered if he was going to be sick, but he quickly fastened his mind on other things.

"There he is!" a childish voice shouted. "He's shaking the tree!"

Faces turned toward him like flowers greeting the sun.

"There he is!"

"Jared! What are you doing?"

"Come down at once!"

"You naughty boy!"

Everybody came running. His father stood directly under the tree, glaring up at Jared. "Come down, son," he said sternly.

Jared didn't really want to disobey, but he seemed to cling more and more tightly to the treetop.

"Do you hear me, Jared? Answer me, I say."

He could have answered, at least.

"If I have to come up there, you'll be sorry, young man."

His mother, too, had returned to the tree. "Don't you dare," she told his father. "You'd break your neck." She shaded her eyes with her hand as she looked up at him. "Please come down, Jerry."

Still he did not seem to be able to move.

"I'll get him down," his Uncle Ben declared. Uncle Ben was a young man, still in his twenties. He tipped back his head and shouted, "I'll count to three. If you haven't started down, I'm coming after you!" Jared liked Uncle Ben, but somehow his limbs had ceased to function. "One . . . Two . . . I'll come up, and if I do, you won't like it . . . Three!" Uncle Ben took off his coat and placed his hands on the tree. "Somebody give me a leg, till I can reach that branch . . ."

He watched Uncle Ben coming up the tree, and wondered what he would do when he got to the top. Would he pull Jared off and throw him down? He was climbing swiftly, almost eagerly, and looked up often as if to check and be sure the boy was still there. Jared's muscles tightened. He began to sway the treetop again back and forth, further and further.

Uncle Ben was close now, a smile of triumph on his face. He reached toward Jared's leg, and then suddenly he stopped as if he had been shot with an arrow. His reaching hand quietly moved back and grasped a branch of the tree. "Don't shake the tree," he whispered.

Jared didn't reply. He noticed that the tree swayed even better with Uncle Ben's weight so close to the top.

"Stop it!" Uncle Ben hissed. "Hold still!" He had glanced down once, and after that he fastened his eyes upward, on Jared. "Don't do that. You'll break it off!"

Jared leaned away from the tree trunk as far as he dared, and then back in close against it, to see if he could make it sway even further.

"O-o-oh," Uncle Ben muttered. He reached beneath him with one of his feet until he was sure it was firmly planted on a branch, then began to back down the tree as rapidly as he could, groping for the branches with his hands and feet and never taking his eyes off Jared. He reached the ground and walked quickly away.

Uncle Clyde thrust himself through the crowd. "Stand back!" he bellowed. "You bunch of grandmothers! Let a little kid buffalo you! What's this world coming to?" He had an ax in one hand, and waved the other to clear people away from the tree. "Stand back! That brat is coming down one way or the other, I promise you that." He swung the ax with both hands, so the head drove deep into the tree trunk. "One way or the other, he's coming down!"

"Stop that!" Jared's mother screamed. "You leave that tree alone." She grabbed Uncle Clyde from behind. He shook her off and continued chopping with great, wide rhythmic strokes.

"Please, Jerry!" his mother cried. "Please come down."

"Stand back!" Uncle Clyde commanded, swinging the ax more and more furiously. White chips flew in a storm.

"Stop him, Alma!" the boy's mother cried.

His father stepped out of the circle of people.

Clyde paused but held his stance, the ax handle gripped in his hands. "Stand back, Al. Less you want to get chopped." He began to swing the ax against the tree again, so rapidly that there was no opportunity for anyone to stop him.

Jared's mother screamed "Oh!" and ran sobbing up the steps and into the house.

"Mother!" Jared cried. "Mother!" He could hear her crying, even from inside the house. "It's all right, Mother. I'm coming!" Quickly he climbed down the tree and dropped from the lowest branch into his father's arms.

Uncle Clyde stood back. "What'd I tell you? You just got to show the little buggers who's boss."

"Mother!" Jared cried and ran toward the house.

His mother sat down on the stairway and drew him toward her, and the smell of talcum enveloped him more closely than did her arms. His face was pressed into the soft curve of her throat. He opened his eyes and found that he could see only darkness, except for a few tiny golden hairs at the edge of his vision where filtered sunlight struck the slope of his mother's shoulder.

"I'll write to you," she said. "Isn't it lucky you've learned to read and write? You can answer my letters, can't you?"

He felt something wet on his cheek, and pulled back, looking up at her. "What's the matter?" he said. "Please don't cry."

Suddenly she stood up, one hand over her mouth. "Oh!" she seemed to say, but it was more a cry than a real word. He saw her eyes, wide and staring, as if he had done something to displease her. Then she turned, hurried silently up the stairs, and closed the bedroom door behind her.

His father came in, picked up the large suitcase and opened the door. "We have to go," he said. Jared lifted his valise.

Outside, his father took him by the hand. People were waving to them as they walked down the path and passed between the giant cottonwoods that stood at the gate. Before they turned the corner Jared glanced back and saw her standing at the upstairs window. She waved, but he could not wave back because one hand held his valise and the other was gripped tight in his father's. Then the hedge came between them, and he continued on, hand in hand with his father.

Separated by a hedge, and then by a thousand miles, and finally by a dozen years, it had seemed that no reunion for Jared and his mother would ever be possible. Now he had found his way back across those miles—could he bridge the years as well?

Behind him he heard the front door of the brick house open. He turned in the swing to see a small, frail man approaching across the lawn. His voice was feathery and cracked. "Yes. Is there something I can do for you?"

Jared stood up. "I'm looking for Lula Fae Roseman."

"She lives here. Come on in."

As Jared followed the little man he heard another echo from the past—the hollow sound of his steps in the brick enclosure of the porch.

He stepped inside and closed the door. The hallway was dark except for a soft light coming down the open stairwell. The man looked at him with eyes that seemed to be unaware of the gloom, or at least unaffected by it.

"Are you a relative?"

"I'm Jared. I'm her son."

The man extended his hand. "How do you do? I am your Uncle Theodore—your mother's brother. If you will wait a moment, I'll tell her you're here." He walked up the stairs, and as he opened one of the doors that ringed the banister, soft light flooded the hallway. The door closed, and Jared was left standing in the shadows.

This was the house where he was born. He looked from door to door around the hallway, remembering which opened on the dining room and the parlor and the kitchen. Behind the kitchen door he heard a clock chime, and then he was conscious of its stately ticktock, like the heartbeat that kept the house alive.

What would his life have been like if he had never left, if all those intervening years he had been here, listening to the chimes of that clock? If that train had never come?

Countless times during his early boyhood Jared had sat on the bank near the railroad and watched the train, had marveled at its hugeness, its whistle, its smoke and steam, its impatient chuffs and clanging bell, and never dreamed that someday it would take him into its bowels and crawl away with him. For all his melancholy, he had not been able to deny his excitement as the train began to move and the houses of the town passed back beneath him, faster and faster.

"Go back!" He did not say it out loud, but inside him the words cried out over and over as the miles and hours passed. All the while his father sat beside him, hat squarely on his head like a Pilgrim, solemnly looking out the train window, or at his son, without speaking.

"Go back!" But as the miles between him and his mother accumulated, and he thought of having to retrace each one of them before he could see her again, his heart sank and he tried to think of nothing. He found that that, too, was not possible.

"Go back!" The voice inside him became fainter as they sped further and further away. It was not that his longing to return grew any less, only that the possibility became more remote.

At noon they ate the lunch which his mother had sent with them, and in the evening they finished what remained. He had explored the train, though there was little for him to see. Only one car was accessible to passengers, so by the time he had been ordered off the platforms fore and aft, checked the washroom, and staggered up and down the aisle a few times, he had exhausted the train's potential for diversion. The land they traveled through was flat and uninteresting. Occasionally, by sitting with his cheek against a sooty window, he could see the locomotive when the train went around a long curve.

They reached the end of the rail line sometime after dark, and took a room in a small hotel.

"That bed will feel good," his father said. "It's been a long day."

But when they had undressed and said their prayers, and his father blew out the lamp and got in beside him, the bed didn't feel good to Jared. All the accumulated fear and longing of the day seemed to gather inside him. His body almost trembled with hatred and despair. He knew it was wrong to hate the man who lay beside him, but he could not help himself.

Uncle Theodore opened the door above him, and again the light streamed down over the banister. "Yes. Will you come up, please? She wants to see you."

Jared climbed the stairs toward his mother's bedroom.

## 2

The room was bright—almost dazzling after the darkness of the hall. The sunlight through the large window reflected on the white walls, white curtains, white dresser, white bed. Lying on the bed, with her hair resting on a bank of pillows, was a plump, smiling woman, looking very much as he remembered her. Her arms rested beside her, almost as pale as the spread on which they lay.

"Jerry?"

"It's me, Mother."

"Come here." She held out her hand. "You've changed, you know."

He laughed briefly, and moved a couple of steps nearer. "You haven't changed."

She pushed at her hair with the hand that was not reaching for him. "Flatterer. You've grown up and I've grown old."

Her hair had turned white, but her skin was as smooth as that of a young woman. "Are you afraid of your own mother?"

He had glimpsed his dusty boots on the white carpet, as if they had been left there by mistake. He felt ashamed to be standing in them.

"Jerry." She still held her arm extended toward him. "Come here."

"I'm covered with dust."

"Come here."

He took her hand, and she drew him strongly toward her. He went down on his knees beside the bed. For a moment she held his face between her hands, then, impulsively, she cradled his head against her. His face rested in the soft curve of her neck, as sweet as the skin of a girl, and around him rose the mother-scent, like a vapor escaping after years sealed in a bottle. Suddenly the past came rushing in on him—the town, the streets, the gate, the swing, the porch, the hall, the stair, the clock. It all came back, not only to his mind, but to his heart; in his pith he could feel it.

"Jerry," she whispered. "My little boy." Her hand smoothed the back of his hair. Softly she began to sing,

"Baloo, my boy, lie still and sleep,
It grieves me sair to hear thee weep . . ."

She stopped there, and he waited for her to continue. He could remember every word, every note, just as she used to sing it when she sat on the bed beside him.

"Go on," he said.

For a moment she didn't reply. Then, "No, that's enough. You're too old now for lullabies."

When she raised his head to look at him, he got up from his knees and sat on the side of the bed. "You look fine," she said. "You look like your father."

He groped for something to say in return. "I always hoped you'd come to see us in Canada."

"I couldn't face it, Jerry. I'm a coward. It was hard enough thinking of Alma with a new wife. Somehow it got to be even worse thinking of you with a new mother."

"You were still his wife."

"Yes, for whatever that was worth."

Jared said, "I wrote to you, you know."

"Yes. I answered every letter. Even when you didn't write any more, I wrote to you."

"They didn't let me see your letters. I guess they burned them."

"Why would they do that?"

"I thought maybe you could tell me."

She shook her head. "What do you mean?"

"I found one of your letters to me a couple of weeks ago, one that hadn't been destroyed. It seemed to say that Father had done something terrible."

"Alma?"

"Is that why they burned the letters? They didn't want me to find out about it?"

"Jared. You mustn't talk this way."

"Have you seen Father, by the way?"

"He used to come every autumn, after harvest. But I haven't seen him for almost six years."

"He didn't come here?" Perhaps it was the long trip from Canada—somehow it seemed to Jared that by now the whole world must know. "He's lost."

"Your father?"

"It happened on his birthday. He started to ride home alone, and vanished. Nobody has seen him since." She did not reply at once. Her eyes seemed to look past Jared, or through him. "Do you know what might have happened?"

She looked down, and with her finger stroked a fold in her bedspread. "How would I know?"

"Somebody must know."

"For me he disappeared long ago." She raised her head. "Plump my pillow, will you?"

He didn't like to touch that pillow; it looked whiter than anything he had ever seen. Nevertheless he took it and awkwardly puffed it and put it down beneath her head again.

"Now you sit in that rocker there and talk to me. I want to learn what kind of man you are."

He backed up and sat in the rocker, rather stiffly.

She said, "Are you going on a mission?"

"I was."

"And now?"

"Now I don't know."

He didn't like the way she looked at him. It was as if his eyes were windows, and by looking through them she could see everything inside of him. He turned his face to one side. "I had my life all charted. I was going on a mission, and come home and get me a farm at Lone Rock and a wife, and a family."

"Can't you still?"

"All at once the wind changed, or something, and I was facing in a different direction."

Her voice sank almost to a whisper. "Yes. I know what you mean." She nodded faintly. "When I was a girl I wanted to sing. I was on my way to New York."

"What happened?"

"I fell in love with your father. I hoped that somehow I could have both—maybe that Alma would come to New York and get a job. But he said, 'What would I do with ten thousand sheep in Central Park?' I finally faced it: I had to make a choice. So instead of singing in Town Hall, I sang in the nursery."

"Are you sorry?"

She mused. "Six of my babies died." She looked up at him. "Sorry? Not for what I have had. For what I missed, yes." She paused. "Except, you see, the way it's turned out, I haven't had either. When I was too old to think of singing any more, your father married a younger woman and took her to live in Canada, took her and took my children. I didn't have a husband, I didn't have my children. If I had known . . ." She stopped talking and lay there looking out the window.

"Why did he marry again?"

"It was the Lord's will—the celestial law of marriage. We talked it over and decided it was what we ought to do. I chose Bessie for him, you know. She was a niece of my dearest friend."

"It doesn't seem to have worked too well."

"Don't be a skeptic, Jerry. It is easy to be scornful of sacred things—easy, and weak. But there is power in reverence."

The white room oppressed Jared. He remembered what his father had told him about the Celestial Kingdom: if a person with a terrestrial body ever landed in the Celestial Kingdom, he would scream to get out. He could not endure its glory. This room, Jared supposed, was as close to heaven as he would ever get.

"How's Grace?" his mother asked.

"She's all right."

"Tell me about her. Is she a happy girl?"

Jared hesitated. "She makes other people happy."

"I guess every mother wants her girl to be pretty." Lula Fae sighed. "She ought to be married by now."

"She's too particular. The men in Canada are a pretty rough lot."

"Has she had the chance?"

"I don't know."

She looked at Jared, and then away. "It's like dying, you know, never to see your children again." After a while she went on. "Do you remember that day you left? You climbed a tree."

"I was thinking about it earlier."

"I hoped you'd stay up there, so they couldn't take you."

"You asked me to come down."

"I was afraid you'd fall, I guess. Afraid they'd spank you. I don't know."

"Why did you let them take me away?"

She opened her mouth, and then closed it on a swallow. "What could I do?"

"Why couldn't I stay here?"

"Alma said it was for the best. He wanted you to ride horses, and learn about sheep and cattle, and how to sleep on the open prairie. He said he wanted you to be a man."

Jared nodded. "There was more to it than that."

Abruptly she said, "How well do you know your father? Did you ever talk together, one man to another?"

"He wasn't a great talker."

"Never has been. You should have heard him propose to me—or seen him, I should say. There wasn't much to hear."

"Ah," said Jared.

"My parents lived in Salt Lake City. Whenever I went to Smithfield to visit relations, Alma came calling, so I started going to Smithfield as often as I could. Once or twice he came to my home, but he had the sheep, you see, and no help in those days—it was hard for him to get away.

"Anyway, when he showed up on our front porch in Salt Lake one afternoon, I was surprised. I guess I was a little scared, too. I knew this wasn't just another call."

"You knew why he was there?"

"My sister answered the door, and called me. When I got there I found your father dressed in his Sunday clothes, standing with a nosegay in his hand and moisture on his face as though he had been working all day in the field. He started to say something, but coughed instead, and looked as if he might drop the flowers and run. I curtsied, and remained so, with my head bent. I thought he could scarcely leave as long as I bowed in front of him. To this day I can remember your father's shoes, and a pair of borrowed spats too big for him."

"Didn't you say anything?"

"I couldn't even squeak. I was in awe of your father then. After all, an eighteen-year-old girl. He was a man past thirty. He wore a beard in those days." She looked toward the window. "My sister invited him into the parlor and left us, and suddenly there we were, alone, facing each other behind closed doors. I waited for him to give me the flowers, but he had forgotten about them. He held them against the front of his coat, gripping the stems so tightly I was afraid the blossoms would pop off. 'Lula Fae,' he said, and that was all. He just stood there, and I stood there, and I think even the flowers started to wilt.

"I heard a giggle outside the door, and I knew my little brother was peeking at us, so I took Alma's arm and drew him to one side, and we stood there listening. Presently I realized that I was still holding his arm, and then he put his hand over mine. And that's all there was to it."

"He never did propose?"

"I don't remember that he ever said anything. He talked to my father afterwards, of course—or at least they went into the parlor together. I've often wondered what was said that time."

"Have you any idea what has happened to him now?"

"Men disappear, you know. They just ride away one day, and that's the last anybody sees of them."

"When they're seventy-seven years old?"

She laughed. "You young men think you're so special. You're the only ones that anything happens to—the only ones to fall in love or run away, or do outlandish things."

"He's lost, Mother. Don't you understand? He's your husband, and he's lost."

"My husband." She laughed again, but shortly this time. "Yes, I married him. I didn't know . . ." She stopped, and turned her face toward the window.

"You didn't know he'd marry another woman and take your children to Canada. Is that it?"

She shook her head slowly against the pillow.

"Then what?"

"Tell me about yourself, Jared. Do you have a sweetheart?"

"You do know something, after all. I thought at least you would help me."

"Of course I would. If I could, I would." She sighed as if a heavy weight lay across her breast.

"I keep thinking of Father. Maybe right now he's waiting somewhere, wondering why I don't come."

She nodded.

"Do you remember that time when Father came to visit us— the time he took me away? One morning I heard you talking —arguing. Father said he couldn't leave me with you—he couldn't trust you, or something like that. What did he mean, he couldn't trust you?"

"You were only a child; how can you question me like this? I don't remember what your father said. I'm sure I never gave him any reason not to trust me."

After a moment Jared asked, "Was it because of persecution he went to Canada?"

"There was more to it than that. You know your father. New land, new opportunities, new beginnings. Alma couldn't resist it."

"What I can't understand is why he took Aunt Bessie. You were the first wife."

"He was thinking of what was best for the family. He wanted children. Six of my babies had died."

"Didn't you want to go?"

"You're talking about things you don't understand. I wasn't well. I couldn't have been a pioneer woman again—not like Bessie could."

"Why did they take Grace away from you?"

"I was too sick to take care of her. They didn't even expect me to live."

"And he left you alone?"

"My family was here, many of them. He had the sheep to take care of, the family. What could he do?"

"Weren't you angry?"

She hesitated. "I don't think so."

"Well, I'm angry."

"Not angry. Hurt, maybe. Lonely. But why should I be angry? There was nothing he could do."

The details of his mother's room were strange to Jared, or perhaps only forgotten, but the atmosphere remained untouched, as if the very air he had breathed at six or seven was still there, waiting to be breathed again. Slowly, with the same languid motion with which those years had passed, the memory of them returned to him. Even then, his mother spent much of her time in this room, in the white bed, and Jared had played on the white rug, and dreaded the chiming of the white mantel clock (still tirelessly ticking) that would mean his time for play was over.

**3** Jared went downstairs. At the bottom step he almost bumped into Uncle Theodore carrying Lula Fae's supper tray. The old man looked up, startled, and backed away. His body appeared almost transparent, as if without clothes he might vanish completely.

"I'm sorry," Jared said.

"Supper's ready, if you care to wash up. I'll serve it as soon as I take this up to Lula Fae."

Jared sidled around him.

"You'll stay with us, of course." Uncle Theodore turned and started up the stairs, his little bandy legs moving with quick precision.

The door to the parlor was open. As he passed it, Jared glanced inside. The old black horsehair sofa was still there, just as he remembered. Its leather arm had been his horse, and together they had galloped a thousand miles a day. He went into the room and sat down, his arm resting on the shiny patch of leather that had been his saddle.

How obedient that leather horse had been. It typified his life at the time—orderly, manageable, serene. But when he walked out of this house with his father, everything had changed. It was as though he had entered a new game, without understanding the rules beforehand, challenging other players on their own court—Aunt Bessie, Rachel, Lyman, and as he grew older, Paula, then finally Lyman and Paula together.

When they moved to Lone Rock, Lyman had been in England on a mission. The day he arrived home, the whole family had gone in the rig to Cardston to meet him. The girls chattered all the way, wondering what England was like, if Lyman had changed in his almost three years away, doubtful if the photograph he had sent them could really be that of their brother. Bessie did her best to reassure them. Lyman would be the same wonderful boy they sent away—a little more grown-up, that's all. And the photograph of the dapper young city man was indeed him—she was able to tell even if they could not. The girls laughed. They knew who it was, of course, but imagine!

They stayed with their old friends the Hayses in Cardston that night, and the next morning at eleven o'clock they were all standing on the platform of the railway station. In fact, half the town was there. The return of a missionary was an event that everyone took pride in, and it didn't happen very often any more.

Belle and Jane announced the appearance of the train when

it was still several miles away, reported its progress as it steadily drew nearer, and almost dissolved in excitement as the locomotive surged past them. After the train stopped, there was a moment or two of hushed silence, just long enough for them to feel that familiar rush of dread—"He isn't on it." Then he stepped into the door of the passenger car, turned to face them, and paused, as if uncertain he had the right stop.

He looked absolutely splendid—dark suit, high collar, bowler hat, button shoes, cane . . . An audible breath went up from the people assembled. Lyman sauntered down the steps onto the platform. Jane, the first to recover, ran screaming into his arms. Bessie and Rachel and Belle and Grace were not far behind, and then Stanley and Alma, and all the friends who had come to welcome him. When the first round of embraces was over, Lyman turned toward the rig and found himself face to face with Jared.

"Welcome home," Jared said, shaking his hand.

"Well, well, little brother. Not so little any more, I see."

"You're looking fine, Lyman."

"I feel fine." Lyman continued on toward the rig, waving, shaking hands, smiling, his sisters clinging to him, the others following like a cluster of leaves caught in an eddy. "Will you get my bags, Jared?"

He had left with one suitcase. But Grandpa Thomas, Bessie's father, who had chiefly financed Lyman's mission, must have kept him in style, for now he had four pieces of luggage, none of them the original. It took two trips for Jared to get them to the rig. By that time Lyman was sitting in the front seat holding the lines, while his parents and sisters climbed in after him.

"Where you going to sit, little brother?" Lyman asked.

"Oh, I'll just run along behind."

Bessie gathered her children in closer. "There's room here, Jared. Come on." Her efforts were ineffectual; the girls did not seem able to compress their billowing petticoats any further. "You can hold Janie."

"For twenty miles? Never mind, I'll borrow a horse."

"Hurry then. So you can ride beside us."

"We'll get started," Lyman said. He swung the team, and

the rig rolled swiftly away up the road, with other outfits following it to the edge of town.

Jared joined the Hays family for lunch, and then borrowed a saddle horse to ride home. He didn't hurry. By the time he got to Lone Rock the rest of the family had finished supper and were seated in the parlor, listening to Lyman. They clamored for Jared to join them, but he had chores to do. He took the pail from the pantry and went out to the pasture to milk the cow.

The next morning Lyman came in for breakfast wearing his missionary suit—even his coat and tie. "You get used to dressing like a gentleman, you just don't feel right unless you are," he said.

"Where's your cane?" Jared joshed. "Ain't you afraid you'll tip over?"

"Jared, don't be impertinent," Bessie reproved him.

"That's all right," Lyman said. "Little brother's turn is coming. Now he can go on a mission."

"Not till we get you weaned away from those clothes," Jared said. "Somebody has to do the work around here."

Lyman looked around him. "Jane, will you bring me a napkin?" With a flourish of linen he seated himself at the table.

The family lingered after their meal, listening to Lyman's tales of England. At last Jared rose and put on his hat. "Thought I might fix that piece of fence," he told his father, "before the cow gets out again."

Alma nodded. "You'll probably have to set a new post."

But when Jared opened the door to leave, he found Paula standing on the step with her hand raised. She laughed. "I almost knocked on your nose."

"You want to go with me to fix some fence?"

"Sure." She hesitated. "Did Lyman get home?"

Jared nodded.

Paula put her head inside the door. "Hello, everybody." She went on in. "Hello, Lyman."

Lyman rose from his chair, looking at her. "Hello." He didn't seem to recognize her.

She raised on her toes and bounced a couple of times. "It's me. Paula. Paula Gibson."

113

"Paula Gibson!" Lyman looked incredulous.

She hesitated, uncertain what to do.

"Well, well." He opened his arms and she stepped into them, then shyly backed away. "You're as pretty as those English girls. How'd you grow up so fast?"

"It wasn't so fast," she said. "You were gone a long time."

"Too long, it looks like. Jared's beat me to you."

"My, you look fine," she said. "Such beautiful clothes."

"He's been telling us all about England," Jane said. "Come on, Lyman, tell us some more. Sit down, Paula."

"Oh, yes." Paula sat on the chair where Jared had been. "Tell us everything about it."

Uncle Theodore came back downstairs, and Jared followed him into the kitchen, where they sat down on opposite sides of the supper table. For a while they ate without speaking. At last Jared said, "Is my mother in bed all the time?"

"Usually."

"Does she have some disease?"

"The doctors aren't sure what her trouble is."

Again they ate in silence.

"Have you seen my father lately?"

"Oh no. It's been some years."

"He's lost, you know."

"Oh?"

"Just disappeared."

"He always was unpredictable."

"There seems to be some great secret that nobody is talking about. Can you tell me what it is?"

Uncle Theodore sighed and wiped his lips with a napkin. "I haven't any idea what you're talking about."

"I think you do know what I'm talking about."

"You are young, Jared. You still think there is an answer for everything. Come, I'll show you your room." The little man rose and led the way down the hall.

At the front of the house, opposite the parlor, he opened the door to a large bedroom. "Just make yourself comfortable." He took a match from his pocket and lit the lamp standing on the table. "What can I get for you?"

Jared sat down on the bed and began to pull off his boots. "All I need is a good night's sleep."

The old man backed through the door. "There are books in the parlor, if you care to read."

"Thank you."

Jared watched the door close. Lying deep in his feather bed in the darkened room, he found that he could not sleep; his mind continued to run on long after it might have begun to rest. The moon rose, and gradually the room was suffused with pale lumination. Finally he slept. Sometime toward morning he woke abruptly. He heard a sound, muted but distinct. The door began to move; he propped the pillow under his head. A filmy white figure came into the room and approached the bed.

"Mother!"

"Alma," she whispered. "So you've come at last."

Jared sat up. "It's me. Jared."

"I've waited so long." She stopped, almost close enough to touch him. "It's been such a long time." She sat on the side of the bed and reached to take his hand. He pulled it away. She was carrying something in her other arm—a book, it looked like. "Why did you take so long? Did you think I was still angry? I wanted to be angry, you know. I tried to be. I didn't understand. I don't understand."

Jared moved toward the other side of the bed.

"I don't understand," she repeated. She uttered a gentle cry and placed her hand over her face, her fingers spread so she could look between them. "Ohhh," she sobbed. "Look what you have done. Look at the little babies. How could you?" She shrank away. "Don't touch me. I don't want you to ever touch me again."

"Mother. You're dreaming."

"I wish I was dreaming. It's not me that has the dreams, you know." She noticed the book in her arm, and held it toward him. "If you don't remember, you can read it. I've read it. I read it every night before I go to sleep. I read it over and over . . ." Suddenly she choked. "We were so happy."

Jared reached to take the book, but she didn't give it up at once, and for a moment they sat, each with a hand on it, gently pulling. Then, abruptly, she let go. "Read it. Then you'll remember."

It was a book about the size of a writing pad, with a very hard binding and one word embossed on the cover. He could see the word, but the room was too dark to read it. He ran his fingers over each raised letter: "Journal."

Another person had entered the room. "Lula Fae?" It was Uncle Theodore. "What are you doing?"

"Don't come in here," she told him. "You have no business coming in here."

He walked slowly toward her and took her by the hand. "Come with me."

"See," she said. "Alma has come at last. Isn't that nice?"

"Come along. You shouldn't walk around in the middle of the night."

She pulled away from him and remained sitting on the bed. "He's only just got here."

"Yes, he's been traveling. He's very tired. He needs to rest, don't you, Alma?"

Jared was uncertain what to do.

"You can visit in the morning."

Lula Fae permitted Uncle Theodore to lead her from the bed, but she looked back at Jared. "It's been so long."

They were at the door before she suddenly ran back and seized the book from him.

"I have to read it," he said, reaching for it.

She clutched it to her. "It's mine."

Before Jared could move, it seemed, they were gone, soundlessly moving into another part of the house. He might have doubted he had seen them at all, except that he could still feel the weight and texture of the book where it had rested in his hand.

For a long time he sat listening, but there was nothing for him to hear.

He slipped from bed and pulled on his overalls. The hallway outside his room was dark and silent, the core of the house, where the full weight of the night was concentrated. When he reached the foot of the stairs he could see soft light silhouetting the banister rail above him.

As he ascended the stairs he found that he was a true nephew of Theodore—he, too, could move soundlessly. The faint light came from rooms whose doors stood open around the upper hallway; his mother's door was closed. Carefully he turned the knob and pushed it open. She lay in her arbor of white, as pale and cool as a figurine. On the nightstand beside her, he saw the book. He moved across the room, gliding like a weary skater, took up the book, and then backed away. When he reached the hallway he closed the door, then continued to move carefully down the stairs and into his room. Once he had the door closed, he lit the lamp and sat on the chair beside it. He opened the book.

**4** On the flyleaf of the journal was an inscription in faded blue ink—an early version of that familiar signature, *Alma Roseman*. Inside, the record began, written in the same hand, with the same pale ink:

May 23, 1870. Yesterday I married Lula Fae Bonett, and afterward enjoyed the hospitality of her father and mother, with good food and the company of many friends. Lula Fae's sister sang for us, and brother Theodore entertained with barnyard imitations and stories etc. Much lafter re: my supposedly advanced age etc. which I bore in good spirit for one scairsly past thirty years. After dinner we drove to Bountiful with much satisfaction to have escaped even that cordial society. I doubt not a good life waits before us. She makes me laugh, which after more than twelve years is like a resurrexion.

May 26. Advice to young men: It is well that you should begin a journal, and even more proper a marriage, but for wisdom's sake do not both on the same day. A new wife and a new record I find to be not compatible, though I have pleased my wife in one respect—that it is the book and not herself who has suffered neglect.

May 27. Arrived home to Smithfield. I went at once to the fields, much gratified to find sheep doing well after my absence of almost a week. Tonight when I returned home imagine my distress to discover my sweet wife in tears, which, though she wept most bitterly, she would not, or could not account for, for all my tender entreaties, but would only say she must miss her mother. Where women are concerned, I confess a vast ignorance, or at least bewilderment. Still, she is my wife, and as such I mean that she shall be respected.

May 28. Today I enjoyed for the first time my wife's society at sacrament meeting, where I was called to preach. I took as my subject our Contest with the Devil, on which I feel perhaps more qualified than some. The congregation's many expressions of thanks etc afterward—though in nowise remiss—were less to me in satisfaction than those of my wife. She voices doubts at my "pretended" wickedness.

June 2. Brought the herd in for shearing, which will start to-morrow. The lambs are fat as ticks.

June 3. Shearing begun. We have a good crue this year, though one of the shearers is careless and cuts the skin more often than he should.

June 4. No work today, in keeping with Sabbath observance, though crue would have worked if I had let them. They are rough men, Godless and profane. I confess I will be glad when they are gone. One of them, who seemed a little less hardened than the others, I attempted to engage in gospel conversation, but only got laughed at. Yet I confess the terrible thought crossed my mind, "Perhaps I am no better than they are."

June 5. Good progress. Held up at noon, because dinner was not reddy. I emphasized as gently as I could the need for prompness etc. but still detected a few tears in the mashed potatoes. (Joke.)

June 6. Shorthanded. One herder cut his hand while sharpening his shears last night, and spent the day in the bunkhouse. He lost enough blood to fill a dipping vat, it looked like.

June 7. Finished shearing. Had planned to buy a new dress for Lula Fae when wool money comes in, but dinner was late again today, and when everybody was gone I was obliged to spank her, which nearly broke my heart, but was not without effect. She seems to see more clearly the difficulty of my position when the crue is kept waiting. Though she cried a good deal, I tried to remember that she is just a child. After it was over, I found that I had earned an increase in her affection, if that were possible, and now as I write this she sleeps upon her pillow most sweetly.

June 8. Today we started the sheep to the mountains for summer pasture. The season promises fine. At last I am making my journal a daily practise.

August 20. So God confounds the wise. It was my hope to make this record an honest account, and so I have tried to understand the cause of my failure to keep it faithfully. First, we had trouble with the sheep, which distracted me, and for a few days I did not write. When I did take up the book again, my eye fell on my boast of June 8, and I was unable to write, no doubt paralyzed with shame. So I have remained these many weeks, one moment resolved, another disarmed, another laughing at my foolishness. Gradually I began to overcome my inward difficulties, until today more than two months later it is finally possible for me to set pen to paper again. How strange are the frailties of the human spirit! How subject to infirmities. And finally, how futile. For if we are unable to rule ourselves in trivial matters, how then shall we ever become masters in things of importance? What an unpromising creature is man; how rash to call himself the infant god!

August 21. Today my bride became unhinged, and wept and swore. I thought my ears would wither on my head before they heard such words from her. The reason for the outcry I did not discover. I suspect that I have been neglectful in my assumption of authority, being too much guided by the tender swelling I feel each time I look at her. But I see that she is an emotional child, easily turned by every breath of fortune, and will require firmness from a stronger hand to steady her course.

September 3. I must confess that four months of marriage seem nigh as long as all the thirty years that went before it. This is difficult to understand, since I do feel for her the most profound affexion, and she for me if I might trust the evidence. But all she wants from life is turmoil, it seems, and all I ever asked for was peace.

October 12. I learned today that I am to be a father—of a son, I've no doubt. Words are unsuitable to express my joy at this discovery. It now appears that all our difficulties shall come to naught, and we shall haply raise our children in fear of the Lord.

January 23, 1871. This morning Lula Fae tearfully confessed to me the root of her fears, to the effect that I had "another" dream last night. Nobody could know better than me that I had another dream, but I supposed it to be private information. What was my horror, then, to have her describe how I would cry and writhe, and sit up in bed wide-eyed and shouting, and then cover my eyes against the blood. Worse, that this has happened many times, almost since the day of our marriage, and she dared not speak of it to me. What horror! That she should see me thus. And worse, that this should all escape its grave, where haply I had long since covered it. Instead of the healing for which my heart yearned, my marriage has done naught but start the wound bleeding afresh.

She presses me for word of it. If she but knew the source of these grim fantasies, then she would understand, so she insists.

And more—knowing, she could heal me. This too she vouches for. Imagine! To be healed!

How small a part she knows. If she but winked one drop of blood with which my soul is splashed . . . What can I do?

June 24. Today our son was born. Tonight he died. I named him Terrance Bonett Roseman.

December 25. Christmas Day. We are in Salt Lake City to spend the holiday with the Bonett family. It was the first time Lula Fae has laughed since our son died. She is by nature a more light-hearted creature than me.

Tonight, when we were alone in our room, she told me that she will not return to Smithfield with me. On one condition only would she consider continuing as my wife—if I would tell her the reason for my dreams. She declares herself on the point of insanity if these night horrors continue without any explanation. The hardest thing to bear is that she has come to doubt my love for her. Tomorrow morning I leave for Smithfield alone.

March 18, 1872. Today my wife returned.

July 7. Today my wife greeted me with a surprise for my birthday. We are to be blessed with a child. Pray God it may be permitted to tarry.

January 3, 1873. Our baby born dead. A very difficult time for Lula Fae. Not even any tiny arms to comfort her. I did the best I could with my rough, awkward ones. When I felt her body tremble, I promised her any treasure that earth contained. She asked only one thing—to hear my story, the secret of my terrible dreams. How could I deny her? Or how could I tell her? In the end, I promised that as soon as she is well I shall tell her everything. She went to sleep then, much releaved. And I have laid all night awake.

March 15. It is over. My oath is broken. But my soul is comforted in the thought that now my wife and I are one flesh—there is nothing that we do not share.

March 17. Today I have brought Lula Fae to her mother's. She wishes to remain and visit for a while.

June 10. Shearing completed. A greater wool crop than I have ever taken. Some thought of increasing my herd. It is said that animals are available in Wyoming.

August 23. A letter came from Lula Fae.

April 22, 1874. A very long, cold winter. Feed scarce. Well that my trip to Wyoming last summer was unsuccessful. It has entered my mind to take another wife.

May 19. Journeyed to Salt Lake City to ask Lula Fae's assistance in choosing a plural wife. My purpose forgot in excitement of reunion, etc. She returned to my house most gratefully, as I am to have her. No longer a girl, but a woman. She has forgiven me. Pray God will do the same.

May 25. My life overflows, as copious in its abundance as recently it was in emptiness.

June 13. What strange human metals are hewn in the forge of life. My wife is a different woman. She daunts and beguiles me in a single instant. I know not what to make of her.

June 16. I think I see it now. She no longer stands in awe of me—having found me to be no more than mortal after all, I suppose. Today I asked her to fetch my lunch to me in the field. She replied with apparent good humor that she was busy, and I could fetch the lunch myself. The result was that the lunch grew stale sitting on the cupboard all afternoon. Thank fortune I did not feel hungry.

October 23. I perceive that there is no living with a woman. I adore her, and yet she vexes me beyond endurance. Would sometimes I had my kitten back.

April 3, 1875. Our third baby. A girl. Born dead.

October 27, 1876. Tonight, while looking through a pile of old books, I came upon my journal. I confess I had forgotten about it. I was of a mind to throw it on the bonfire, but hesitated long enough to glance through it. After this time it strikes me as more pretentious than profound, yet I felt unwilling to destroy it. Neither have I the will to extend it. I shall leave it, I suppose, as a half-finished memorium.

We have had yet another stillborn child, and it begins to appear that I shall never have posterity.

Jared turned the page. There was one more entry in the journal, set by itself about halfway down the sheet of paper, almost as a divider between the full pages and the empty ones:

June, 1877. Had word today that Bro. John D. Lee was executed at Mountain Meadows. A hard thing, after twenty years.

**5** Jared thumbed through the remaining part of the journal to be sure his father had not continued the account further on, but all he found was a small piece of folded notepaper that had been tucked between the pages. It was a letter dated at Cedar City, Utah, March 26, 1897:

Dear Mrs. Roseman: I received your letter and read it with considerable interest and amusement. You obviously don't know anything about Mountain Meadows. You seem to have the quaint idea that it would be possible for me to grant your husband some kind of blanket forgiveness. Do you realize what you are asking? I can't even extend my own forgiveness—what right have I to offer anyone else's? Or what right have you to ask? You aren't Jesus, you know. You can't atone for anybody else's sins. It is your husband who must seek absolution. But tell him not to look for it here.

Obediently yours,
Gladys Wells

Jared folded the letter. Almost twenty years had passed since it was written. It seemed like something inscribed by another people in another age, like Scripture. He put the letter in his shirt pocket.

When Jared returned the journal to his mother's room, it was growing daylight. She did not appear to have moved, nor did she move now. Her face looked strangely young and fair, luminous, unmarked, as if her heart had chosen to suffer privately, hiding its pain not only from the world, but from her own flesh. Even as he stood there, the morning seemed to blossom, strewing her room with petals of sunlight that fell through the branches of the willow tree outside her window.

He wished he was back in Canada, with Lyman and Tom and the others, riding through fresh pine forests in his search for Alma. Surely by now they had found him, lying in a remote alpine meadow—injured, or even dead perhaps, but purified somehow, innocent, like the wildflowers that bent above his body.

Jared got out his horse and headed south. That evening he reached Salt Lake City, a place he had never been before. As he came around the mountain he saw the city spread before him, a gauze of commerce and forested domesticity floating close above the desert, airy as a dream, but pinned to the earth by the tabernacle dome and the granite spires of the temple. Once it had been no more than a dream. How close, he wondered, did this brick-and-stone reality come to the vision of Brigham Young?

He stopped to visit Temple Square. As he walked through the gates, bronze memorials to Mormon history stood around him larger than life—the sea-gull monument, the handcart company, the Prophet Joseph Smith, Hyrum, his brother. Jared sat on a bench and felt his heritage gradually press down on him. That weight had been with him all his life, but always before he had felt it as a stabilizer holding him on course; now it was a burden. Somehow it seemed that he had started to drift.

It was after sundown several days later that he rode into Cedar City. It was not a big town, and especially in the darkness it seemed diminished by the lightly wooded hills among which it lay. The day's heat still hovered above the ground, slowly dissipating. The air was thin, and so clear it might have been a glass cover that protected the town like a specimen case.

Jared took a room for the night at a hotel. The next morning, following the directions of a townsman, he was able to find his way to the home of Gladys Wells. It was a two-story house, so narrow that it looked as if a strong wind might tip it over. A sharp-faced little woman opened the door to his knock.

"Yes?"

"Mrs. Wells?"

"Yes."

"My name is Jared Roseman. I wonder if I might see you for a moment."

"Roseman?" she said. "Any relation to the Willard Rosemans?"

"He was my grandfather."

She stood in the door, scarcely five feet tall, with thin arms folded across the front of her body. "What do you want?"

"My father has disappeared." He took from his shirt pocket the letter that she had written to his mother, and handed it to her. "I wondered if you might be able to help me."

She glanced at the letter. "I don't know how."

"Can you tell me what happened at Mountain Meadows?"

She cocked her head to one side, and then tipped it back so she could look him in the eye. For a moment or two she didn't speak. "Come in," she said at last.

He entered the hall. The house was a repository for bric-a-brac—figurines, jugs, vases, clocks, dishes . . . He was afraid to move, almost; his elbow might strike something. The lady closed the door and glided past him, leading the way into the living room. "Sit down."

He sat where she indicated, and she took an easy chair opposite him, sinking so deep into it that he almost feared she might slip behind a cushion. "Somewhere your mother got my name and wrote me, I don't know why. Something about her conscience. Her conscience? What about her husband's conscience? Why didn't he write the letter?"

Jared remembered his hat, and quickly took it off. "Maybe his conscience was clear."

"Alma Roseman!"

"My father was a good man."

"Hah! That makes a pile of difference. If there was only some way we could make sure only good men go around murderin' people."

Jared looked at the little woman. "What are you talking about?"

With a quick twist of her body she was off the chair and standing on the rug. She took an old album from a drawer of the desk and handed it to him—newspaper clippings, photographs, pages from books, notes written in pen and ink. One was a clipping from a newspaper, dated June 11, 1877:

> John D. Lee was executed by a firing squad today at Mountain Meadows, the scene of the massacre which he was convicted of leading twenty years ago. Sitting on his coffin, Lee insisted to the end that he was only carrying out the order of his superiors. Then the guns fired, and he fell backward without a sound.
>
> On approximately September 11, 1857, an emigrant train on its way to California was wiped out in an Indian attack. Only a few small children survived. It was later learned that white men were involved.
>
> Mountain Meadows is a remote area located about thirty-five miles southwest of Cedar City.

The papers of September 1857 that were kept in the album were small, curious-looking tabloids containing long discourses by church leaders, many of them having to do with the United States Army then marching on Utah. News items appeared in a section of the paper between the sermons and the classified advertisements. On a page near the back of the September 26 edition, a brief account was circled in black:

> Word was received today of the ambush of an emigrant train at Mountain Meadows in Southern Utah, by Indians. The entire company of more than a hundred men, women and children was annihilated. The emigrants were mostly from Missouri and Arkansas, on their way to California.

Jared glanced up. Mrs. Wells had returned to her chair, and sat staring at him as if she in her look alone could compel him to read. He needed no compulsion; he seemed unable to stop himself. One account of several pages had obviously been clipped from a book and fastened in the album so that both sides of the page could be read. It was marked with a pen: *Bancroft.*

It began with a description of the emigrant party, mostly from Arkansas, though there were a few Missourians, some of whom called themselves the "Missouri Wildcats." They were orderly, sober, thrifty, and among the group, suffered no lack of skill and capital. They were driving six hundred cattle, thirty wagons and thirty horses and mules. The value of their property was afterward estimated at sixty to seventy thousand dollars.

In testimony following the massacre, however, the emigrants were accused of abusing women, poisoning wells, destroying fences and growing crops, violating city ordinances at Cedar and resisting arrest.

Meat from cattle poisoned at the wells was said to have killed a couple of Pah Vant Indians. This was perhaps the principal cause for the Indian attack. The reasons for the assault by the Mormons was not so clear, other than those already mentioned, plus the fact that the previous spring Parley P. Pratt, a favorite Mormon apostle, had been brutally slain while serving on a mission for the church in Arkansas.

But the evidence was contradictory. The Indian Affairs

superintendent said that the emigrants had acted with propriety.

On September 5, 1857, the emigrants had encamped at Mountain Meadows, an area on the divide between the Great Basin and the watershed of the Colorado River. When the Indians attacked, the emigrants drew their wagons into a circle and tried to fortify themselves behind dirt banks. Their defense was spirited enough to hold the Indians off for more than four days, though some of them were wounded and they suffered desperately from thirst, since they had camped a short distance from the stream.

After four days a couple of Mormons came into camp with a proposal for their escape, which they accepted. Their desperation can be guessed by the terms of the proposal: that they give up all their arms, as a gesture of peace toward the Indians, and walk to Cedar City under Mormon escort.

On the next morning a large company of Mormons arrived at the embattled wagon train. The men cheered their supposed deliverers. While the implementation of the agreement proceeded, a rider came urging haste, as the Indians were threatening to renew their attack. The wounded emigrants were placed in a wagon, along with all the weapons of the defenders. The small children occupied a second wagon. Then the wagons started off, closely followed by the women and older children. The men followed at a distance, each one accompanied by a Mormon escort. At a certain point there came a shout, "Halt! Do your duty!"

Each Mormon thereupon shot the emigrant beside him. At the same time the Indians attacked and killed the women and older children. Seventeen children presumed to be too young to act as witnesses were permitted to live.

A few of the Mormons, unwilling to kill, had been instructed to stoop down, a signal for their men to be dispatched by the Indians.

After the massacre the Mormons went back to camp for breakfast, later returning to bury the dead.

Bancroft's account continued:

Over the last resting place of the victims was built a cone-shaped cairn, some twelve feet in height, and leaning against its northern base was placed a rough slab of granite, with the following inscription: "Here 120 men, women and children were massacred in cold blood early in September, 1857. They were from Arkansas." The cairn was surmounted by a cross of cedar, on which were inscribed the words: "Vengeance is mine; I will repay, saith the Lord."

Jared looked across the room at Mrs. Wells. "My father was there?"

She stared at him, her eyes bright and unblinking. "Your father was there." She dipped her head firmly, rearranged her dress, and looked up again, straightening. "My father was there too, you know, at the other end of the gun. My father and mother both."

"But this couldn't have any connection with my father's disappearance?"

She shrugged, staring at the floor. "There have been men die, or disappear—men who broke the oath of silence. The wolves turning on each other, you see." Her eyes were like knobs on a cupboard door; she never seemed to blink them. "But they're nearly all dead now. I've watched 'em die off one by one."

"You've kept track of all of them?"

"That's what I come back to Cedar to do, when I was just a girl."

"Well, there's been a mistake. My father never killed anyone."

"I know its hard to accept." She raised her jaw and again she twisted out of her chair.

"Maybe my father was one of the ones who stooped down."

She stood before him. "Saints! Saints, you call yourselves!" She spat out of a dry mouth. "You killed my father—my mother. Your own father did it. He was there. Don't fool yourself about that." She stopped, and her knobs of eyes began to gleam with tears. "You complain to me about losing your father! I lost my father when I was three years old."

"I'm sorry," Jared said. "I . . ."

She tossed her head; the motion was a dismissal.

"I didn't even know . . ."

She crossed the hall and held the door for him, and closed it quickly as he stepped onto the porch.

6

The next morning Jared woke in his hotel room. He rose slowly toward consciousness, at first uncertain if the soft grey light which shrouded him belonged to the hours of darkness or day. Even the smoke of his dreams clung around him, oppressive and dark; sleeping and waking seemed different only in degree. It required great effort to crawl from bed; his covers might have been made of iron.

Beneath the window grey wagons moved slowly by in the skim-milk-colored street—the town and distant hills were obscured in fog, an element that muffled the vision but seemed to sharpen and amplify the creak of the wagons and the ring of the blacksmith's hammer across the street.

Sitting on the edge of the bed, he began to dress himself—his hat, his socks, his shirt. He seemed to have difficulty with the buttons, as if his fingers were as fat and stiff as cucumbers. He stood to put on his overalls, thrusting in first one leg and then the other, hitching them around his hips, tucking in his shirttail, buttoning, buckling, sitting again to pull on his boots. On the nightstand was a porcelain basin and pitcher embossed with figures in royal blue that depicted a forest scene. Beneath the trees a knight in armor looked toward a distant castle which stood among the clouds.

Jared washed and shaved, took his coat over his arm, closed the room, and walked down the hall. The open stairway of the little hotel had been built to give a feeling of spaciousness; he stopped on the landing to look at the mounted animal heads that ringed the walls of the lobby—an elk, a deer, an antelope, a moose, a bear, a buffalo.

There was a clerk behind the desk, his large frame strangely at odds with the cramped office, almost as if he, too, were a trophy dragged in from the forest and fastened to the wall. As he watched Jared descend the staircase his eyes held the same luminous opacity as those of the stuffed buffalo.

Jared placed the key on the desk in front of him. "Good morning."

The man did not reply. He stood with forearms crossed on the countertop, his head thrust back slightly, so the line of his jaw merged with his stovepipe neck. Only his chin protruded.

Jared asked, "How far is it to Mountain Meadows?"

"That's out past Pinto," the man said. "Thirty-five, forty miles, I guess." His hand moved across the counter top and enfolded the key. "Why do you want to go to Mountain Meadows?"

"Curious. Just want to see what it looks like."

"You pick any tree you pass and look at it—you'll be seein' more than you'll ever see at Mountain Meadows." He reached and hung the key on a nail beside the others. "The Pinkertons couldn't find that place today—not till the fog lifts."

The air outside was moist and cool. Next door to the blacksmith shop was the barn where Jared kept his horse. *Aaron's Stable* the sign said. *Horses for hire.* A man stood in the doorway of the barn, picking his teeth with a straw.

As Jared saddled his horse, he asked, "Can you tell me how to get to Mountain Meadows?"

"I could tell you," the stableman said. "But it wouldn't do any good. The road's grown over now, crisscrossed with trails."

"I'll find it." Jared took the reins and mounted. "Do I head south?"

"Head west. You'll be all right as far as Pinto. Ask somebody when you get there."

Jared turned his horse and started down the street. The fog seemed to have drifted into his mind, blurring thought and memory; he moved through an endless haze. By the time he reached Pinto the air was clear and the sun shining; it would soon be hot. Still nothing touched him—heat or cold or bright or grey. He rode steadily on, aware of the things outside his skin but untouched by them, as one might stand behind a window and watch the world.

Once he met a man on horseback, and another time overtook and passed a family in a wagon. Traveling through wild, forested hills, he inquired of anyone he saw, and followed the directions he received from one lonely ranch to another, along country roads that slowly descended to flatter, drier territory; the landscape turned grey-green—the color of sagebrush. Finally he stopped at a remote ranch house—the most isolated he had seen.

As he drew near he saw a woman sitting in the shade of the house, shelling peas with her large, ungainly hands. Two young children played in the dirt nearby. Jared tipped his hat, "Ma'am."

She popped a peapod and ran her thumb down the length of it. The peas fell into her pan with a tiny rumble.

"I'm looking for Mountain Meadows," Jared said.

"You're here."

"Here?"

"Mountain Meadows Ranch." She closed her hand over her mouth, then pulled it away and opened it above the ground as if the words offended her.

Jared hesitated. "Can you show me where it happened?"

She looked down at her work, and nodded. "You mean the massacre." She disposed of the words with her hand.

"Yes."

She pointed toward the southwest. "Yonder."

"How far?"

"Only half a mile."

"Can I tell the place?"

"You can tell. There's a pile of rocks." Again the strange motion with her hand. It was somewhat as if she were picking a hair out of her mouth. "The soldiers were sent out after, you see, to bury them proper—all in one grave. In the same hole they'd dug to fight the Indians. All in one grave."

"Thank you, ma'am."

"They covered it with rocks." The woman looked down at her hands and began slowly rubbing them against each other, as if perhaps she could wear down the large knuckles. She nodded her head without looking up at him. "You'll see it. The grave." Again she gathered the words in her hand and dropped them on the ground.

Jared turned his horse and rode in the direction she had pointed.

Mountain Meadows was a long grassy flat lying between low sage-covered hills. A deep arroyo, fringed with trees, cut through the meadow. The air was full of bird calls, varied and low but unremitting. Far down the valley a calf bawled for its mother. He came to a place where the trees grew a little higher, and he could hear a spring gush from the earth at the bottom of the arroyo.

The breeze dipped, the hum of crickets faded, the sun was like an orange floating motionless in the great pool of the sky. But even in the glare of that desert sun, a shadow seemed to fall across the land. He rode his horse down through the steep arroyo.

On the opposite bank was a heap of stones—rugged roan-colored rocks, mottled with lichen, yellow and sea-green, lying in a pile perhaps twenty feet by ten feet. The mound was somewhat flattened now, no doubt from having sunk into the earth by its own weight and the decomposition of the massive grave beneath it. As he watched, a small lizard skittered from a crevice in the stones and darted away. The oak cross was gone.

Did he hear shots? Galloping hooves? The cries of women? Somehow those ghostly echoes seemed more real than the soft ring of his bridle bit or the creaking saddle. The cries came up to him from skulls lying within this piece of ground, and when Jared thought of them his body shrank. He got down from his horse and knelt—not in supplication, really, nor in penitence, nor even in mediation for his father, but in awe, staggered to his knees by the weight of happenings too dreadful to forgive, or even understand. A misty cold permeated his heart. He knew then, and he would always know, that men had died here, and other men had killed them.

**7** When Jared arrived back in Smithfield, Uncle Theodore somberly welcomed him to the house. "Your mother's been asking for you."

"How is she feeling?"

"She's asleep right now." Uncle Theodore led the way into the parlor and sat stiffly on the piano stool, pushing himself back and forth with the tips of his toes.

Jared took his seat on the sofa, where his hand could caress the shiny black saddle. For a few moments neither of them spoke. Then Jared began, "Was Father an unlucky man?"

"Well, he had his misfortunes, it's true. But then, haven't we all?"

"What sort of misfortunes?"

"You know them as well as I do."

"Not really. My father was fifty-seven years old when I was born. What misfortunes were you thinking of?"

The piano stool squeaked softly as Uncle Theodore twisted it back and forth. "The babies, for example. Lula Fae's first six babies were born dead, or died the same day. Maybe it was seven."

"Many women lost their babies."

"That's true."

"Father's misfortunes were not the same kind that other men have."

"Perhaps not."

"Take Mountain Meadows, for example."

"As a young man your father did very well—became rich, I'd say. But later he lost his herd."

"Did he ever talk to you about Mountain Meadows?"

"I think I hear Lula Fae. Let me tell her you're here. She may want to comb her hair."

A few minutes later Jared mounted the stairs and again entered the glistening room.

"Hello, Jerry."

"Hello, Mother." He bent and kissed her.

"Where did you go?"

"Looking."

"Still looking for your father?"

"That's what I'm going to do until I find him."

"Don't waste your life, Jerry. Your father wouldn't want you to."

"Aren't you worried about him?"

"Of course I'm worried. I just don't want you throwing your youth away."

"Tell me about Mountain Meadows."

"Where did you hear of Mountain Meadows?"

"From the newspapers. It's not such a great secret as everyone supposes."

She nodded.

"How come you never told me?" Jared asked.

"Why would anyone want to tell it? Or hear it, either?"

"But it happened. You can't just sweep it under the rug."

"That's where it's been for sixty years, until people like you start rummaging around."

"And I intend to keep on rummaging."

"You young people! You hold nothing sacred."

"What is sacred about murder?"

"Jared!"

"Well, what was it? I don't know. If it wasn't murder, what was it?"

She looked away with a shrug. "How would I know?"

"There is something you know that I don't. Does that make you more wicked than me? Or more righteous?"

"More burdened."

"Then let me share it."

"There's no need for you to know."

"I could never understand what separates the hiders and those who are hidden from. Are the hiders so much wiser that they can live with information that would wither the hidden from?"

"Please, Jerry. Let's not talk about it any more."

"Did Father ever live in Cedar City?"

"I thought you knew that. He grew up there."

"Was he involved in the massacre?"

"Of course not. He was only a boy."

"He was nineteen, almost as old as I am."

"Why are you doing this, Jared? What difference does it make?"

"If Father was there, it may explain what happened to him."

"I don't see how."

"There have been men enforcing the oath. Some of those who talked died."

"You're suggesting that your father would break his oath?"

"He was there, wasn't he?"

"Not until later. After the massacre some of the men went out from Cedar City to bury the dead. Your father was with them."

"Ahh."

"The Indians had stripped the bodies naked, mutilated them. He could never forget it. Over a hundred men and women they had to bury . . . Your father used to have nightmares." She shuddered. "Let's not talk about it any more."

"Did Father ever tell anybody about it? Besides you?"

"Never. Your father was an honorable man."

**8** Jared's horse was jaded from weeks of travel. He himself was tired: tired of looking, tired of riding, tired of a search that he could neither abandon nor end. He seemed no more able to stay in Smithfield than to leave it. At last, in a sort of mindless desperation, he sold his horse and caught the train north.

It was a slow journey—days passed before they reached the last few miles, rolling into Cardston. He found Alberta still bathed in the amber glow of Indian summer.

Jared was the only passenger; he sat alone in the railway coach, his bedroll and saddle on the seat in front of him. Though the railroad was new, the passenger car seemed a hopeless relic; he saw the old coach stretch and shorten in the corners as it swayed swiftly along the track. Outside the window, the telegraph line ran beside him, its burden of wires born on a myriad of rushing shoulders. He passed an occasional snow fence made from vertical boards placed a few inches apart, so it looked like the backbone of some long-dead buffalo lying over the hump of the land.

The ground dropped away beneath him; he felt the sudden thrill of flight, and found himself soaring above the river. Even the sound of the train was left behind, huffing anxiously along somewhere beneath him. For an instant he escaped the world and looked down upon it like a god—at the deep green water and bleached stones, and cattle drinking.

Suppose he could be a god? The thought frightened him. He had no desire to hold the fate of nations in his hand, or worse, the life of a single person. What would he do, for example, with a young man who had spent his missionary fund in a fruitless search for his father? Well, if he were a god he would understand. And if he understood he would forgive, wouldn't he? He would look into people's hearts and know there was a reason for the foolish or wicked things they do. Wouldn't he? He would have to forgive everyone.

With a rush and a clatter they reached the further end of the bridge, and the ground rose up again under the wheels.

The train rolled swiftly on, seeming to float, almost, and to lift its wheels each time it crossed a break in the rails, so its heavy click became a rapid *tick, tick, tick*, as if they were coasting home. Then as they began to slow, screeching and thumping, Jared craned to look forward out of the window. It seemed that he had been gone for a long time. With a dying shriek the train stopped, its last shudder running back through the cars like the weary quiver of a horse at the end of a long day.

Late that evening Jared rode into Lone Rock on a borrowed horse, and approached the house he had helped his father build. By the lamplight in the window he could see the family moving about the kitchen—Bessie and Lyman, Grace and Jane. He put his horse in the pasture and went inside.

"Jared!" Grace said. "Welcome home."

He kissed her lightly. "Thank you, Gracie."

"So you decided to come back?" Lyman said.

"Yes." He looked around the room. "Still no word of Father?"

135

Bessie shook her head.

Jared took a chair. Grace sat down across the table from him, but her eyes were on the handkerchief that she twisted and retwisted in her fingers.

"In Utah they don't know anything about him," Jared said.

Bessie asked. "Did you see Lula Fae?"

"Yes." Then he added, "I wish things had been different— that we all could have been together."

"That's what your father wanted," Bessie said.

"He did?"

"It's what we all wanted, really. That was the whole idea, for him to rule as a patriarch with his wives and children around him."

"Then why did he leave Mother?"

"The law forced him to do something. You can't imagine what it was like—sheriffs swarming over the country; people afraid to answer a knock at the door; fathers hiding out in the hills, sneaking home to visit their families when they dared; men in jail like common criminals simply for taking a second wife. It was either move to Canada or Mexico, or go underground." She paused. "So he came to Canada."

Lyman said, "And now he seems to have gone underground."

"It's nothing to joke about," she told him.

There was an awkward silence.

"How did the harvest go?" Jared asked.

Lyman started to laugh, and stopped abruptly, as if he had sucked in a fly. He coughed. "I'm glad you're interested."

"Of course I'm interested."

"Now that it's all in, you'd like your share, is that it?"

Suddenly Bessie faced Jared, for the first time since he came through the door. "Didn't you respect your father?"

"Yes. I respected him."

"How could you? How could you respect him, and still run away from the work he left undone?"

Jared didn't know what to say.

"I'm sorry to talk to you this way," she went on, "but I can't help it. You've had me so upset I couldn't sleep. Running off right at harvest time . . ."

"I was looking for Father."

"All this time?"

"I'm still looking."

"Do you know how hard your brother has worked?"

Jared rose from his chair.

Grace jumped up. "Where are you going?"

"Out." He put on his hat.

"Well, just a minute, little brother," Lyman said. "You might wait until we finish talking to you."

"There's more?" Jared asked.

"Go ahead, Mother. Tell him."

"Tell me what?"

"Don't argue with him," Lyman told his mother. "Just tell him."

"Yes," Jared said. "Tell me."

"All right." Bessie tossed her head. "You certainly have a right to know."

"Then tell me."

Still she hesitated.

"It's about the farm," Lyman said. "Since you ran away, those of us who were here had to decide what to do."

"About what?"

"About who would run the place. Somebody had to make decisions, be responsible, keep the bills paid up."

Jared sat down again.

Lyman glanced at Bessie.

"Go ahead," she said.

"Well," Lyman said, "I don't have to tell you that Father was not a rich man. But he was a good man. We already have our chief inheritance from him—a good name and a proud heritage."

"You talk as if he were dead."

"In Father's absence, it seemed to me we should be guided by the thought of what he would want if he were here. I'm sure his first concern would be for Mother. As the eldest son, I will stay and assist her in the management of the place."

"But Stanley's the eldest son," Jared said.

"I have talked to Stanley about it. You know how he hates the farm."

137

"You've claimed the estate, and you don't even know if Father's dead. Or do you?"

"What does that mean?" Lyman asked.

"You left the birthday party right after Father did." Jared turned toward Bessie. "Remember? He started home early to do the chores."

"So?" Lyman asked.

"But when I got there hours later, the chores still weren't done. Where were you, Lyman? Where did you go in such a hurry?"

Bessie gasped. "Stop it, Jared! I won't hear another word!"

"Did you kill my father?" Jared asked.

"He was my father, too," Lyman said. "You talk as though he were private property."

"No, Trash. That was you. That's how you thought of him—private property, something you could buy and sell. Or trade. Something you could trade for the farm."

"Jared!" Bessie cried. "Stop it. Do you hear?"

"You don't think I can find Father, do you?" Jared went on. "But you're wrong. I'll find him if it takes a thousand years."

"Good," Lyman said. "You need something useful to keep you occupied."

Jared started for the door.

"Just one thing," Lyman said firmly, "I want you to understand. When you return to your senses, don't come crawling back here."

Jared paused. "Are you trying to tell me something, Trash?"

"I am telling you. There's nothing here for you."

"You think you can run me off."

"I don't have to run you off, little brother. Nothing here belongs to you."

"I helped Father build this house, break this land . . ."

"We don't have to give you a thing."

"Give? Give? It's not yours to give."

"In Canada, Father has only one wife. Legally, you and Grace are bastards."

Lyman's words echoed in the abrupt silence that filled the room. Bessie breathed a single word "Lyman!" in horrified reproach. For a moment Jared stood silent, unmoving. Inside his body something burst, and strange, bitter liquid gushed up in his throat. He flung himself headlong across the room, and blind as Samson, grappled with Lyman. He seemed to sense blows falling on his face, but wiped them off like raindrops. Again he plunged forward, over table and chairs, into the corner and back. The floor sloped under him, the walls pitched, slowly turning; he felt a jar, and saw Lyman arched above him, falling. He rolled. There was another thump, and a scuffle. Arms tore at him, fists struck him, shouts deafened him close by, and from a distance he heard the shrieks of the women.

Somehow he got the floor under his feet, and pushed upward. He saw Lyman rising too, fists out in front of him like red flags waving, red with blood. Dimly through his armor of rage Jared felt the first faint scrape of pain. Again he lunged, and hurled the body of his brother back against the wall. Lyman's blurred, sweating face appeared before him, so close he seemed to catch the smell of dread it breathed. He thrust his open hand against the face and pushed it hard until it struck the wall—once, twice, three times. The world careened. Like falling comets they went across the room end over end, trailing a clatter of falling furniture and kitchenware. Jared landed on top, seized Lyman by the hair and began to smash his head against the floor.

Screams, arms, bodies flowed across him, plucking, punching, fumbling, leveling him at last, even pinning his limbs. As he lay there a kind of consciousness slowly returned to him. First he was aware of the pain in his body—in his bludgeoned face and aching bones, and in his chest, which seemed to roar like the inside of a burning tower. For several minutes he lay gasping. When he opened his eyes he saw Grace and Jane sitting on top of him.

"You almost killed him," Jane said.

He turned his head. Lyman lay not far away, needing nobody to hold him down. Rather, Bessie was bathing his face, which appeared strangely discolored under the blood that smeared it. His eyes were closed.

"If we let you up, will you behave?" Jane asked.

He felt a sense of peace, a strange detachment, as if he had no connection with the other people in the room. They moved in a different element, torpid and heavy, like water at the bottom of a deep river. "I'll behave," he said. His voice sounded strange, his hearing was fuzzy, his sight blurred. Even his pain seemed to come from a long way off. He slowly rose, groped around the room for his hat, and left the house.

The night air was restorative, putting an edge on his pain at the same time it fed life back into him. He crossed the dark yard, and saddled his horse, Summer. As he prepared to mount, he became aware of a pale image floating in the night not far away. He turned, and it moved toward him.

"Jared?" It was Grace. In the darkness she appeared not to touch the ground as she walked. "Where are you going?"

"I don't know."

"You don't have to go tonight."

"I can't stay here."

She hesitated. "You're not coming back, are you?"

"No."

"What about your things?"

"I don't have anything. Didn't you hear Lyman?"

"You don't believe him, do you? You'll fight him? You won't let him get away with it?"

"Fight him how? In court? Go to court to prove I'm not a bastard?"

"Oh, Jared."

"I won't give him that satisfaction."

"If you leave, you'll be doing exactly what he wants."

"I know. But I won't fight with anyone over my father's bones."

She timidly drew closer. "You're all I have, Jared. We only have each other now. Isn't that true?"

A swift stab of loss pierced him. "Yes. I guess it's true." As much as any orphan, he felt alone in the world. Painfully he climbed into the saddle. "Good-bye, Gracie." He turned his horse down the lane.

**9** As Summer galloped into the night, Jared realized that left to himself, the horse would take the road to Cardston out of habit. Jared didn't want to go to Cardston, not tonight. He had no stomach for quiet firesides and familiar, pious faces. What he needed was noise and darkness, some cellar reeking with the sweat of sin. Hickory Jack's dance hall—that was the place he yearned for. He remembered the plump, perfumed woman who had whirled him around the room. If he could find her tonight . . . Too bad his father had burned the dance hall down.

But that woman was somewhere still, drinking and dancing. His mouth felt dry with unholy longing for her.

Or Paula. Even the thought of her caused his heart to drop. Nothing that happened could completely take away the memory of their first day together—that misty, far-off, half-forgotten dream.

That had been the morning of July 24 when Jared was seventeen. He had curried his horse, Summer, then galloped down the main street of Lone Rock. The whole town was joined in the celebration of Pioneer Day—the day when Brigham Young first saw the Salt Lake Valley. There was music and speeches and comic readings at the meeting house, followed by sports and activities down by the river. The last event of the day was the horse race.

Down a long stretch of river flat they had laid out a race course. The ground was level, but marked by shallow swales and clumps of buckbrush. At one end the group gathered, and two girls were assigned to hold a slim rope which would mark the finish line.

As Jared mounted Summer, the horse seemed to catch the mood of the event, and side-stepped nervously. Jared jerked the reins slightly, and then gave a steady pull. "Hup! Hup, boy!" Summer backed a short way, neck arched and tail high, then briefly raised his front hooves clear of the ground, and again, and then reared almost straight up and walked three steps backward before he came down. The ladies squealed their approval, while Jared bowed in the saddle and waved his hat to them.

He was suddenly aware of Paula Gibson standing by his horse. "Jared!" she cried. "Where did you learn to do that?" He was fascinated by Paula Gibson, but he was not sure that he liked her, really. He turned his horse.

"Wait!" She held her handkerchief up to him. "Carry this for luck."

Taking off his hat, he slipped the handkerchief under the band, so that one lace corner fluttered in the wind. "Ya hoo!" he yodeled, and galloped off to the starting place. Just as he turned Summer into line with the other horses, the starter cried, "Go!"

He sank his heels in Summer's ribs and arched his body close above the saddle horn. The horse lunged forward so swiftly that for an instant the saddle seemed to lift above his back. Hooves fell on the sod, staccato at first, almost with a hesitation between them, then sounding more and more closely, until the noise was a steady drumming beneath and all around him. The snorts of the horses, the squeak of their bellies, the thunder of their hooves, the shouts of the boys enveloped him—bore him along, it seemed, like the crest of a wave. And far down the river flat he saw the crowd gathered in two bright clusters, with the white thread of rope stretched between them.

"Hah! Git!" He lashed Summer's sides with the bridle reins. The pack had thinned as slower horses trailed away behind him, but Hyrum Wills on his bay mare stayed up even, stride for stride, so close that twice their stirrups clicked.

The sound of the two horses, and their speed too, seemed to approach the line in a rushing crescendo that swelled unendurably and then climaxed in the scream of the girls as the horses touched the rope and swept it free.

But Jared had reached it first. As he loped back to the group, he saw Paula running out to meet him. All the force and fury of the race still surged inside his body. When he reached her he drew Summer to a stop, then while the gelding wheeled he kicked his foot free of the stirrup, reached down for Paula's hand and lifted. Her foot caught the stirrup, and she was up behind him, mounted sidesaddle. He felt her arms tight around his body.

Someone shouted, "Come on, you two. It's time to eat." But Jared wasn't hungry. His mouth was dry with a strange excitement, not new exactly, but beyond anything he'd ever known before. He rode Summer through the swift, roiling current of the river, and into the trees that fringed the water on the other side.

The place was still. All they could hear was the rush of the water, the rhythmic whisper of Summer's hooves falling on the soft earth, the caw of a crow and the sound of his wings as he flapped up from a cottonwood.

"When's your birthday?" Paula asked suddenly.

"April."

"April the what'th?"

"Tenth."

"You're an Aries. That means you are passionate and unruly, sure of yourself . . ."

"Hah!"

"I'm a Pisces. I'm cuddly." Reaching, she pulled the bridle reins. Summer stopped. "Come on. I'll show you."

Her foot kicked his leg. He lifted his left boot free, and then, with her arms even more tightly around him, she began to slide down, her toe stretched toward the stirrup.

"Wait," he said. He unclasped her arms from his body, and with a quick twist, threw his leg over the saddle horn and jumped to the ground, turning just in time to catch Paula as she slipped helplessly from her place behind the saddle. For a moment he held her free of the ground, then let her slip through his arms. Even after her feet were firmly on the ground, she clung to him.

"Where did you go?" she chided.

"I was going to lift you down."

"You almost had to lift me up." She pulled out of his arms, and bending, led him by the hand into a thicket of black birch. There she sat in the deep grass, her arms around her knees, and looked up at the lacy canopy of their arbor. Presently she said, "Aren't you going to sit down?"

He tried to speak, but his mouth wouldn't work. He sank to his knees.

"Not way over there, silly. Here, beside me." She indicated the place with her hand.

He advanced, walking on his knees.

"What are you scared of?"

"I'm not scared."

"I won't hurt you." She took his arm and drew him close beside her. She raised her face toward his. "Just hold still." She slipped one hand behind his head and drew him down. He felt her soft, warm lips come against his, then draw away. "There. Did that hurt?" He realized that he had closed his eyes; he opened them and saw that she was watching him. "You're all tense," she said. "You have to relax. Your mouth feels like somebody's elbow."

This time when her lips touched his they didn't draw away again. One of her hands was still behind his head, the other around his shoulder, drawing him down. She bent backward, slowly, languidly, turning, stretching. He found that he was lying partly across her body, his lips still pressing hers. She pulled back slightly. "Put your arms around me," she said. He felt ungainly, still he did as he was told. They rolled to permit his arm to pass beneath her.

"Isn't that better?"

"Yes."

"Aren't I cuddly?" She had begun to breathe in quick little gushes, her arms tight around him. His body surged in an involuntary spasm. She gasped, and lay utterly still. "Jared. What are you doing?"

"I don't know."

"What did you have to spoil it for?" She pushed him away and sat up, smoothing her skirt down over her ankles.

"I'm sorry."

"You boys are all the same."

He realized, and it seemed to come as a surprise, that he was not the first to have kissed her or felt her firm young body in his arms. "I never kissed a girl before."

She laughed. "You don't have to tell me that." She got quickly to her feet. "We'd better go."

"You're not mad, are you?"

"Of course not, silly."

He caught Summer, and they rode slowly back to the picnic. Paula didn't speak, but Jared was feverishly aware of her arms circling him, and her breath warm through the back of his shirt.

Now, as Summer galloped steadily on, Jared was riding alone, and the Indian Reserve seemed broad as the plains of Hades, but empty, without inhabitants. He turned east, toward Lethbridge. He didn't need Paula. There were plenty of girls in the world—houses full of them: light-hearted girls anxious to please a man, so Jared had heard, not torment him; not lie in the dark meadow with him, murmuring, "You don't have to worry. I'll stop you."

Tonight he didn't want to be stopped. Somewhere he'd discover a dark pool of wickedness, and bathe himself in it, wash away this crust of piety that covered him like a coat of mail. Perhaps at last he'd find peace, rest from this infernal labor of righteousness.

As he came over a height of land, Jared saw a few distant lights faintly winking from the earth, like reflections of stars. He flicked Summer's sides with his heels, and the horse broke into a gallop down the slope of a ravine. His front hoof slipped into a hole, and he was flung forward so quickly that Jared could not free himself from the saddle. Summer's upending body trapped his head against the ground. He gave a squeal of pain. Jared landed on his hip and shoulder with a whipping motion that snapped his head against the hard earth. His skid was stopped by his foot caught under Summer's body.

He was dazed for a few moments—only seconds, probably. The weight of Summer's body on his leg was the first thing he noticed clearly—the weight and the shaking. The horse's hind legs were kicking convulsively; Jared could hear the hooves drag on the ground. He squirmed, trying to free himself. The shaking stopped. Summer lay still. Jared realized that he was dead.

The bulge of the horse's belly lay on Jared's leg just below the calf. The ground beneath him was almost bare of grass. He scraped at it with his fingers, but all he did was wear out his skin. When he had exhausted himself, he lay back, breathing heavily.

He needed some kind of tool to dig out the ground under his trapped leg. If he could reach the bridle and get it off, perhaps the shank of the bit would be sharp enough. But he was lying at an angle away from Summer's head. He stretched, twisting, thinking perhaps his leg might slide sideways, but it didn't move at all. It might as well have had a stake through it. He lay back to catch his breath, and realized that even in this cool hour of the night he was sweating.

He decided to wait for daylight. Maybe in the light some obvious solution would become apparent. He lay back and tried to relax.

Around the Pole Star the Big Dipper turned, carrying with it all the stars of heaven, like some gigantic construction of lights. He had heard that some stars were so distant that a thousand years after they had burned out, their light would still be traveling toward earth, still visible. He might be looking at a star that no longer existed. Tonight Jared felt like that, as if he no longer existed but because of some lag in the cosmos he remained visible.

He couldn't lie on his back for very long because that twisted his leg, and when he rolled onto his side his bruised hip and shoulder hurt. At last he crossed over, twisting at the waist, so he lay partially on his face. It was the most comfortable position he could find. When it had grown light enough to see around him, he rolled back and raised on his elbow.

He lay on the slope of a shallow ravine, which still had a little water trapped in its cup, a watering hole. When the water had been higher, the cattle had trampled the edges of the pond bare of grass, and now the place where Jared lay was pocked with hoofmarks as hard as mortar. He turned his body first one way and then the other, studying the land. The furthest he could see in any direction was not more than half a mile.

He began to pull on his leg, pushing against the saddle with his other foot—twisting, tugging. After several minutes he stopped and lay over on his face again.

As the morning progressed, he prayed—not necessarily for

deliverance at first, only for the strength to meet this test, whatever it was. He felt unworthy to ask for more. But as the sun continued its slow progress across the sky, he prayed for forgiveness, and finally for rescue.

No angels came. He hadn't expected them. He didn't know what he did expect—nothing, probably. But he reminded himself he must have faith. Surely if the Lord wanted to save him, He could think of a way to do it.

The air was heavy and stale, especially there beside the body of Summer. Flies had begun to buzz around the horse's head. Jared became aware that he was actually dozing. Stiff, cramped, pained in both his leg and body, unable to lie comfortably, he still felt the weight of the day pressing him down beneath the level of consciousness. He didn't know whether to yield to it or try to stay awake. Was it possible that while he slept, some opportunity for rescue might pass him by? Even as he thought of it, he drowsed.

He noticed a noise coming from somewhere. It seemed to reach him through the earth rather than the air—a sort of rustling, stirring, stepping, cropping . . . He turned and looked behind him. A few cattle had grazed over the hill and were making their way down to the water. By now they were quite close to him. There was something disturbing about them, something almost cruel in the life and freedom which they seemed to regard so lightly. Then one of them, raising her head to chew, noticed Jared and Summer lying close in front of her. She snorted and jumped to one side, her tail out straight. Instantly all heads were up, all eyes on Jared. The herd veered to the right, except for a large roan bull who stood fast and brought a low strangling moan from so deep in his throat, it shook his wattle.

The cattle came slowly forward, heads lowered and eyes wide, sniffing. Jared swung his arms. "Hah!" he cried. They stopped. A couple of them dodged back. The bull came through the front rank, his great shoulders swaying each time he planted a hoof. He stopped scarcely twenty feet away and looked at Jared. Another moan escaped him. He reached forward with one front hoof, scraped it swiftly back and sent a spray of dirt arching over his back.

Jared could see the bull close above him: the horns, white with shiny black tips; the cluster of hair on the brow of the head; the eyes, bright with fury; the smooth, dished face; the white muzzle, partly open, dripping slaver.

As the animal took another step, Jared flipped the leather loop from his saddle horn, grabbed his lariat, and tied the end of it around his body just under the armpits. Then he managed to shake out a small loop in the other end of the rope, and twisted as far as he could to face the bull. "Okay, bull," he said. "Come and get me."

The rest of the cattle were drawing closer. The bull lunged forward and scooped with his horns, then stopped again. Jared threw the lariat. The rope whipped through his hand, the loop spread; his aim was good. Now if he only had the length to make the distance. The rope played out and the loop seemed to hesitate, diminish, even lift slightly as it hit the end. Then it fell over the bull's horns. For a moment the loop lay there like a low-fitting garland around the tufted head, across the nose, just under the angry little eyes. Jared shook his rope; the bull shook his head. The rope slipped lower. He waited, giving it all the slack he could.

The bull snorted and tossed his head. The loop fell over his nose. Jared jerked, the rope came tight; alarmed, the bull edged backward and swung away. Jared had an excruciating moment in which he saw his body parting in the middle, the top half dragging after the bull and the legs remaining trapped under Summer. The rope was like a steel wire cutting into his chest, and his leg felt as if it were being drawn down in an auger. Then suddenly he was free, and being dragged over the sod faster and faster as the bull tried to escape its strange burden. The other cattle ran alongside them, hopscotching and bellowing. As they converged on their leader, he slowed and turned. Jared felt the rope fall slack. He jerked it over his shoulders and flung it free.

The bull stared at Jared for a while, then turned and led his harem away, the rope still trailing from his neck. They had not gone far before they were grazing again. Some of them turned back to drink at another part of the pond.

By the time his pain had begun to subside, Jared realized

that the sun was gone. He lay for a while, hoping that some-how his body could restore itself. He was parched, hungry, pained and weary.

He managed to pray again—to thank God. He was alive; he could stand the pain. But as the hours passed, doubt set in. Just because he had prayed, and not died, did that mean the two things were connected? He remembered the story his father used to tell about the man sliding off the roof who hastily said a prayer. At that moment his overalls caught on a nail and stopped him, so he cried, "Never mind, Lord. I can manage myself this time." Was that the kind of man Jared was?

He was ashamed of himself for praying—he would have preferred to feel that his victory had been his alone. The prayer didn't prove anything, anyway. If you could live through the same experience twice, one time praying about it and the other time not, and then compare results, maybe you could prove something.

At length he rose and made his way down to the stagnant water, bathed his head and drank. As he glanced back, it seemed that already the dead horse was beginning to swell; he returned and unfastened the cinch. Then he began to cross the dark plain, Summer's body like a great anchor dragging fur-ther and further behind him.

**10** He walked all night—walked and rested by turns. It was not walking, really; he hobbled, and so his prog-ress was very slow. When at last the light came, it revealed, far down the slope of the prairie, a small log house. That cabin became his objective, though whether it was inhabited seemed doubtful. Indian families did live in such remote places, but he could not imagine where they got water or firewood. As he came closer he was able to see other things besides the house—a wagon and a small canvas tent pitched nearby.

It seemed as though hours passed. The sun rose high. The

distant line of the river appeared to enlarge through the glass of the heated air, and wavered, watery and mystical. But the house seemed as far away as ever. He hobbled on.

In time, as he drew near, three dogs rose up from under the wagon and ran toward him, barking. A small child came out of the tent, and was followed by other people. They stood looking in Jared's direction. The dogs came running straight toward him, two of them barking. The third, a brindle greyhound, ran ahead of the others. A few feet away he stopped and walked around Jared, staring, head and tail curled downward. The others bounded up, snarling and yapping.

Jared stopped too. The eyes of the greyhound seemed hollow, like holes in a cave. Jared could see the firelight reflected on the walls inside the dog's head. When he started forward again, the dogs moved too, the silent one circling, the others backing in front of him, barking. It seemed to require physical effort to push them back, and he had none left. He stopped; he felt his body sway. He wanted to sit down, but he was afraid if he did the dogs would attack. All at once the landscape blurred and the world began to turn. He had no sensation of falling, but he knew by the tilt of the horizon that he no longer had his feet under him. He didn't even feel his body hit the ground.

He woke to a heavy, sweet smell, compounded of living flesh and buckskin and hot canvas. He was lying under the tent. Around him several dark, solemn faces stared down, children and adults. Jared tried to say something, but found that he could not. One face—that of an old man—moved forward from among the others and spoke a few Indian words. His voice was soft and fluid, almost without consonants, the syllables flowing over each other like waves in the river, hesitating, continuing, and then falling away to a sibilant whisper, and dying. He began an odd ritual, a sort of combination witchcraft and massage. Jared was not sure whether he was giving him first aid or performing last rites.

Sometime in the course of the afternoon they took him outside, where a team of horses stood hitched to the wagon— no more than ponies, really, with collars too big for them. The horses' faces peered from deep behind the blinders. The

150

grandfather, sitting on a board at the front of the wagon, indicated that Jared should sit beside him.

Jared demurred. Unsteadily he climbed over the rear wheel and crawled full-length onto the floor of the wagon. There he was joined by the squaws and children, who somehow seemed to sit comfortably on the hard boards. The wagon moved away, its box shaking solidly with each movement of the wheel. Jared lay on his back on the jiggling floor. The children stared at him with wide eyes.

The miles and hours rolled away, almost in unison it seemed. Somewhere on the road Jared passed from consciousness.

He woke when the wheels began to joggle even more violently. He could hear the rush of water under the wagon box and the splash of the horses' feet. They must be bouncing over the stony bottom of the St. Mary's River. A short distance further the wagon stopped. Jared could see a rustic sign hanging from the high pole above them: *Arrowhead Ranch.* One of the squaws opened the gate, and they drove on in. Jared raised on his elbow to look over the side of the wagon box. The old man stopped his outfit in front of the ranch house. A dark-haired girl stood in the door.

Jared apologized. "I didn't know where they were bringing me."

She studied him. "You're a mess. What in the world happened to you?"

"My horse fell and pinned me."

"And smeared blood all over your face?"

For a minute he didn't understand what she was talking about; it all seemed to have happened years ago. "That was before. I had a little scrap with my brother."

"Can you walk?"

"I think so."

"You'd better come in and rest."

Jared climbed painfully out of the wagon. For a moment he steadied himself against the wheel. "Thanks," he said, and waved feebly. The Indian family drove away, down past the barn, their three dogs trotting at the rear with their heads in the shade of the wagon box.

151

**11** As Jared mounted the steps to the bunkhouse a great weariness came over him, like a disease. He began to shake. He stumbled across the room and sat heavily on the edge of the bunk, pulled off his boots, and stretched out. The girl said, "Is there anything I can bring you?"

"I'm thirsty," he said. But while he waited for her to return with a glass of water, he went to sleep.

It was after dark when he woke. He thought at first it must be the middle of the night. As he lay there, though, the door opened, footsteps crossed the floor, a match struck and flickered, and the soft light of a coal-oil lamp filled the room. The girl came toward him, carrying the lamp. Behind her walked a tall man with eye sockets like old wounds. Jared's heart lurched. It was Hickory Jack.

"You're awake," the girl whispered. "Here. Have a drink."

He raised on his elbow and drank from the glass she handed him.

Hickory Jack stood behind the girl, his shadow looming up the wall and halfway across the ceiling. "What happened?" he asked.

"My horse stumbled," Jared said. "Broke its neck. Pinned me."

"You got anythin' broke?"

"Just lost some hide off my hip. And my leg's pretty sore where he laid on me."

"We better look at it," Hickory Jack said. Jared pulled off his shirt and rolled on his side. "Yah, you're missin' a little meat," Hickory Jack told him. "But you made it up with dirt."

They brought a washtub from the ranch house and emptied the teakettle into it, then the girl stirred in cold water until the temperature suited her. She laid a towel on the chair, and left them. Jared finished undressing and gingerly settled himself into the washtub, with his arms and feet hanging over the sides. Very slowly he soaped and rinsed himself, first on one portion of his body, then another.

Hickory Jack sat on a chair nearby, puffing his pipe. "You one of the Roseman boys?"

"Yes. Jared."

"Where you headed for?"

Jared tried to remember his circumstances just before Summer stumbled. He shook his head. "No place."

"Just figured we ought to let somebody know why you didn't get there."

"Nobody was expecting me."

For a while Hickory Jack sat puffing on his pipe and watched Jared wash himself. One corner of his lips made moist little sucking noises as he puffed. "They ever find your pa?"

"No."

As Jared stood up in the tub Hickory Jack passed the towel to him. "That's a wicked-lookin' scrape you got there." He left the room, but was back in a few minutes with a dark-colored bottle. "You get blood poisoning in that, we'll have to amputate your rear end." He laughed. "You lie on your belly."

Jared stretched across the bunk, and felt cool liquid daubed along his wounded back and hip. As it seeped into the flesh it began to burn, rather dully at first, then with quickly increasing sharpness. "This might smart a little," said Hickory Jack. "Mostly I use it on wire-cut horses."

Jared grabbed a fistful of blankets at the edge of the bed and squeezed with all his might. Still he could not hold back a quick exclamation of pain.

"How'd old Hungry Dog come to bring you here?" Hickory Jack asked.

"I don't know," Jared said, and tried not to reveal the catch in his voice, though as more linament was spread on him he winced and gasped. "I guess it was the closest place. I didn't even look—I thought he was taking me to town."

At last Hickory Jack quit swabbing on the firewater and pulled the covers up over Jared's shoulders. The girl came back into the room, carrying a plate of supper for Jared.

Later, after Hickory Jack and his daughter were gone, a young man came into the room and crossed the floor to the bunk in the other corner. As he sat on the bed unbuttoning his shirt he didn't look at Jared, but acted as if he were alone in the room. Completely naked then, he rolled a cigarette, lit it, and crossed the room with long flat-footed strides and blew out the lamp. The red tip of his cigarette returned through the darkness, pulling the pale figure of the man behind it. He got into bed and lay there, his features dimly illumined by soft red light each time he drew on his smoke.

The next morning when Jared woke he was alone in the room. He dressed and hobbled up to the ranch house. Hickory Jack and the young man were seated at the table, while the girl worked at the stove.

"Just set anywhere," Hickory Jack said from his armchair at the head of the table. Jared took a place across from the young man.

The main room of the ranch house was a kind of combination kitchen-parlor. It contained a stove, cupboard, table and chairs, an old couch, a rocking chair and a fireplace. A random collection of coats, sweaters, hats, caps and scarfs hung on nails behind the door. On one wall was a large red calendar with a picture of a couple of hunting dogs. The rest of the space on the walls was taken up with mounted deer and antelope heads, skulls, antlers and guns.

The girl set the coffeepot on the table, and several heaping plates—one of fried eggs, one of crisp brown potatoes, one of bacon, one of pancakes—and to her father she passed a bowl of thick gravy made from milk and bacon grease. Hickory Jack stacked a couple of slices of bread on his plate and covered them with gravy. Around the side he added several strips of bacon, a pile of potatoes, three or four pancakes with butter, two fried eggs on top of them and a slosh of syrup over that. He rolled his sleeves a little higher.

"Go ahead," he told the others. He sank his knife across a corner of his meal and carried it dripping to his mouth. Again. And again. He paused to chew, and looked around the table. His eyes stopped on Jared. "Eat up there, young feller. You need your strength."

The girl was still at the stove frying pancakes, but she glanced over her shoulder. "Daddy enjoys his breakfast," she said.

Hickory Jack motioned with his knife. "That girl of mine. 'They don't eat like that at Buckingham Palace,' she says. What do I care how they eat at Buckingham Palace? This sure and certain ain't Buckingham Palace, is it? Can you tell me how a left-handed idiot on his day off could mistake this for Buckingham Palace? It ain't possible." It was uncanny how he could keep food going in and words coming out simultaneously. "But I don't mind. She can nag all she wants, as long as she'll swing a skillet like that, eh? I know what the scientists say—we got taste buds at the top of our mouths for honey, and buds at the bottom for lemon, or is it the other way around? Mister, I got taste buds all over my mouth, and I use ever one of 'em with ever bite I take." He looked down. His plate was empty. He seemed a little disappointed. He consoled himself by skating chunks of bread around it on the end of his fork, wiping it clean. Then he raised his coffee cup and slurped from the rim. "Where'd you leave your horse? Maybe we can go get your rig today, before the Indians beat you to it."

"I'd appreciate that."

"Can you tell me how to get there?"

Jared tried to think. "There's a pond. It's a shallow ravine, and a sort of natural dam has made this pond."

"Up above Hungry Dog's?"

"That's right. It seemed like I walked for miles, but it likely isn't far."

"I think I know the place. Whit and I will go and have a look."

The young man stretched back in his chair. "Don't send me to fetch no greenhorn's saddle. Don't take no two men, anyways, to get no greenhorn's saddle."

"Might be a might tricky, gettin' the saddle off without scratchin' the leathers."

The girl said, "I can go with you, Daddy."

Hickory Jack stoked his pipe and fussed with it, getting it going. "All right."

Whit rose, took his hat from a nail behind the door, and left the house.

"That Whit's a moody devil," Hickory Jack said.

Jared didn't quite know what to say. "I appreciate your help."

"I'd do the same for any lame Indian." Hickory Jack went outside.

The girl had taken a place at the table and was quietly eating her breakfast.

"Is Whit your hired man?" Jared asked.

She nodded. "He just rode in one day, looking for work."

"So really, there's just you and Hickory Jack?"

"For a while there were three of us. Mother died when I was four."

"Don't you get lonesome, way out here?"

"Not really. But it's nice to have company sometimes."

"I'm not sure your father thinks so."

"Oh, don't mind Daddy."

There came a shout from the direction of the barn. "Kelly!"

"I guess I'd better go," she said. "Can you make it to the bunkhouse all right?"

"Sure. I'm all right."

At the door she looked back. "You're welcome to stay as long as you need to," she said. "I can manage Daddy."


**12** Jared didn't leave the Arrowhead that day, nor the next. The third day he spent most of his time down at the corrals, watching the men break horses. Hickory Jack had a contract to provide remounts for the Army, and it kept him and Whit going to break them fast enough to meet the terms of his agreement.

One morning at breakfast Jared said, "I guess I'm ready to start traveling again, if I can borrow a horse."

"Sure," Hickory Jack said. "You can take Snowball."

"You're not ready to travel yet," Kelly told him.

"I'm feeling pretty good. In fact, I was wondering if I could help you break horses for a few days to sort of work out my board."

"We don't need no help," Whit said.

But Hickory Jack told him, "Come on down to the corral and let's see what you can do."

Jared was sitting on the top rail of the corral when Hickory Jack and Whit drove the herd galloping in from the prairie. The lead horses reached the open gate and stopped, circling nervously, snorting. The riders crowded the herd, pressing the leaders until they started through the gate. The others followed easily.

With one man working the gate to the adjoining corral then, and the other on horseback acting as cutter, they began to mill the herd, peeling off the horses they wanted and driving them into the next corral. They left behind the ones that didn't carry the Arrowhead brand, or that were too old, too young, too small or too heavy, and when the cutting was complete, turned them back onto the prairie.

They had about twenty-five head of horses left—mature, healthy animals, all Arrowhead stock. It was midafternoon. At last the work of breaking could begin.

Adjoining one of the large square corrals was a small octagonal one with a snubbing post in the middle. At one time the post had been thick, as could be seen by its size where it came out of the ground, but the top portion of it was half worn away, gouged and routed, and polished to a soft gloss by countless lariats, so it gleamed like some cherished wood antique. While Jared manned the gate to this small corral, Hickory Jack cut a bay gelding from the bunch and hazed it in. As soon as it found itself separated from the others, the bay trotted back and forth, stretching its neck to look across the six-foot gate at its comrades.

"This one's mine," said Hickory Jack. Already he was down in the corral with his lariat, his right arm across the front of his body, holding the loop low so it dragged behind him on the left. As the bay turned and moved to the right, Hickory Jack brought the loop quickly across in front of him and threw a hoolihan, or inverted loop, from below shoulder level. The bay didn't even know the rope was on its way, so low and quietly did it begin. It rolled up like an iron hoop, coming out of nowhere. Before the horse could stop, or turn, or even nod, it had plunged headfirst into the loop. Hickory Jack took a swift dally on the snubbing post, and when the horse tried to plunge away, it was brought up short at the end of the lariat.

Then, while the bay sashayed back and forth, Hickory Jack drew in each ripple of slack it gave him, working it closer and closer to the post. With every loss of ground the bay hung back more desperately, wringing its head from side to side. The rope around its neck tightened. Its nostrils flared, the horse's breath rasped out and in, loudly at first, then more shrilly and quietly as the loop was drawn tighter and tighter. Bit by bit the rope advanced, and in a matter of minutes the bay's head was tight against the post. Its whole body was bent like a bow, its legs trembling. When Hickory Jack snapped a sack at it, it seemed to go straight up about four inches.

"Easy does it," Hickory Jack said, flipping the sack. "This ain't gonna hurt you now. You're a fine fella, you are. Just easy there, Jasper. Slow. Slow . . ."

For several minutes he sacked out the bay, talking all the while, moving closer, slapping it with the sack on the neck and body and legs, finally walking all around it, dragging the sack up its flank and under its tail. Gradually the horse's arched, resisting muscles softened. Hickory Jack touched it with his hand, patting its neck and talking quietly. As the bay stood, more quiet now, he slowly worked some slack into the rope, slid a loop forward through the noose around the horse's neck, and deftly passed a half-hitch over its nose. Then he slipped the rope off the post.

Gingerly the bay backed a step or two, and then turned to go. Hickory Jack pulled on the rope—the "nerve line" that he had created—and the loop tightened on the horse's nose. The bay faced around in some surprise. "You come with me," Hickory Jack said. The bay backed away, then started forward as the nerve line tightened over his nose and under his jaw. "Be a good boy now, and this won't hurt you."

The cayuse stood uncertainly. Again it edged away, and as it felt the rope tighten, suddenly reared backward on dancing legs. It squealed and wrenched its head, fighting the pain. Hickory Jack gave ground, but held the rope tight. Suddenly the bay plunged forward, almost upon him.

"That's right, Jasper. Be a good boy. Easy. Come with me."
Quivering from head to toe, the bay dared not move. Hickory Jack walked two or three steps to the left, pulling the rope. The bay shifted. He went back the other way. Again the horse turned. "Don't get in a tug-of-war with him," Hickory Jack said to Jared. "You can move the biggest horse in the world to the side. That's the way you start him following you." Presently he began to move a step or two ahead of the bay, and it came. Within a few minutes it was following him around the corral at a trot.

"Well, Jasper," Hickory Jack said. "You ready for a canter?"

Jared jumped down into the corral, and while he held the nerve line, Hickory Jack fitted Jasper with a hackamore that had a wide leather brow band on it. He slid the band down so it acted like a blindfold. Jasper stood, trembling slightly, but unwilling to move unless he knew what was going on around him.

Hickory Jack sacked him out a little more, until he seemed to accept the touch of the sack any place on his body. Then he placed the saddle blanket. The weight of the saddle caused Jasper to sag and step nervously. He reacted again when Hickory Jack pulled the cinch tight, but as long as he couldn't see he dared not move or kick.

Jared slipped the lariat off. Hickory Jack passed the hackamore rein over Jasper's head, then with the reins firmly in his left hand, he took the saddle horn with his right, raised one foot to the stirrup, and mounted. The movement was unhurried, yet so quickly and smoothly done, with Hickory Jack's body so close to the horse, the stirrup scarcely sank under his weight. Jasper staggered slightly and turned his head. Hickory Jack reached forward and pulled up the blindfold.

There was no immediate reaction. Jasper needed a moment or two to try to understand what was happening. Then Hickory Jack moved his legs out and in slightly, causing the stirrup leathers to slap the horse's sides. Jasper crow-hopped experimentally. The weight on his back remained. He bucked higher, and then higher; finally, with a squeal of rage and frustration, he sank his head and threw himself upward with all his strength, twisting his body in midair.

"Yah-hoo!" yelled Hickory Jack.

Jasper landed, ran two jumps and bucked again, and finally fell to plunging wildly around the corral. Hickory Jack stayed with him. "Yah-hoo!"

Within a few minutes the horse grew weary. His lunges diminished. Twice he stopped, bucked a little more, and stopped again. He stood with head down and sides moving in and out. Hickory Jack slid the blindfold down and dismounted.

They unsaddled Jasper and turned him into a corral by himself. "We'll give him another lesson tomorrow," Hickory Jack said. "Three lessons and he gets a diploma."

The days that followed were delightful to Jared. He liked the excitement of the milling horses, the glint of their coats in the sun, the occasional wild whinny of one, followed by a shrill, bugling reply. The dust that rose around them filled his nostrils, and at night he seemed to breathe it in his dreams— the gentle, acrid scent of horses.

One night Jared wakened and found that the other bunk was empty; Whit must have taken a midnight stroll. He started to doze again, but he heard a voice from somewhere beyond his bunkhouse window and realized it was that sound which had disturbed him.

"I thought you weren't coming." The voice was scarcely more than a whisper, but he could tell at once it belonged to Whit. A reply seemed to breathe out of the darkness, too softly to be understood. "I just wanted to talk to you," Whit went on. He continued to speak, with occasional pauses during which a responding murmur came to Jared more and more clearly.

"About us. About life," Whit said. "I don't know. Just to talk to you alone, without anyone around."

Murmur.

"You're a very pretty girl, you know."

Jared came fully awake.

Whit softly expelled a sample of his dry, unamused laughter. "I can tell a pretty girl when I see one, all right."

There was a pause.

"Is old Hickory Jack really your daddy?"

This time the reply was audible. "Of course."

"Your mother must have been a looker."

The voice faded again, too low to hear.

"How long you been keepin' house for your daddy?"

"Fourteen years."

"Fourteen years! Isn't it time you found another man to take care of?"

"There aren't any men any more."

"That's what your daddy tells you. But how do you know, stuck out in this hole?"

"I know."

"Listen. There's plenty of things I could teach your daddy."

"Like what?"

"I been to Texas, you know. New Mexico, California."

Silence.

"I think I'll go back to San Antone. After spending a couple of years at the center of the world, this place is like the outside edge of hell. How do you stand it?"

Murmur.

"I mean. Them Texas girls are pretty, but if you was to ever put on a dress, you'd paint 'em right out."

"I don't have a dress."

"Listen. Next time I go to town I'll get you one."

"You will?" Then the voice changed. "Please don't do that."

"Man, you're jumpy."

"Don't, please."

"How old are you?" he asked.

"Old enough."

"Hah! You're not even old enough to hold hands."

There was a long pause. "I'm eighteen," she said.

"And you've never held hands?"

"I didn't say that."

"I can tell if a filly has never been rode before."

"I'm not a horse."

"You ought to be. Then you'd have some company other than that old billy goat of a daddy."

There was a brief scuffle outside the window. "Let go of

me!" The words were spaced and emphatic, though still very quiet.

"Promise not to hit?"

"I don't make promises."

"All right."

There was another scuffle. "I'll call," she said.

"Call, then." He laughed again.

"Keep away from me. Let me go!"

"You're all mixed up," he said. "It's not wicked to kiss a man."

"Stop it!"

"It won't hurt."

"No! Stop it!"

"Don't be silly. It's what you wanted all along."

"It is *not!*"

"That's what you tell yourself. But why else did you meet me?"

"I don't know. I wish I never had met you."

Again he laughed. "You're crazy, can't you see that? You're a crazy old woman, a crazy old maid with crusty lips and dried-up breasts. Eighteen years old! Judas Priest, *I* must be crazy to waste my time with you."

The door to the bunkhouse opened and footsteps crossed the floor. Whit slipped off his clothes and crawled into the bunk across from Jared's. He lay wide-eyed, his hands behind his head, staring at the ceiling. He glanced at Jared. "You awake?"

"Yes."

"That woman's crazy." Jared had wondered why Whit chose to have his tryst so close to the window. Now he saw that it titillated him to think he might have an audience. "I mean, you look at her and you think there's a nice bit of fluff, but she's like a suit of armor." Whit swore. "That was the only thing that made this job tolerable—the thought that someday I'll get her on the floor."

The next morning, when Kelly had finished her work in the house, she saddled her pinto and rode over to the corral to watch, and occasionally to laugh or cheer at the men who struggled in the dust.

As they worked Jared heard a scream and turned. For an instant the world seemed to stop as if caught in a photograph, every element of the scene sharp and clear: Whit standing beside his saddle horse outside the corral, his face turned in alarm toward Kelly on her pinto; Kelly strangely contorted, body thrown back over the cantle and arms over her head; the pinto itself in a mock epic equestrian pose, head up, bridle reins trailing, haunches flat, front legs curled as if at a hurdle. It might have been a bronze tableau; then, in the same instant that Jared's eyes glimpsed it, it burst its mold and leaped into action. The pinto ran, head turned and one wild eye on Kelly; she herself clung by her boots, but her body lay back along the horse's side, hair and arms trailing. She screamed again. Before the scream ended, Whit was in the saddle and riding after the pinto.

Jared ran the width of the corral. Hickory Jack stepped on a pole and hooked his arms over the top rail to watch the runaway.

The pinto raced across the prairie, dodging this way and that, as if to escape its peculiar burden. It had a strange, deer-like gait—it seemed to run by jumping. Kelly screamed repeatedly, her head flip-flopping in the horse's flank.

Whit's horse quickly overtook the pinto, but as he rode alongside and reached to lift Kelly, the pinto changed direction, and Whit nearly lost his stirrup. He had to right himself in the saddle and stop his horse before he could set off again. The pinto circled back. It was a mystery to Jared why Kelly didn't fall off.

Again Whit galloped close and reached for the girl. She grabbed his wrists, screaming. When the pinto turned again, the riders were stretched for an instant between the horses. Before they broke, Whit was almost pulled from the saddle. Again he reined in and set himself, looking after the galloping pinto.

Hickory Jack was quietly laughing. "Glory, that girl can ride."

Whit spurred his horse and once more rode up beside the pinto. This time, though, he made directly for the horse's head, grabbed the bridle, and jerked it to a stop. The pinto sidled away from the girl hanging almost completely upside down in its saddle. She was silent now. Whit dismounted and carefully lifted Kelly in one arm. Her boots came free from the stirrups and she slipped against him. He carried her over beside the corral and laid her on the grass. Her eyes were closed, her face flushed. Whit, kneeling beside her, looked up at Hickory Jack. "I got her as quick as I could."

"Yah," said Hickory Jack. "That was close."

The girl's body twitched.

Whit looked down at her. "Do you think she's hurt bad?"

"Hard to say," Hickory Jack said.

"I'd better take her to the house," Whit said. He bent beside the girl again.

A sound burst from her lips, like a muffled thump. Then, slowly at first, her torso began to move in and out. The expression on her face hardened, her lips drew back tight. It might have been the beginning of a convulsion; in fact, it was a convulsion of a sort. Kelly was laughing.

"What!" Whit exploded.

Kelly opened her mouth and the laughter rolled out, pumped by her shaking body. She looked up at Whit. "My hero!"

His face grew suddenly dark. "You slut!"

Hickory Jack was laughing too, and then Jared.

Whit stomped away, mounted his horse, and rode toward the bunkhouse.

Later, as Jared and Hickory Jack worked together, Jared said, "She can ride like a Sioux Indian."

"Better," her father replied. "She didn't have a mother, didn't have any dolls, didn't have any friends. All she ever had was horses. She can crawl all over a running horse, saddle or no. Under the neck, anywhere. Walk on it in her bare feet. She scares the daylight out of me sometimes." He paused. "Wonder what she was huntin' old Whit for."

"She wasn't just funnin'?"

"It isn't fun for Kelly unless it's fun for everybody. She was serious, for all she laughed."

When they went in to supper, Whit was gone.

**13** Jared stayed on at the Arrowhead. Hickory Jack needed a man; Jared needed work. Together they completed the Army contract. During the winter months there was not as much to do as in the summer, but the days were short and there were fewer hours to do it in. The range horses looked like woolly wild animals in their winter coats. They were tough, and as independent as if they were wild, eating snow to survive and pawing through winter's icy crust to reach the nourishing buffalo grass. But the cattle required care, and the two men spent part of every day out in the cold or wind, sometimes urging their horses through chest-high drifts to feed the cattle and open a hole in the ice for them to drink. In the evening they kept the fireplace roaring to thaw their chilled bodies, while Kelly baked or mended or made candy. Then Jared would run through the snow to the bunkhouse, bank up his puffin' billy, and go to bed.

The winter passed, and one spring night Jared sat on the step of the bunkhouse listening to the sound of the river. It seemed that after a few months on the Arrowhead he had begun to understand the lure of this country. Many people felt lost in a world which had no edges, but to Jared that unbroken sky had become a shelter. It reminded him of Alma's sheep lease.

For the first time since Alma disappeared, the two came together in Jared's mind—the man and the land. His father had loved that lonely place. Was it possible that somehow he had returned to it?

The next morning he prepared his bedroll, borrowed a horse, and waved good-bye to Kelly and Hickory Jack. He didn't tell them where he was going—he felt too unsure of his purpose to try to share it.

He traveled south and a little to the east. There were no landmarks, no trees or streams—only grass-grown wilderness rising toward the Milk River Ridge.

Still, his direction was true. Toward late afternoon he came in sight of a set of abandoned buildings. Approaching, he recognized the remains of the bunkhouse, stable and corrals that had once been headquarters for Alma's sheep operation. Now the roof of the stable had collapsed and the bleached poles of the corrals lay crisscrossed on the ground. Over the grass and out and in among the decaying timber, the west wind moved with a hollow sound.

The door of the bunkhouse was gone, the windows broken. The grass had begun to grow up through the floor. The table was still there, and two or three chairs, warped and broken, lying on their backs. A few mildewed magazines lay about, their pages stirring in the breeze from the open door. In the lean-to that had served as a kitchen, the corners of the cupboard were sprouting tufts of grass. The rust-colored stove sagged under its crust of neglect.

And then, in that grey and rust and ocher room, a flash of scarlet caught his eye. He actually jumped. It was a soup can, sitting on the cupboard, its jagged top half raised as if in greeting. A can opener lay beside it. He opened the cupboard door and found other cans of soup and beans and evaporated milk. Then he noticed an unwashed saucepan sitting on the stove. His skin prickled with sudden apprehension.

He carefully surveyed the larger room. There were some things he had missed in his first casual glance—dust-covered articles on the table and a litter of clothing strewn across the floor by one of the bunks.

He approached the bed. Nothing could be discerned among its snarl of blankets, but on its pillow rested the head of a man, his eye sockets, cheeks and temples gaunt and shadowed. The face seemed bloodless, its skin almost transparent, like the scraped deer hide that old time trappers used for panes in their cabin windows. Jared's heart lurched. "Siwash!"

"Eh?" The old man's body responded with a small, swift tremor, and then lay still again. The eyes were almost closed— would have been, it appeared, but that the skin wouldn't stretch far enough to permit it.

"It's me. Roseman."

"Eh?"

"You know me. Roseman."

"Roseman," he said reflectively, and then with more firmness repeated it. "Roseman." The pale blue eyes were wide open now, looking at Jared. The face, as grey as ashes, slowly glowed with a sense of recognition. "Roseman!" It was almost like a resurrection, the way the old man's body took on vitality. A blush of color suffused his face; the eyes began to burn. He raised one hand, weak, but hard as a talon, and grasped Jared's arm with it. "How about a little drink, Roseman?" There was part of a bottle of whiskey on the floor beside the bed. Jared held it to the old man's lips while he drank. He ran his tongue back and forth outside his mouth to be sure nothing was wasted.

"What are you doing here, Siwash?"

"My home, Roseman. I come home to die." Briefly he let his eyes close again, but maintained the pressure of his hand on Jared's arm.

"Looks a little drafty to me."

The eyes opened, the thin lips smiled. "It's old, Roseman. No windows. No door. Like me. My eyes, my ears, my teeth, my bowels—all windin' down like a French clock. One of these days they'll stop. Was you ever settin' in the room when the clock stopped? When it's runnin', you don't hear it. Ticktock, ticktock, ticktock . . ." Siwash paused and ran his tongue across his lips again. "Then when it stops, you hear it—not with your ears but in your head. Ticktock, ticktock. It's crazy."

"You all by yourself?"

"You're the only friend I ever had, Roseman. You and your daddy."

"I'll get you to a doctor."

"No. I don't want no doctor. I've seen everythin'. I've done everythin'. I've did things that never happened, Roseman, but I've run out of dally. I wish I could let go 'fore I catch my thumb."

Jared couldn't think of anything to say.

"Did you ever find your daddy?"

"Never have. Horse, saddle, man—gone!"

"I wish I knew how he done it. I'd disappear too."

"I came here looking."

"Don't look no more, Roseman. No use. You'll never find him."

"Do you know where he is?"

For a long time Siwash lay without speaking, his face turned away as if he were looking out the window. Finally his frail chest rose, and he said, "I guess we're all sinners. We sin by what we do and what we're scared to do."

"I don't understand."

"He made me promise I'd never tell. Maybe I should have told you right at first, but I'd give him my oath." He shook his head from side to side. "I don't know. All these years I've suffered for somethin' that waren't my fault at all."

"What wasn't your fault?"

"Did your daddy ever tell you about the massacree?"

"No."

"He told me about it—over and over. Said he had to let it out, had to talk to somebody." His face became flushed; he was speaking more and more quickly, as if driven by some reckless engine. "Made me promise never to tell. But I got to tell you, Roseman. You got to leave it alone—give it up, quit this infernal searchin', searchin'. And there ain't nobody to tell you after I'm gone."

"Tell me what?" Jared asked.

"I'se scared, I guess. But I'm through with tryin' to forget." The old man laid his head back on the pillow and stared at the ceiling with watery eyes. "It's all so long ago."

"Siwash. You have to tell me about it."

"Yes I do, don't I? I give my oath, but now I'll have to break her." He gulped. "I guess that means I'll go to hell for sure."

"You think the devil would want you puttering around down there?"

Siwash opened his mouth as if to laugh, but scarcely any sound came out. "Maybe he'll let me herd his sheep. Or goats, or whatever." He dropped his head, and his teeth came together with a click. "I don't mind, though, if your daddy's goin' to be there."

"Why would Father be there?"

"That's where he said he was goin' to end up. Always said it."

"Because of Mountain Meadows?"

Siwash squeezed his eyes shut; his whole face grimaced. "He was only a kid. He done as they told him, that's all."

"All he did was help to bury them."

"That wagon train brought upon itself the wrath of God," Siwash said.

"Then why didn't they let God handle it?"

"God did, your daddy said. Called himself a what . . .? Chosen instrument."

"But it wasn't Mountain Meadows made him disappear."

"Your daddy took an oath too, you know. If a man ever told what happened, the others'd kill him."

"Father never broke his oath."

"He told *me*." The water in the old man's eyes slowly welled up, brimming against the scanty lashes. "When I heard your daddy had disappeared, I knew that was it. They'd got him at last." He sighed, and tried to raise his head. "What could I do? I thought I was doin' right. But if I'd told you then, maybe there was something you could have done; maybe Al would still be here."

Siwash's body winced and began to arch under the blanket. The skin on his face stretched tighter, drawing down the corners of the lips and showing clenched tobacco-stained teeth. Sweat appeared on Siwash's face, like moisture on a jug. "Roseman!"

"Yes. I'm here."

Siwash motioned with his clawed hand. "Get my gun."

A Winchester carbine rested on a couple of nails on the wall. Jared took it off and moved the lever down. There was a shell in the chamber.

"Shoot me, Roseman."

Jared was stunned.

"It's easy. You can do it."

"How can you talk of such a thing?"

"Give me the gun. I'll do it myself. I'd have done it long ago, but I had to tell you first." He tried to sit up. As the blanket slid back, Jared saw that he was naked. His shrunken chest was dark, and out of the skin there welled a long, ugly roll of ulcerated matter, like a serpent breaking the surface of calm water.

"Tell me what?"

"Put the pillow over my face, Roseman. Nobody'll know."

"What are you talking about?"

"Finish me, I don't care how. It'd be a mercy."

"I can't do that. I'm not God."

"You could be. That's what you believe, ain't it? You Mormons? You're all goin' to become gods?"

"Not like that."

"Then how?"

"By slow degrees. By doing things that God would do, I guess."

"God gives life, don't He? And He takes it away."

"What do you know about it? You don't even believe in God."

"Hah, Roseman. You think you Christians invented God? You got a patent on him?"

Jared didn't reply.

"What do *you* know about God?" Siwash insisted.

When he was a boy Jared knew God. He was a friend. Many times the boy prayed to Him, and the prayer was answered. But when he was fifteen Jared moved to Lone Rock, and somehow he and God lost touch with each other. It didn't seem that twenty miles should make that much difference to the Lord.

Siwash lay back heavily. "I get to the happy hunting ground, I'll send you a smoke signal—tell you all about it."

After a while Siwash's pain seemed to ease, and he said, "I'm glad you come, Roseman. I never minded bein' alone till now."

As the hours passed, his energy slowly subsided, his hand relaxed on Jared's arm and fell away like fruit at harvest time. His eyes closed. The sound of his breathing grew steadily fainter. Sometime—Jared could not be sure when—he passed from consciousness. By morning he was dead.

Jared found a rusty old spade lying among the ruins of the stable. On a sandy knoll not far from the bunkhouse he began to dig a grave. He was not certain if it was proper, or even legal, for him to bury Siwash in this forsaken place, but where better for him to rest than in the land he called his home?

When the grave was ready, he placed the tall black hat on

Siwash's head, wrapped his naked body in the blanket, and carried him out of the bunkhouse. He could not have weighed more than a hundred pounds. With the body resting in the grave, hat and face still exposed, Jared stood for a moment looking down. He had no Bible in his pack. In the days of his preparing for a mission, he had read the Scriptures faithfully, but his memory was poor. There came to his mind a passage from the writings of the prophet Alma in the Book of Mormon: "It has been made known unto me by an angel that the spirits of all men, yea, all men who have lived upon the earth, as soon as they die, are taken home to that God who gave them life . . ." He knew these were not the exact words, but he repeated them aloud, and added, "Amen."

He drew the blanket over Siwash's hat and face then, and covered the body with earth. It took him a couple of hours to gather enough stones to make a heap above the grave. He didn't place any other marker.

# 14

Jared spent a day in Lethbridge, and the next evening traveled back down the road to the Arrowhead. All around him the prairie shimmered like the tawny skin of an animal. Patches of wild flowers lay among the buffalo grass in ponds of limpid color—yellow, blue, purple and pink. The sun was low. The sky arched overhead, faintly tinted, flawless. At the edge of the world the horizon blurred, blending with the pale, luminescent air until the line between earth and sky almost vanished.

Slowly he unsaddled his horse and turned her in the pasture. He dropped his bedroll at the bunkhouse.

When he entered the cabin he found Hickory Jack in his rocking chair and Kelly busy at the stove.

"That was a long vacation," Hickory Jack said.

"Too long," Jared agreed.

"But you still hit it just in time for supper."

"I could smell it for twenty miles."

Jared tossed his hat on a nail beside Hickory Jack's. The coal-oil lamp hung on a wire in the center of the room, unlit as yet, though the cabin was filled with shadow. Familiar as it all seemed to Jared, he felt a little awkward for some reason, like a guest rather than a hired man.

Hickory Jack hitched his chair toward the table, sniffing happily. "Hot biscuits! S'prisin' how company inspires the cook."

Kelly, busy serving the meal, appeared to Jared to blush faintly, though her color could have been from the heat of the stove.

As they began to eat, Hickory Jack asked, "You do any good?"

"Not what I intended," Jared replied. "But yes, I guess I did some good. I was glad I went."

"And glad to come back?"

"Yup."

For a moment the formal air of the occasion seemed about to disperse, then thickened again like fog as minutes passed when nobody could think of anything so say.

All at once Hickory Jack began to talk. "I remember when I was a young feller. How old are you, Roseman?"

"Just turned twenty-one."

"I'se a little older than you, I guess. I rode horseback to Mexico City, alone. All the way there and all the way back. One night I'se settin' there by the fire eatin' my beans, and these bandits come ridin' up in their big sombreros—roughest-lookin' crowd you ever see. Three weeks' whiskers on their chins, dirty as a country road—laughin' and talkin' till you'd have swore there was fifty of 'em. They's only five, really.

"Well, I ain't too happy seein' 'em, but I reckon it's a mis-take to let them find out, so I invite 'em to supper as best I can. They don't savvy my lingo no more'n I do theirs. I guess they've already ate; anyway, they sure ain't interested in my beans and bacon and bread. They takes my gun and my pocket watch. One of 'em grabs my hat, and they all take turns tryin' it on, but it comes down so far it bends their ears over and near blinds every one of 'em, so they give that back to me. My wallet has a five-dollar bill and a few ones in it, and before they divide that up I think they's goin' to be another Mexican war.

"Then they look around and one of 'em spots my horse tied off in the trees. They all head for the pony—saddle, bridle, the whole works. In ten minutes I'm stripped—gun, horse, money, grub, all gone; two thousand miles from home and I don't even know what time it is. Next mornin' I start shufflin' down the road afoot. A couple of hours past sunup, here them greasers come back, laughin' and whoopin', and I figure sure they've decided they let me off too easy. But they're leadin' an old broke-down cayuse with a scrubby-lookin' Mexican saddle and halter on him. He is the meanest-lookin' beast I ever see—blind in one eye, so no matter which way he stands, his head's cocked lookin' off toward Fisher's. He's got a sway back, shad belly, long legs and hooves like a set of plough shares. You'd swear his nose come off a bull moose. His head is bald as a suitcase, with little carrot ears stickin' ever which way on top of it. They ain't enough mane left on his neck to braid a watch fob. He walks with his tail between his legs and his flank tucked under, so he always looks on the edge of settin' down. They's more scars on his hide than hen-tracks in a Shanghai Bible.

"Well, maybe he ain't the prettiest horse in Mexico, but I tell you he looks plain beautiful to me. I've walked two miles, and already I've got blisters. I figure these 'cano boys feel bad for what they done to me, so they hopes to make it up by lendin' me a cul for the trip home. But I no sooner fork that weasel than I catch on they's still just funnin'. Ol' Sandpaper feels me on his back, he twists his neck double to see what he's got. First he almost falls down laughin', but the 'cano boys is hollerin' at him to remind him what he's hired for. Man, he sets to work. It ain't that he just goes up and comes down, mister. He come all apart, pieces flyin' east and west till there's nothin' left to sit on but the saddle. I see the ground way down below me somewheres, and those 'cano boys with their faces in the sky laughin' at me, and I says to myself, 'Okay, Hickory. It's stick this squirt of vinegar or walk to Utah. You takes your choice.' Ever few minutes he gathers in all the pieces from where he's scattered 'em over thirty-seven acres of desert, and puts 'em back together and starts again. I've rid more horses than you've ate Van de Camp beans, and I tell you, I never see anything to touch that old cannon. I swear he kicked me in the head with his hind foot. "But I stick him. Lord knows how, I don't. Those 'cano boys follow me for miles, wa'hooin' and yodelin', but they's gentlemen, for all their faults. They see that Sandpaper and me has struck a bargain, they just backs off and waves, laughin' like turkey gobblers, and let me go. By this time he has given up on unloadin' me, and travels along all right, though he walks with a sort of whoop, like a man with a wooden leg. We travel. I don't leave the saddle for three days, until I know he ain't ever goin' to give me a dance like that again. They ain't nobody envies me my mount no more, and I ride him clean home to Utah."

Hickory Jack finished his supper and lit his pipe. "I'se lucky with Sandpaper, though, 'cause another time I hit a horse I couldn't stick, and he wasn't a patch on Sandpaper when it come to originality. In fact, he was just a colt. It was when I had the dance hall out of Cardston. You don't remember that."

"Yes. I remember," Jared said.

"I used to set bear traps up in the mountains—collect the bounty from the ranchers. Well, one day I rid this colt up to check my traps; and sure enough, I'd caught a big black feller all right. The colt was pretty upset, but I tied him a little ways off in the trees while I hided the bear. He was a handful, and time I got the skin off him it was after dark. I folded the skin and tied it on behind the saddle, bein' careful to keep the colt's nose upwind. Everything went fine till I forked that cayuse and turned him toward home. The breeze fetched the smell of that green bearskin to him, so close I guess he knew it was ridin' him, and he just lost his mind. I reminded myself that it was twenty miles home, but it don't do no good. That horse was changin' directions so fast I never got set in the saddle after the first jump, and the next thing I know I'm out the back door and he's buckin' off down the mountain without me. By the time I got home my feet was so sore it was three weeks before I could walk again. But the horse never recovered. He was deranged permanent, and I traded him off first chance I got." Hickory Jack sat for a while, finishing his pipe. Then he pushed back his chair. "Well, I don't know about you two, but I'm for turnin' in." He went into his bedroom and closed the door.

Jared stood up. "You know, the first time I saw this ranch I thought it was the end of the earth."

"Maybe it is," Kelly said.

"But riding in today was different; it was like coming home. Not Lone Rock, or Cardston, or Utah. The Arrowhead. Can you imagine?"

She nodded.

"Wait here, will you?" he said. "I'll be right back."

"Where are you going?"

"Just wait. I have something . . ." Jared hurried out to the bunkhouse. He didn't stop to light the lamp—he knew what he was after and where it was. He unrolled his blankets, and from the things he carried inside, he quickly identified the package he was after by the noise of its paper wrapping. With that package in his hand, he hurried back to the house.

Kelly was standing at her bedroom door. He hurried in, and stopped, holding the package behind him.

"You're being very mysterious," she said.

"I have something for you. I didn't know whether I dared to give it to you or not." She didn't reply, but stood with an expression of alarm on her face as he crossed the floor and extended the package to her. He hadn't realized how travel-worn it would become. The paper was all crinkled and the ribbon soiled. "It's been in my grip," he explained.

She appeared uncertain whether to take the package or not. He thrust it toward her.

She stood holding it in both hands, as if she had just taken it out of the oven. He heard her sniffle. "What is it?" she asked.

"Open it and see."

"I never got a present before."

"Never?"

"Not a wrapped present. All Daddy ever gives me is horses." She crossed in front of him and sat down with the package on the table in front of her. Her fingers languidly strummed the ribbon. "Jared. This is the most beautiful thing that ever happened to me."

"You don't even know what it is."

"It doesn't matter what it is."

"But don't you want to know?"

"I'm dying to know. I just can't stand to open it."

"Well, I can." He strode to the table and began to pull off the ribbon.

Kelly sat watching him, then pushed him away and finished unwrapping it herself. As she folded the paper back she gasped, "Jared!"

It was a dress. She took it by the yoke and raised it, stood and turned away from the table so it fell full-length. "Jared. It's beautiful." She held it against her body, one arm drawing in the waist, one leg extended, and looked down at it. "Oh, Jared."

"Aren't you going to put it on?"

She sat down, still clutching it to her. "First I have to catch my breath."

"I hope it fits all right."

"I can make it fit." She took the lamp and the dress, and went into the bedroom, leaving Jared in the dark.

After what seemed like a long time, he called through the door, which she had left slightly ajar, "Does it fit?"

"It's fine. I just have to pin it a little."

He waited, pacing in the darkened room. "Can I help you?"

"No. No, I'm finished."

The door swung open. She stood there with the lamp in her hand. She'd unpinned her hair and brushed it loose around her shoulders. The room behind her was dark; her hair and eyes and sash were dark. But in the lamplight her dress glowed like phosphorus, its eyelet tiers cascading down as white as traceries of snow.

**15** At supper the next evening Hickory Jack ate without speaking—something Jared had never seen him do before. He attacked his plate with special ferocity, even for him, and in a few bites demolished his meal. It was unnerving to Jared, just when he needed all the confidence he could get.

Hickory Jack pushed back his plate and wiped the back of his wrist across his mouth. "Well, what you goin' to do?"

Jared almost jumped. "About what?"

"I can tell when the wind changes. Nobody knows what makes it change; just slam-bang! and there it is, straight out of the east." Hickory Jack leaned back and stared at Jared. "I need a cowboy, but I don't need no more relations. You get my meanin'?"

"I'm not sure."

He glanced at his daughter. "Hah! You get it, all right. The air around here last night was like sparks off a grinder—the whole room full of lightnin'."

Hickory Jack began to build a fire in the fireplace.

"It's hot tonight," Kelly said. "What d'you want to build a fire for?"

Hickory Jack piled on the logs. "I want to look at it."

"You'll roast."

He brought a bottle from some little-used cache that he kept somewhere in his room. "I'll open the door."

"That's silly."

"Did you ever watch a fire through the bottom of a bottle? Prettiest thing you ever see. I could look at it by the hour."

"What are you depressed about?" she asked.

"Me? I ain't depressed." He laughed out loud to prove it. "I'm old jolly knockers himself, ain't I, Roseman?"

"You're a wonder, all right," Jared agreed.

Hickory Jack moved his armchair to face the fire, then sat in it with a thump. He opened his bottle. "Now you take Roseman there—got a face as long as a clothesline. He should see a doctor, find out if there's anythin' they can do about it. Maybe take out a couple of inches between the proboscus and the obdoola oblongata. That's what they call a physiognomyectomy. That's what they call the operation. Physiognomy-ectomy. How'd you like that one, Roseman? Not bad for a grade-three education, eh?"

"You're drunk already," Kelly said. "And you haven't had a drop."

"It's the anticipation," he gloated. He passed the bottle under his nose. "Just thinkin' about it drives me wild."

"Well, if you're determined to make a fool of yourself, I'm going to bed."

Hickory Jack had been rubbing his palm around and around the mouth of the bottle. Now he raised it and took a quick swallow. "Ah . . ." he sighed. "That's a good girl. I prefer drinkin' alone. It goes further that way." He looked over his shoulder at Jared. " 'Less, of course, you want to join me."

"No. You go ahead."

"You don't drink, do you?"

"No."

"I knew there was something I liked about you." He took another drink. "Seems like there's somethin' I don't like about you."

"I don't know what it'd be," Jared said. "I'm the nicest guy you'd ever want to meet."

"Goodnight," Kelly said. She went into her room and closed the door.

Jared moved his chair close to the fire. For a long time he sat beside Hickory Jack, staring into the flames.

Hickory Jack extended the bottle toward Jared. "Nobody's goin' to know."

"No, thanks."

"You ain't all that mighty a Mormon that a little swig's goin' to scotch your chances?"

"I don't suppose."

"You don't drink whiskey, you don't smoke cigarettes . . . you won't even have a cup of coffee. Is there anything you do do? Must be somethin' you want."

"I want to ask you a question."

"Ask me no questions, I'll tell you no lies," said Hickory Jack. He reached forward, half out of his chair, and tossed a couple of more logs on the fire. The sparks flew out, fluttered, and then rushed up the chimney. "Well, spit it out. Anythin' I can't abide, it's pussyfootin'."

Jared turned toward Hickory Jack and took a deep breath. "I want to marry your daughter."

Hickory Jack didn't move. His expression didn't change. Then the bottle slipped in his hand and he jerked forward to save it. "Did you say what I think you said?"

"I want to marry Kelly."

"Hah! You know why I have to fire all my hired men? 'Cause they all got eyes for Kelly, so I send 'em down the road. I'm disappointed, Roseman. I figured we was safe with you. I thought you fellers only married Mormon gals."

"Usually we do."

"Can't you find a Mormon?"

"I want Kelly."

Hickory Jack set his bottle on the floor, took his pipe down from the mantel, and lit it. Then he leaned back and stared at Jared through the smoke. "Like I say, Roseman, I need a cowboy, but I don't need no more relations. And Kelly sure don't need a husband."

"Can I talk to her? Let her decide?"

"You think you know what she'll say?"

"I think so."

"Maybe you've talked to her already."

"No."

"S'posin' she says yes and I say no?"

"Then I'll take her any way I can."

"If that's the case, what are you askin' me for?"

Jared hesitated. "I want this to be a proper wedding. I'd like for you to give Kelly to me."

"I'll tell you this, Roseman. If I don't want you to have her, you'll never get her."

"Well, do you or don't you?"

"I ain't decided. I never thought of you in the family." Hickory Jack took the pipe out of his mouth long enough to put the neck of the bottle in, and drink. He returned the bottle to the floor, the pipe to his mouth, and leaned back with his

179

eyes closed. "Why does a man have to stop smokin' 'fore he can take a drink? The feller that invents whiskey-tobacco will make a fortune."

"If he doesn't choke to death on his way to the patent office," Jared said.

"Reformers!" snorted Hickory Jack. "How I hate 'em!"

Jared took his hat from the nail behind the door. "Goodnight, Hick."

"Goodnight."

**16** In the days that followed, the work of breaking horses resumed, Jared working and watching, and listening to all that Hickory Jack could teach him. "A horse is a creature of habit. He likes his home and his friends, just like a man does. He'll graze the same piece of country and herd with the same bunch. You take him away from it and then turn him loose, he'll usually go back." Hickory Jack seemed to think like a horse, as if he must at one time have worn horsehide—and by the look of his weathered face he had never taken it off. He appeared to know all the grazing areas, their approximate boundaries, and about where any particular herd would be at a certain time of day.

"Never fight him," the tutor would say. "He's stronger than you. Just wait him out and make him work for you." . . . "Keep your loop small. You don't set a bear trap for a badger." . . . "Horses are scared of being hurt. As soon as he gets scared of that nerve line, put your hands on him. Pat him. When he finds out you're not going to hurt him, he'll follow you." And finally, "You've got it, kid. Horse sense. First thing you know, you'll hear 'em talk to you."

Occasionally Kelly moved from the top rail and came down in the corral to help with the horses. She handled a rope with skill and assurance, and talked to the horses as if they were rowdy children. While Hickory Jack worked with a colt at the snubbing post, Jared found himself gazing through the rails to the next corral, watching Kelly. There was a purity of movement about the way she handled horses, as if where strength was lacking, poetry might win.

One morning, as they rounded up a fresh band and started back to the corral with them, Jared noticed a black filly loping slightly apart from the herd. Her eyes were wide apart, her face dished. She had a deep chest and strong legs tapering to firm slender ankles. She galloped easily, with neck arched and tail high.

When they got back to the corral and paused to size up the bunch, Jared climbed onto the fence beside Hickory Jack. "I've been looking for another horse," he said. "Ever since ol' Summer broke his neck."

The black filly galloped clear of the bunch, raised her nose across the top rail, and whinnied sharply.

"And that's the one?" Hickory Jack asked. "I been watchin' her since she was a foal. She's a duchess."

"Is she going to the Army?"

Hickory Jack shook his head. "Too small. Too small for me, too. I'd have to use roller skates 'stead of stirrups."

"Is she for sale?"

"Hadn't thought about it."

"I'd like the chance . . ."

"She's a duchess. I don't know." Hickory Jack rode his horse into the corral and started cutting out strays. Jared noticed, though, that he didn't cut out the black filly.

As the day progressed the mare was all over the corral, in the men's way, dodging between them and the horses they wanted to work with, whistling, stamping and stirring up trouble. At last Hickory Jack said, "Tarnation animal! Another five minutes, I'll put a bullet in her head."

"Don't shoot her," Jared said. "Give her to me."

Hickory Jack cut her into the breaking corral. "Think you can ride her?"

"I'd sure like to try."

The older man stood watching the black filly. She didn't look at the men; her attention was directed toward the distant prairie.

"You ever skinned a wild horse, kid?"

"I don't know what you mean."

"Without a saddle or bridle. Nothin' but mane and tail and fingernails."

"I never heard of it."

"You skin her, you can have her."

"How long do I have to skin her for?"

"Till one of you quits."

"Nobody can do that."

"I've done it."

Jared looked at Kelly sitting on the corral fence. "Did you ever hear of that?" he asked.

She smiled, and nodded. "I've heard of riding a bicycle over Niagara Falls, too."

"If she throws me?" Jared asked.

Hickory Jack replied. "If she throws you, you ain't man enough for her, anyway."

"You don't give a fellow much chance, do you?"

"That's more chance than I'd give any other mortal."

Jared turned to get his lariat. "I'll take it," he said, "if we can spare the time."

Hickory Jack, sitting on the corral fence beside Kelly, laughed. "This won't take long."

Jared let fall a couple of coils of his lariat; a false cast or two fed the slack into his loop. "What's the secret of skinning a horse?"

"I'll tell you all I know," Hickory Jack said. "But I don't reckon it'll do any good—not with that filly."

"Tell me all you know."

"Number one, tie down your spurs. Number two, get on her if you can. Number three, take a fistful of mane, dig in your heels, and say your prayers. After that only God can help you, and He might prefer standin' clear." Hickory Jack laughed. "Number four, where do you want to be buried?"

"Oh, I'm going to live," Jared said. "Chim and I plan a long life together."

"Chim?"

"That's her name. Chimney. Look at her."

"You skin her, mister, you can call her anything you want."

Jared faced the mare, the lariat in his hand. "Are you ready, Chim?"

The black filly nodded at him and switched her tail. He started toward her, feinting to his left. She backed a step and swung to the right. He spread his hoolihan; running, she ducked right into it. He took a dally on the snubbing post, bringing her up short. She turned to face him.

"Oh, ain't you pretty?" he said softly. "Oh, you're a pretty girl, you are." He began to work with her, holding a steady tension on the rope.

He worked her slowly, not with the quick impatience that they used with the other horses; he edged her in by almost imperceptible degrees. All the while he talked to her, his voice low and reassuring. "You're a pretty baby. Now, come on, Chim-girl. Don't be scared, baby. Come on. Come. Come. Come to the church in the wildwood, Chim-baby. This isn't gonna hurt. You and I'll get along fine . . ."

When he had her head tight against the post, he picked up the sack and began to sack her out. "See, baby. That doesn't hurt, does it? I wouldn't hurt you, Chim-girl. We're gonna get along fine."

"You're stallin'," Hickory Jack shouted.

"Hush, Daddy," Kelly said.

"If I'm gonna lose my horse, ain't I entitled to a little fun?"

"You said you're not going to lose her."

"Not by a jugful, I ain't. He'd use his time better poundin' nails in mud pies."

When he had Chim so familiar with the sack that she scarcely flinched when it touched her, he started with his hands, patting her neck and shoulders, then her head and along her back and over the curve of her rump. "Ah, you're a good girl, Chim-baby."

"It'll be dark soon," Hickory Jack said. "I think you're scared, Roseman."

It was still early afternoon, but maybe there was some truth in what Hickory Jack said—perhaps he was stalling. He wrapped the sack around Chim's head and tucked in one corner. Her body, which had been hanging back, rose slightly, and the rope around her neck loosened. Her wheezing stopped.

She turned her head as if to check the limits of her blindness. When she found the whole world was dark, she stood almost as if she were frozen.

Jared went to the side of the corral and tied down his spurs with a couple of rawhide thongs, so the shanks were immovable, as fast to his boots as a talon. Then he returned to the little black mare. Her mane was heavy and long. He took a good handful of it, stepped back, and swung himself up. Her back dipped under his sudden weight and her hooves minced quickly a time or two. She snorted nervously.

"Well, Chim-girl. Are you ready?"

"Are *you* ready?" Hickory Jack asked.

Jared reached forward with both hands and loosened the lariat still more, to a loop big enough to slip over the mare's head. Then he ran the fingers of his right hand through her mane just above the withers, and closed them so it formed a sort of knot. His left hand took firm hold of both the sack and the lariat, and with a sudden forward movement, pulled them off over Chim's nose. She started to one side, then hesitated. Jared felt her body quiver against his legs. He threaded his left hand in the mane above his right. For a moment or two she didn't move. He leaned back, his legs hanging loose.

"I'll open the gate!" Hickory Jack called.

Jared heard the familiar creak of the gatepost turning in its iron ring, and glimpsed a hundred miles of uninterrupted prairie. His cry of betrayal and outrage was cut short when Chim's body surged beneath him. She rushed through the open gate and for a short distance ran flat. He used that moment to set himself, body leaning far back, heels tight in her sides. Suddenly she broke, and started to buck with a violence that seemed as if it must dismember her. Somehow her center held; perhaps it was Jared's limbs clutched tight about her that kept her together, for he felt as if he, too, were about to be torn apart.

The flying mare squealed and thumped, twisting high above the ground. Each vibration seemed magnified ten times when it struck Jared. But stubbornness had fastened him to her, and now nothing could pluck him free; he would not give Hickory Jack that satisfaction. And when all was said and done, he wanted this horse—wanted her more certainly with every agonizing jump.

Luckily her most furious bucking was over before she started to become slick with sweat. He slipped about more then and his punishment increased, but he was still somehow able to hang on.

All at once she whirled and started to run. Over his shoulder he glimpsed the ranch buildings growing further and further away. A bitter despair took hold of him. Just at the moment when it appeared he had won, his victory became empty, for though he might ride Chim to kingdom come, how would he ever prove it to anyone?

After the first few miles she ran more slowly, her breath rasping into her lungs in deep quick huffs that seemed to keep time with drum of her hooves. Jared's legs were soaked from her gleaming skin. When they came in sight of a few horses some distance away, Chim stopped abruptly.

Jared felt like a seasick traveler finally reaching shore. The release of tension on his arms and legs was like a blessing, though he did not dismount and he dared not relax.

He looked back; the ranch buildings were out of sight. He had expected someone to at least ride after him. Here he had fanned the mare to a standstill, and there was nobody on hand to witness it.

Keeping one hand on the mane, he unbuckled the belt of his chaps, unsnapped first one leg and then the other. Finally he pulled them free. Chim crow-hopped half-heartedly, and then stopped again, her sides going out and in like a concertina, feeding the squeal of her breathing. Jared slapped the chaps at one side of her head. She jumped sideways, then stood there with her head up, one white-fringed eye cast back at him.

He still kept one hand knotted in her mane. "Don't worry," he told her. "It's gonna be all right. You just do as I tell you . . ."

He nudged her with his legs, and she moved forward uncertainly. But the chaps flapping at the side of her head caused her to turn one way, then the other. Gradually they began to move in the direction of the ranch. Chim was exhausted and unwilling to move very fast, but that suited Jared well enough.

Patiently he patted her, urged her forward, turned her, told her what a good girl she was.

Presently her pace picked up, and once or twice she acted as if she might try to unload him again. Should she so much as shudder, Jared thought, he'd roll off on the ground.

By the time they approached the corral, the shadow of the high pole gate stretched far across the prairie. The glare of the sky had softened, the hush of twilight was upon them. Hickory Jack turned and walked to the side of the corral, watching Jared and Chim approach. Kelly came running from the house. A short distance away, Chim stopped.

Hickory Jack dropped the saddle he'd been holding in his hand. "Well, I'll be damned," he said. "The kid's half horse."

# THE ARROWHEAD RANCH
## JULY, 1922

**1** The Arrowhead Ranch was like an island in the world. Over the years Jared had come to treasure the distance that separated him from other men, even his own family. Though he and the Rosemans visited back and forth at times, these times had become more and more rare as the feeling of estrangement continued unrelieved. He had not been back to Lone Rock for a long while.

The kitchen at the Arrowhead was little changed. Jared had built a new cupboard for his bride, but by now it was sufficiently worn to blend harmoniously with the rough wooden walls and log rafters of the room. Recently Kelly had been asking for a new stove, but until Jared had time to fetch it from town, the old one sat in the corner as black as a battleship. From it, Kelly still served the same hearty breakfasts. But there were four at table now—Hickory Jack, Jared, Kelly and their son John, not yet six.

Jared still retained one simple custom from his days in his father's home—he always asked a blessing on the food. He did so now, and when he finished, John asked, "Who is Heavenly Father?"

"You'll have to answer him, Jared," Kelly told him as she took her place at the table. "I don't know anything about God."

Hickory Jack helped himself to a piece of meat. "Might as well live in a monastery," he muttered. He delivered a large bite to his mouth, like an emergency measure to keep him alive until he could be served fried potatoes, gravy and scrambled eggs, and homemade graham bread. "Pray to get up, pray to lay down, pray to turn sideways."

Jared looked at his son. "You have two fathers," he said. "One on earth and one in heaven."

"It's a disease," Hickory Jack said to nobody in particular. "Religion and hydrophobia, all the same thing. People with rabies runnin' around the country tryin' to bite everybody they see . . ."

"Your Heavenly Father loves you just as much as I do," Jared went on.

"How do you think I feel?" Hickory Jack asked. "A stranger in my own house. Can't smoke, can't swear. Can't even spit without a certificate. Might warp the little bugger."

"Daddy!" Kelly scolded. "If you prefer, Jared and I can build a house of our own."

"Don't start that again. I'd have to keep roarie-eyed drunk twenty-four hours a day to stand livin' in this place all by myself."

"Then quit complaining."

"Fish, complainin's the only thing I got left."

Hickory Jack pushed back his plate. "Well. Looks like a good day to start haying."

"Can't hay today," Jared said. "Got to get those cattle up in the hills."

"Well, you go ahead and take 'em," said Hickory Jack. "You know I can't ride no more. John and me'll mow hay." The realization that he was too old and stiff to ride horseback all day had come very painfully to Hickory Jack, but now that he had accepted it, he waved it like a banner.

"Can't drive today," Jared said. "Not till we go to town and get some rock salt to take up there with us."

The old man's eyes turned toward Jared, and began to gleam. "That's right, ain't it? Never even thought of it."

Jared went on. "So you and John mow hay and Kelly and I'll fetch the salt."

"Hah!" snorted Hickory Jack. "Not much. You ain't goin' to town without us, eh, Johnny?"

John shook his head till his hair billowed. "Uh-uh. Me and Grandpa want to go too."

"All right," Jared agreed. "Today we go to Lethbridge. Tomorrow we work."

Half an hour later the democrat with its four passengers passed beneath the high pole of the Arrowhead gate, the team trotting smartly, their haunches winking in the slanted light of the early sun. About noon they drove into Lethbridge, a city of perhaps fifteen thousand. They shared the street with other horse-drawn outfits, and with automobiles as well. The team shied nervously at these ungainly vehicles, which for some reason always looked to Jared as if they might suddenly tip up on their noses. He chose a place to hitch the team on a quiet side street where cars seldom passed. He unbridled the horses and fed them a couple of armfuls of hay he'd thrown in the democrat.

John jumped down and ran away in the direction of Fifth Avenue. "You wait!" Jared shouted. "You'll get lost." The boy stopped far down the street and leaned against a post, fidgeting while he waited for the others to catch up to him.

"Where shall we eat today?" Jared asked.

"At Conklin's," John replied.

"You go ahead," said Hickory Jack. "I got better things to do."

"I never knew you to turn down nourishment before," Jared told him.

"I'll get it," Hickory Jack replied. "The kind of nourishment I need." He started off down the street.

"We should go home early," Jared called after him. "Say we leave about two."

Hickory Jack stopped and looked back. "Two o'clock? Fish! A man can't do no good in a couple of hours."

"You'll have to work hard at it today."

"It ain't no fun if you have to work at it."

"We'll pick you up at the Alex about two. Kelly and I need to get an early start tomorrow."

Hickory Jack shuffled on his way, grumbling.

They walked into the restaurant, John tugging on his father's hand. "I'm going to have a bread of veal cutlet," the boy said.

As they settled into a booth, Jared said, "It's almost Father's birthday."

"Friday," Kelly said. "I was thinking about it this morning."

"Seven years," Jared said. "I wonder what happened to him."

The waitress came, and they placed their orders.

"I should have kept looking, I guess," Jared said. "I shouldn't have given up."

"What more could you have done?" Kelly asked.

Jared didn't look up from the table. "I don't suppose we'll ever know, now."

"How old was he?"

"Seventy-seven. He'd be eighty-four next Friday."

Later, at the store, they bought eight blocks of salt, two sacks of flour, a sack of sugar, a bag of potatoes, since the ones in the root cellar were going soft and the new crop wasn't ready yet, some fruit and other groceries, new gloves for the men, and straw hats all round to wear in the hay field.

While Kelly selected fabric for a new dress, Jared and John went to get the outfit. They found the team patiently nodding in the sunshine and switching at flies. One horse nuzzled at the remains of the hay, which lay on the ground like balls of fluff. Jared bridled the team, then together he and John drove down the main street and pulled up in front of the store. They tied the team while they loaded. Jared had to make several trips, shouldering the hundred-pound bags of sugar, flour and potatoes, and then launching them into the democrat with a flip and a thrust. Most of the other things were packed in cardboard boxes, but John was pleased to find one thing he could carry—the paper bag that contained the straw hats and the gloves. As he picked up the last box Jared called to his wife, still standing among the dry goods at the back of the store, "We're ready."

"I'll be right there," Kelly said.

A man burst into the store, puffing. "You Roseman?"

Jared turned. "Yes."

"Come on. They's trouble at the hotel." The man headed for the door, glanced to be sure Jared was coming, and then ran into the street and back the way he had come. Jared followed, and heard the footsteps of his wife and son behind him until he outdistanced them or their sound was covered in the confusion of other hurrying feet.

It was a block and a half to the hotel. Long before he got there Jared was out of breath, but he tried not to slacken his pace. He overtook and passed the man who had come to get him.

The door to the beer parlor was open and crowded with men trying to see inside. Jared ran into them almost unchecked, thrusting with his hands and shoulders, ignoring the angry reactions thrown against him. When he got through the circle of men he suddenly stopped. A couple of tables were overturned, leaving a small cleared space on the floor of the beer parlor, where Hickory Jack lay spread-eagled on his back, his hair awry and a smear of blood across his cheek. A sweating young man in a black shirt knelt straddle of his body, one hand holding down Hickory Jack's left wrist, the other raised with a knife in it. The blade of the knife had a slim red line along its polished surface, and hung like a thirsty bird, ready to dip for another taste of blood. Hickory Jack's right arm, braced to hold the knife hand away, had a dark stain around a slash in the shirt sleeve.

"Wait," Jared said softly.

The young man didn't take his eyes away from Hickory Jack's face, so close beneath him. "Can't wait," he hissed. "He'll die of old age and cheat me."

Jared started toward him.

"Stand back!" the young man said. "You come another step, I'll slit the old fool's throat."

Jared stopped and looked around, finally at the man standing behind the bar. "What happened?"

"Nobody knows. Just suddenly they was fightin'. Old Hickory Jack was doin' all right too, till the kid pulled a knife."

Jared said, "What's the trouble, kid?"

The young man's lips were trembling. "Ask this old fool."

"I'm asking you."

"Ask this old fool."

"You're not going to kill him, are you?"

"You damn right I'll kill him."

"Then what you waitin' for?" asked Hickory Jack.

"I want to see you shake."

Hickory Jack smiled. "You better order a sandwich, kid. You got a long wait."

The knife plunged an inch or two against Hickory Jack's restraining arm.

"Come on," said Hickory Jack. "Can't you even finish off an old man? It's cold on this drafty floor."

The kid raised slightly, both his body and his hand with the knife in it.

"Hold it," Jared said. He moved a couple of steps nearer to Hickory Jack and measured the remaining distance with his eye.

The kid flashed his knife down again. "If you don't stand back, he's dead." He tried to sound resolute, but his voice shook.

Jared didn't move.

By now a policeman had joined the group in the beer parlor. "Put down the knife," he advised, "before you get in trouble."

The young man said, "I been in trouble all my life."

"Not like this. You ever killed anybody?"

"Sure." He laughed, a shaky, querulous giggle. "Didn't expect that, did you?"

The policeman took out his gun. "Put down your knife." There was the click of a hammer going back.

"He ain't goin' to do anything," said Hickory Jack.

The kid plunged the knife downward, but still Hickory Jack held it back.

The policeman took aim. "I'll shoot."

Jared felt an arm around his shoulder, and looked down to see Kelly standing beside him, and beside her, John. "What can we do?" she whispered.

"Get John out of here. He's crazy. He might do anything," Jared said.

"I'll shoot at the count of three," the policeman said. "One . . ."

Suddenly John ran forward, straight for Hickory Jack.

The young man glanced at him. "Stay back!" he cried.

John squatted, right above the old man's face, looking down. "Does that hurt, Grandpa?"

"Naugh!" said Hickory Jack.

"Get out of here, kid." The young man's voice was high and loud. "You get out of here."

John looked at him. "Why? This is my own grandpa."

"I'll get him," Jared said, moving to take John.

The kid feinted with the knife. "Stand back!"

Jared stopped.

"Two," the policeman said.

John stood up and looked into the young man's face. "Mister. Don't hurt my grandpa."

The young man took his eyes away from Hickory Jack's face; he looked at John, and his gaze held. "Hah!" he breathed.

"He's my grandpa, and he gave me a pony for my birthday."

The tight lips of the young man softened and slowly turned tremulous, twitching upward at the corners. For a moment he sat staring at John, then he started to laugh. At first Jared could not be sure what was happening, but gradually the laugh became audible and he could see the young man's shoulders moving. Then the sound changed and the shoulders began to shake more violently. The kid lunged to his feet, flung the knife so the point sank deep into the wall, and staggered from the room, roaring. The people in the doorway moved back to let him through. Kelly rushed forward and knelt beside her father.

An hour later Jared and his family were on their way back to the Arrowhead, the democrat loaded with supplies and Hickory Jack's arm wrapped in bandages.

"What did you say to him, anyway?" Jared asked.

Hickory Jack snorted. "Nothin'. It was what he said to me."

"You mean you started it?"

"He started it. I took the first swing. He was surprised. I dang near finished him right there."

"Well then, what did he say to you?"

"I don't recollect."

"Must have been something strong."

"I don't recall."

"Don't be silly, Daddy," Kelly said. "Of course you recall."

"That fight knocked it right out of my head."

"Tell us what it was," Jared said.

Hickory Jack looked around at them. "If you really want to know, he got started swearin' at Mormons."

Kelly laughed. "You've been swearing at them all your life. I'm surprised you didn't buy him a drink."

"They ain't as bad as they used to be."

Jared said, "So you go ahead and get yourself killed."

"He wouldn't leave it alone," Hickory Jack went on. "I told him to shut up, but he just got louder and fouler." He snorted. "So I stopped his mouth."

"And he almost stopped your gizzard."

"Fish! There was nothin' to worry about with that twerp."

**2** By the time they reached the ranch, it was evening. The long hot day had finally wound down to that last hour of half-light, hanging in the sky after the sun has set. Jared stopped the democrat in front of the house, and he and Kelly helped Hickory Jack climb down over the wheel.

The old man's face was grey. "I ain't some stretcher case," he said, shrugging at them. "Leave me be." Still, he rested a hand on the porch rail as he mounted the steps one at a time. John weaved behind him, almost asleep on his feet.

Jared unhitched the team and turned them into the pasture. As he stood by the gate watching them roll in the dust, he heard the rapid little *chuff-chuff* of an approaching Model T. He watched the road. The sound of the engine swelled, and under the silent sky, seemed to become impossibly loud before the silhouette of the car appeared on the hill, dipping and rising with the gentle undulations of the land. With almost unabated speed it swung around a bend, rushed into the yard, and stopped in front of Jared, all its activities controlled by the firm, fat hands of its driver.

"Hello, Jared."

'Lyman!" Jared said. "I sure wasn't expecting you."

Lyman looked as if he had gained at least fifty pounds since their days on the farm together. "We're having a memorial service for Father this week."

"What? They've found him?"

"No," Lyman said. "You recollect it's his birthday. After seven years we can have him declared legally dead."

"Oh."

"Then we can clear up the estate—get things settled."

"Oh."

"Believe me, it's hard to have the responsibility but not the authority."

"Yes. I can see that." For some reason he could not explain, Jared felt peevish. It was uncanny after all this time, that in the course of speaking a couple of sentences they could nettle each other in the same old way. They were like two musicians who had been sitting through a musical rest for seven years, marking time with their heels, and now continued in perfect unison the same discordant melody they'd played all their lives.

Jared took a package of Ogden's Fine Cut from his pocket. "How is everybody?"

"Fine. Mother, Grace, Paula—all fine. You should come back more often. It isn't far, you know."

Jared licked along the edge of his cigarette and twisted the ends together. "You've no idea how far it is, Trash." He flicked his lighter and bent to the flame.

Lyman watched him. "It's funny to see you with a cigarette in your mouth."

Jared didn't reply.

"You're the last person I would have expected to leave the church."

"Who told you I'd left the church?"

Lyman shrugged. "What else am I to think, I see you smoking a cigarette?"

"I haven't left the church. We just got separated, is all—it's at Lone Rock and I'm out here. As long as you don't tell on me, I'm all right."

"Don't be silly."

"Are you the bishop yet?"

Lyman laughed shortly. "Maybe next time. I'm still pretty young."

He got out of his car and stood leaning on it, the knuckles of one hand thrust against his hip to hold back the side of his coat like a theatre curtain. He was dressed in a dark suit, with a necktie and a bowler hat. A gold chain looped across the front of him, from one vest pocket to the other, as if to prevent the further spreading of his girth. As the twilight deepened, the final remnants of light seemed to be caught along the chain in tiny rosettes that moved back and forth across it as he breathed. "Little brother, it's hard to imagine you living in this Godforsaken place."

Lyman took a briefcase out of his car and from it handed a document to Jared. "I thought you might like to sign this declaration; you know, to the effect that you haven't seen father for seven years. It's not required, but we thought it would be nice for everybody to sign—as a gesture of family unity."

Jared glanced at the document. "Suppose Father is still alive? Does this mean I can finish him off with a quick stab of the pen?"

"Don't be silly," Lyman said. "This simply admits the legal premise that a man lost for seven years isn't likely to show up again."

"It seems like giving up."

Lyman laughed. "Same old Jared. Come on. You don't think signing this paper will change anything, do you?" He snapped a fat red pen out of his vest pocket and handed it to Jared. "It only means we all agree."

"You've forgotten, Trash, I don't agree. You wanted to write Father off seven years ago."

Lyman reluctantly gathered his things back—his pen, his document, his briefcase, his smile. "I can't understand you. You won't talk sensibly about anything."

A wind came across the yard and blew the breath of rain in Jared's face as it passed. The shirt against his body felt suddenly cold, and he shivered. "Better come in and have some supper. Meet my family."

"I have to get back to Lethbridge tonight."

"You're welcome to sleep in the bunkhouse."

"No, thank you. The court hearing is tomorrow. I can't afford to miss it." He closed his briefcase and returned it to the car.

"Well, stop and eat, anyway," Jared said. "Kelly has supper ready."

They walked to the ranchhouse, and Jared held the door for

his brother. Lyman stepped into the lamplight, stooping slightly as he passed through the opening. Inside, he seemed to hunch his body, as if he felt crowded by the log walls and the ceiling so low above him.

John, who sat at the table, cried, "Hello, Uncle." His face twisted. "I can't remember your name."

"Uncle Lyman," Kelly prompted.

"Hello, John," Lyman said, and nodded to Kelly and Hickory Jack.

In the lamplight Jared saw that Lyman was colored grey from head to foot, coated with the fine Alberta dust that lay thick at the bottom of the wagon tracks he had driven in; his shoes, his clothes, the hat which he had removed and now held in his hand, all grey as paint. In a grey face, and beneath fluffy lashes, his eyes moved like colored buoys on a grey sea. The top of his head, where the hat had been, was untouched, as if he had been saved at the last moment from sinking into a grey pool.

"Care to wash?" Jared indicated the old wooden washstand with its pail and tin basin, and a fresh towel hanging from a nail beside it.

Lyman slipped off his coat and hung it carefully over the back of a chair. In the rustic grey tones of the cabin the collar and sleeves of his shirt seemed to glow with an almost unnatural whiteness. He advanced toward the washstand, rolling up his sleeves along the way. "How's the horse business these days?"

"It's fine," said Hickory Jack.

"We're running more cattle all the time," Jared explained.

"The horse is dead, all right," Lyman said. "In ten years it'll all be tractors."

"Heh!" wheezed Hickory Jack. "And when the tractors get stuck, who's gonna pull them out? Horses."

They sat down to eat.

"Are you rich?" John asked.

Lyman laughed. "Me? No, I'm not rich." He took the watch out of his pocket, snapped open the case and checked the time.

John sucked in his breath.

"We're comfortable," Lyman went on. He closed the watch, and with a deft motion, returned it to his vest pocket. "Not rich by any means, but we have a nice place. Why don't you tell your dad to come out to Lone Rock and see us one of these days?"

"Can we, Daddy?" John asked.

"How about Friday," Lyman suggested. "The memorial's on Friday."

"What memorial?" Kelly asked.

"It's been seven years," Jared said. "They can declare Father dead now."

Lyman shifted in his chair. "We thought it would be proper to have a memorial service."

"That was your grandfather," Jared explained to John. "The man I told you about—the one who disappeared."

"Then I could see my grandma in Lone Rock, too, huh?"

"That's right."

"I want to see my grandma."

"We will one of these days."

Lyman pushed back his chair. "I'd better be going." The wind blew a branch of the maple tree against the window. "Maybe I've waited too long already." He rose and put on his coat, and took his hat from the nail. "Thank you so much," he said to Kelly. He nodded to the room. "Goodnight."

"Good-bye, Uncle," John said.

Lyman marched to the door and stepped outside, where he seemed to swell on space and fresh air. In the shelter of the veranda he paused to put on his hat, then hastened down the steps and away into the darkness. The others had followed him onto the porch. They heard the car start, saw its little red taillight appear and then rush off up the hill, bobbing nervously.

Not far above the treetops black clouds rushed through the sky, moist and heavy. Almost as soon as Jared and his family got back in the house they heard the rain. The sound of scattered drops increased until it became a solid drumming on the roof. Lyman would never make it past the creek in this rain. Jared put his hat on and took his mackinaw down from the nail. As he opened the door a skein of misty wind rushed in, darkening the boards of the kitchen floor. He pulled his hat down and stepped out, slamming the door behind him. The rain came against him, soaking his face, and almost at once he could feel the weight of the waterfall pouring from the brim of his hat onto his back. He made his way by instinct and long familiarity with the ranch yard. His eyes were no use to him except once, when sheet lightning revealed the stable and corrals in a strange new light, as if they were glimpsed through a burning window curtain. He strained against the wind, but his boots slipped on the glaze of mud that covered the ground, and twice he almost fell down. When he reached the stable he stepped inside its quiet warmth and closed the door against the storm. There was the soft click of hooves as his horse turned in her stall and nickered out of the darkness. Jared's left hand found the lantern hanging from its nail, even before his other struck the match, and as the wick flamed up, the stable seemed to fill with blooms of light turned toward the lantern, each with its own slanting black shadow.

Quickly he threw the saddle on his mare. As he led her to the door and opened it, she swung back on the bridle rein like a kite, then plunged forward, her hooves skating on the stable floor, and pulled Jared into the whirling night. He seized the horn as it passed, and tried to get his place in the saddle before the rain had soaked it, but the mare was turning like a four-footed ballerina, and by the time he got his boot in the stirrup and raised himself, the cold, wet leather came up against his underparts as keenly as if he were naked. The mare broke into a lope, with the rain at her back, and he had to turn her to face it, toward the road for town.

From time to time as he rode along, the lightning revealed a strange white landscape gleaming with rain and completely empty. Then suddenly the mare shied, and Jared realized they had reached the creek—the car was right in front of them, its lights out, its motor dead.

"Who's there?" Lyman shouted.

"It's me. Jared!" He got down out of the saddle. He could see Lyman standing by his car, or parts of him at least. He appeared in segments, like a dismembered body, as the rain glittered fleetingly on his face, or wet clothing, or the fender of the Model T. "Come on back!" Jared shouted. During a flick of lightning he saw that the wheels of the car were deep in mud on the further bank of the creek.

"I can't," Lyman replied. "I've got to get to town tonight."

"You're stuck. You'll never make it."

"Why don't you pull me out?"

"You'd be stuck again in half a mile."

"Then I'll have to walk."

"That'll take you all night."

"I'll make it."

Lyman turned to start away, but Jared seized him by the shoulder. "Take my horse at least." He thrust the bridle reins into Lyman's hand.

Lyman hesitated. "I don't ride much any more."

"You can come and get your car tomorrow."

Lyman took the reins and closed both hands over the saddle horn. Hitching himself, he lifted one foot into the stirrup and hopped on the other as the mare sidled away, then floundered upward uncertainly to his place in the saddle. He swung the mare and urged her into the storm. The rain fell noisily on the fenders of the Model T.

By the time Jared walked back to the ranch the sound of the rain had faded until all he could hear was a faint crystal murmur, part the distant deluge, part the whisper of single drops landing near at hand.

In the dark, empty kitchen he shook down the ashes, laid a fire and lit it, then stood holding his hands to the stove, as if the crackle of the new flames could somehow warm him.

Shivering, he began to pull off his clothes. They clung to him, as wet and heavy as if he had just been saved from drowning. Kelly came in dressed in her nightgown, put the copper boiler on the stove and began to fill it from the pump in the corner.

Between clenched jaws Jared muttered, "The boys in bed?"

"The 'boys' are in bed—John and his grandpa. They almost went to sleep at the table." Then she chided, "You'll catch pneumonia."

"I'm all right."

"Did you find Lyman?"

"He was stuck up to the axle, just like I knew he would be."

"But he wouldn't come back with you?"

"He has to be in court tomorrow. I loaned him my horse." He peeled off his long underwear like a second skin.

Kelly sat him naked on a chair and began to rub him with a towel. "Just because he doesn't know enough to come in out of the rain is no excuse for you."

"I have you to look after me."

"Lucky thing."

"But what will happen to poor old Lyman?" Jared was able to speak better as Kelly's rubbing dried and warmed him; still his words passed awkwardly between set jaws. "Well, the mare'll get him there all right."

Her touch grew more gentle. "Can I go to the mountains with you tomorrow?"

"Whether you like it or not."

"John will want to come too."

"He's still pretty young. Besides, I want to be alone with you."

She laughed. "I'll bet you say that to all your wives."

"Yes I do. To you and you and you." The stove had begun to heat up a little, and Jared felt its breath on his skin. "It's funny. I used to wonder why my father would want two wives. Since I got married, I wonder even more."

"It's that bad?"

"One wife is all I can handle."

"You do all right."

"It *must* have been because he thought it was the will of God." Kelly put down the towel and drew a blanket around his naked body, clasping it under his chin like a hood. He pulled her onto his lap. "I'm glad those days are over, Kelly. I never want anybody but you."

"It's a good thing." She waggled the knot of the blanket under his chin. "Hold this." Then she rose and dipped her fingers in the boiler. "Still cold."

"It'll take hours," Jared said. "Just fill the hot-water bottle from the kettle and let's go to bed."

"Is that what you want?"

"If you don't mind sleeping with the unwashed."

"You've been washed by the rain."

He stood, and drew her under the blanket with him. He could see her face, pale in the darkness, ethereal, illusive. Her softness was real enough, though, and her warmth. He lifted her in his arms and carried her into the bedroom.

"You forgot the hot-water bottle," she said.

"Who needs a hot-water bottle?"

**3** The next morning the sky was clear. The world shone in the early sun; grass and trees and fences sparkled with clinging drops of rain. In a square of sunlight on the kitchen floor Jared prepared the bedroll and grub box for the trip to the mountains.

"Can I go?" John asked.

Jared said. "You stay with Grandpa this time. Next year you can help me drive the cattle."

John paused to consider.

Hickory Jack said, "You figure by next year I'll be dead, Rosie?"

"No. Fish, Hick, I don't know if you'll ever die. But next year you'll have to stay home alone."

"And I can come with you?" John said.

"Yup."

"I'll be a big boy next year, huh?"

"And I'll be dead," said Hickory Jack.

Jared spread several blankets in a pile on the kitchen floor, rolled them up, and tied them with a small, stout rope. Then, while he got the horses ready, Kelly finished loading their grub box. The bedroll, grub box and blocks of salt were placed on the packhorse, along with a small coil of barbed wire and tools for fixing fence. Soon they were mounted, ready to leave.

Hickory Jack lifted John onto his shoulder, where he was high enough to kiss his parents good-bye.

"You boys take care of yourselves," Kelly said.

"We'll be all right," replied Hickory Jack. "We'll have a great time, won't we, John?"

"What'll we do, Grandpa?"

"Well. First off we'll take the .22 and shoot some gophers."

"Oh boy, let's go." John ran toward the house.

"See you in about three days," Jared told Hickory Jack. They turned their horses and started for the south pasture, the packhorse following.

The cattle drive was one of the high points of the year for Jared. It was not a great distance and there weren't many cattle, and they often drove along fenced road allowances; still it stirred his imagination.

Sometimes he and Kelly rode drag together, following the herd and popping the rumps of laggards with the tip of a lariat. But often, when the road forked, or they passed a homestead, or some obstruction or diversion threatened, one of them rode to the front of the herd to steer them past the difficulty. The air was fresh after the rain; the day was not too hot and the herd moved easily. They camped that night on the St. Mary's River not far from Cardston.

The next morning they were moving along the road adjacent to the town before most people were out of bed. Children ran outdoors to watch them pass; dogs barked at them. One early bird who was hanging out her wash stopped and shaded her eyes against the sun.

At Rachel's house the blinds were drawn, the chimney inert, without the wisp of fresh blue smoke that rose from some of the other houses. Tom had apparently learned the secret of how to make money without rising early in the morning. "Looks like we're too early for breakfast at Rachel's," Jared said. "Maybe we can call in on our way home." On the peak of the roof the iron rooster still faced the wind, shifting gently.

Kelly said, "This is where your father disappeared."

"You remember?"

"Of course."

"And I." Yet he had forgotten, or become occupied with other things.

The sun was about in the middle of the sky when they reached the pasture. As they turned the cattle in through the gate, Jared said, "I think I'll check the fence and set the bear traps before lunch. I should be ready in a couple of hours."

He took the grub box down and set it on the ground, then, leading the packhorse, he rode upward through the trees. Already the herd was spreading across the meadow at the lower end of the pasture.

In a grove of spruce at the top of the hill, he found a place where three large trees grew close together, forming a triangle. He chose a crevice between these trees, at the far point of the triangle where other animals could not step, to set one of his traps.

The bear trap was a huge metal jaw, with teeth clamped now like those of a grinning monster. Jared fastened a piece of fresh meat to the iron tongue. All his weight and strength were needed to press down the springs and pull the jaws apart until they lay flat, teeth upward, bait between them, waiting for their prey. Gingerly he pushed the trap back into the crevice between the trees. He had once witnessed the moment of a bear's capture. He would never forget the roar of the animal and the anguished lunges which seemed to shake the whole mountain. He hated these traps, but he could not afford to have a hungry bear turned loose among his cattle. He anchored the chain to a log, small enough that the bear could pull it without tearing off his foot, but large enough that he could not drag it far. Satisfied, he went to the other end of the field and set his second trap.

On his way back he followed the fence line, making repairs as needed. As he approached the camp he stopped in a nearby clearing. Above the bank he found ancient blackened logs half buried in the sod—all that remained of Hickory Jack's dance hall. He stopped his horse and got off. He remembered his father's face that night when he swung the lantern against the wall. It had been an act of almost holy retribution—Alma had never doubted the rightness of that arsony. And yet, his life after it was forever changed, dragged down and finally obliterated as though God himself could stand the sight of him no longer.

Where was justice? Not in this world, certainly. And what restitution in the hereafter could compensate a man for a mortal life that had been nullified?

Jared balanced himself on the edge of one of the timbers and looked around him. The breeze dipped, the rustle of leaves hushed; the clearing seemed to hold its breath, still awed by the memory of that night of flame. Even in broad daylight Jared felt the hair on his body lift. But what was there to see? The grass, the trees, the water, the sky; the black relics of that awful night.

As he led his horse into camp he heard a sound, and straightened, listening. It was quiet and distant at first, but quickly drawing nearer. The indistinct rumble swelled, its component noises growing sharper every moment—the drum of hooves, the squeak and rattle of spinning wheels, the clink of harness rings; the one-syllable sounds of an urgent voice, repeated at intervals.

"What is it?" Kelly asked.

"Somebody coming."

They watched the place where the road came around a small hill a short distance down the creek.

"Hah! Git!" the voice cried.

"It's Hick."

When the outfit rounded the corner Jared saw that the horses were almost lunging, too weary to run, but still whipped to a frenzy by Hickory Jack's lashes. They careened headfirst toward the fire, then stopped with a surge that almost ran the democrat against the horse's heels.

"Where's John?" Kelly cried.

"He's lost!" croaked Hickory Jack, his voice dry from shouting at the horses.

"Lost?"

Hickory Jack clambered unsteadily over the wheel. Jared moved to help him. "Don't ask me how," the old man said. He stood on the ground, slowly marching in place, as if to get his legs moving again. "I thought I'd never get here."

"Tell us what happened!" Kelly cried.

"What happened?" He shook his head and rubbed his hand across his eyes. "I don't know what happened. This morning he was gone. That's all I know."

"You got drunk last night, didn't you?" Kelly exclaimed.

"He's all right," said Hickory Jack. "He can take care of

himself." Then, as if by way of explanation, "I came as fast as I could."

His daughter repeated, "You were drunk."

Hickory Jack straightened, perhaps to slough off the rebuke in her voice. "We had a little party, John and me."

"And what happened?" Kelly asked.

"No," Jared said. "That doesn't matter. Not now. We still have three or four hours of daylight . . ."

"That's not even time enough to get home," Kelly said.

" 'Tain't no use goin' home anyway," Hickory Jack said. "He ain't there. I scoured that place upside down." He wiped his sleeve across his face.

"Where would he go?" Jared asked.

"There ain't no place for him to go," replied Hickory Jack. "They's no place on earth he knows but the Arrowhead."

"Would he try to follow us?" Kelly asked.

"He's never been here," Jared said. "He'd have no idea even which way to go."

"Lethbridge?"

"He doesn't know anybody there. Did he say anything, Hick? What did you talk about last night?"

"I hardly recollect." He shook his head. "I'se so sleepy."

"You've got to think," Kelly told him. "Remember."

Hickory Jack stared at her. "He did talk about his grandma in Lone Rock."

"The silly little kid," Jared said. "Would he set out for Lone Rock?"

"I can't imagine," Kelly said.

Jared reflected for a moment. "All right. As Hick says, he's a tough boy. He can take care of himself. I think that probably he went riding somewhere on the Arrowhead. He's likely back home by now, wondering where Grandpa is."

"I didn't know what to do," Hickory Jack said.

"There is a chance, though, that he tried to get to Lone Rock, so this is what we'll do. Kelly, you go back to the Arrowhead. Hick, your horses have gone as far as they can today. You tend the camp in case he finds his way out here. I'll go to Lone Rock. One of us will find him."

**4** Jared cut directly across the Indian Reserve, his horse galloping steadily, for a time almost effortlessly. Beneath her hooves the grass blew light and dark, whipped by the wind into twisting sheets of reflected sunlight. It seemed a different wind from the one that blew at the Arrowhead; this was fresh off the mountains, still carrying the scent of pines. When Jared watched that bending grass, and felt the cool wind on his cheek, it was as if he had never been away.

But as the miles passed, the mare began to flag. Her coat turned black, and foam collected on her neck where the bridle reins rubbed. Her breathing became loud and heavy, tuned to the increasing effort of her slower and slower gait.

It was late afternoon when Jared rode over the broad hump of the Indian Reserve and saw before him the cup of earth that had nourished his youth—not actually a hollow, but made to appear so by the mountains that ringed it on the west and south some thirty miles away. His flesh seemed to burn with the thrill of forgotten beauty suddenly restored. Home. The word came to his mind unbidden, unwelcome even. He had lived here only four years out of his life—why should he call it home?

At last he rode out on the hill above the river. Lone Rock lay beyond, hot and quiet in the late-afternoon sun. Jared urged his horse down the hill, though now at a walk, across the bridge and up the other side. Years ago he had left a collection of small houses huddled on the prairie, exposed and, it seemed to him, transitory, as if they never could survive. He came back to a town rooted like an ancient garden. The wild prairie had been trapped in a net of roads and fence lines, broken by the plough, tamed with fields of wheat and alfalfa hay, tethered to farmsteads and clumps of poplar windbreak, until it seemed that the only thing to escape was the wind.

Jared remembered ploughing with his father, four horses and a walking plough, with Jared at the handles. Mixed with the heat of the dry air, the cry of the sea gulls that wheeled above them, the jangle of the traces, the moist aroma of the freshly turned earth; mixed with these physical things that he could see and hear and smell, Jared had felt a powerful sense of continuity—of carrying forward a pattern. He glanced across at his father, leaning back against the pull of the lines as he walked beside the plough. Alma was past seventy, but still vigorous and powerful. His face gleamed under his hat brim, and a wide band down the front of his shirt was dark with sweat.

"Whoa!" Alma called. The horses stopped, and stood slowly puffing, sweating, nodding, snorting, switching at the flies.

In the midst of the flat furrows Alma's coat lay humped over a water jug wrapped in burlap. The two of them walked over to it. Alma pulled the cork, twisted his palm over the mouth of the jug, and tipped back his head to drink. Then he handed the jug to Jared. "It's wet, anyway."

They returned to the outfit, and as they stood for a moment on the unturned sod, Jared stepped up on a loaf-sized stone, then to another close beside it. He paused. There were several such stones nearby. They seemed to be lying in a line, and as his eye followed it he saw that the line formed a circle, enclosing an area about the size of a large room. With his arm he indicated the circle to his father.

"Some Indian tepee," Alma said. "Must have weighted the skirt with rocks." They turned over a couple of the stones. Each rested in its own little pit of earth—they had lain there for a long time.

Jared was stirred. This land belonged to Alma under title from the King, but still bore the symbols of the dispossessed. The ring of stones on its slope was the muted tongue of a fallen people, like some ancient monument—a prairie parthenon.

As he rode into town, the first building that he recognized was the school, a two-story square frame place with a fire-escape slide from one of the upper windows. It had been the first building of any consequence in the town, and the cause of much community pride at the time of its completion. Now its paint had faded; in a few years it had grown old, like the rest of the village.

He stopped his horse for a moment to get his bearings. The

whole town lay in shadow, except for Beckett's windmill, whose softly-turning blades still winked the light of the setting sun.

He saw a woman gathering vegetables in the garden that grew beside a karaganna hedge. Jared dismounted, crossed the fence, and walked toward her. She looked up, a red-haired, freckle-faced woman, her body billowing grotesquely under a cotton tent-dress as she worked. When she noticed Jared she turned and stood with one hand on her hip, looking at him. Her eyes flared with the shock of recognition; her body seemed to contract, pressing a startled wheeze from her lips. Her hand went to her mouth. "Jared!" She began to sink.

"Gracie!" He rushed forward to grasp her, but she twisted out of his arms and sank to the grass in a crumpled heap, her face covered with her hands. He couldn't tell if she was laughing or crying.

He sat on the grass beside her. "Aren't you glad to see me?"

She nodded, and gradually the shaking of her body subsided. "Shame on you—staying away so long." She came partway out from behind her fingers.

"Yes. I know I should have come to see you more often."

She reached her hand to touch him, a child's hand it looked like, emerging from the pale wattles of her arm.

"Have you seen John?"

She hesitated. "Your John?"

"He ran away last night. I wondered if he may have come here."

"He's only a baby."

"He's five now."

"That's only a baby. How could he find his way here?"

"I guess he couldn't. I just don't know where else to look."

She gathered her brows into a nest of dimples. "Poor Kelly must be worried sick." And then she smiled again. "Never mind, Orville will go and help you look. Maybe I can leave the children with Aunt Bessie . . ."

"No, Grace. He's probably safe home by now, but I just want to check around Lone Rock while I'm here."

"Well, I never!" With deceptive nimbleness she got to her feet. "I have to run and fix supper. Will you eat with us?"

"Maybe after dark; after I have a look."

She followed him to the fence. "It won't be ready for a while."

"All right."

"Well, I never. I kept waiting for you to write, even."

"After a while I was too ashamed."

"You know about Daddy's funeral?"

He nodded. "Lyman came out to the ranch the other day."

"You'll have to stay. It's just till tomorrow."

"I don't know. I'll see."

She hitched her shoulder. "But you'll come to supper. You promise?"

"I'll be there."

She turned and started her body into motion. It seemed to have a thousand moving parts that worked in double time to propel her slowly across the ground.

Jared carried out his search, up and down the streets of the town, but he did not find John's pinto pony. It was almost dark when he stopped in front of Grace's house, a small dark cottage barely afloat in a sea of disassembled machinery. Around a nucleus of old car bodies lay scattered every kind of wheel, gear, pedal, chain or engine block imaginable. Over most of the dooryard no grass grew; the earth was black with ancient oil drippings, the air heavy with its stale vapors. At the back of the lot an old shed seemed to sag beneath the weight of metal shards that encrusted its walls.

A small boy answered Jared's knock and admitted him to the kitchen. Grace was busy at the stove. She glanced over her shoulder. "You didn't find him?"

"No. He must be safe at home by now."

"Well, come in. It'll be ready in a minute."

In the center of the room a large man sat at the table, one forearm resting in front of him as if he were waiting for someone to put a fork in his hand, and the other balancing a plump baby that straddled his thigh. He nodded at Jared, and rising slightly in his chair, reached forward to greet him. Jared could feel the grime, almost like a polish on the huge, meaty hand.

"Hello, Jared."

"Orville."

"Introduce Jared to the children," Grace said.

Orville gestured with his hand. "These are the kids, Jared. Kids, this is your long-lost uncle."

Still at the stove, Grace complained, "Tell him their names, for heaven sake."

"What for?" Orville asked. "He couldn't remember them, anyway." He extended his arm. "Just set down there anywhere. We're goin' to have something to eat here in a while."

Jared selected a chair and sat down. Opposite him, a small boy stood, his only visible parts his head and his fingers on the edge of the table. The other children, briefly diverted by the arrival of their uncle, returned to whatever it was they had been doing before. Their noise made it hard to hear, but Orville didn't seen aware of the difficulty. He continued to talk, looking up at Jared, and then down at the table, and then up again. Jared caught a few words here and there—sufficient to satisfy him, and nodded his head from time to time, which seemed to satisfy Orville.

In time the table was set, the food was ready, and the family sat down. The noise subsided briefly while one of the children said the blessing, then almost instantly swelled again.

Grace still cooked a great meal, anyway. It was marvelous to Jared that somehow she could move through this welter of human bodies and week-old food stains, and appear at the table with a supper that tasted so good.

While they ate, Orville talked on, hesitating only to fill his mouth or drink from his water glass. Jared contented himself with eating and looking about him. He noticed that his sister, once she had helped her children serve themselves, withdrew from the bedlam—her mind was far away, while her abandoned body quietly took on nourishment.

For the next hour Jared felt as if he were being nibbled to death by worms—children and Orville, separately or all together, spilling their questions or food on him, and licking off the answers or crushing them on his sleeve. "Why don't you get a haircut, Uncle Jared?" "You a cowboy?" "I got a pet beetle." "You still in the horse business, Jared? Horses are dead as the Dodo, you know. You take my advice, you'll sell while you can. Get yourself a good garage."

As soon as the meal was over, Jared excused himself.

Grace said, "Please don't go yet. The children will be in bed soon. We can visit . . ."

He put on his hat. "Maybe sometime. After I know where John is."

He hurried out through the door. Grace followed him. The quiet of the evening sky was like a sanctuary, to which even the children responded as they came running out of the house behind them.

Moonlight glittered on a thousand shiny surfaces, till Orville's dooryard had begun to look like the inside of Ali Baba's cave, but the effect was spoiled by the fetid air.

"Where will you look now?" Grace asked him.

"I don't know. I'll go home, I guess. But first I want to talk to Aunt Bessie and Lyman—see if they've heard anything."

He mounted and turned toward the road.

"Bye!" they all cried.

He urged his horse to a gallop.


**5** By daylight Lone Rock had looked as tacky as ever, only in a different way than when he was a boy. Then it had been tacky-new: ungraded roads, unfinished houses, uncultivated land. Now it was tacky-old: falling-down barns, houses needing paint, yards gone to weed. The town looked better by moonlight—all its scars and ugliness were hidden in the shadows.

He stopped at the gate to Bessie's cottage, which Lyman had built for her when he and Paula moved into the family home. The house was set far back on the lot, attached to the rest of the world by a plank sidewalk that lay white in the moonlight. Three large willow trees grew in the yard like a private forest. The windows of the house were black as openings in the earth.

He pushed the gate, and the hinge creaked plaintively, then sighed as it swung back. He started down the plank walk. It must be later than he thought.

He knocked at the door.

From somewhere inside the house he heard faint movements, and presently footsteps scuffed across the floor. A voice from behind the door said, "Who's there?"

He knocked again.

"Who is it?"

The door wasn't locked; it couldn't be locked. Lone Rock had no locked doors.

"Who's there?" The voice was close to the door now, almost as though she was bending toward it, but the tone was impatient. "Who's there, I say. I won't open this door until you tell me."

"A friend."

"Some friend! What do you want?"

"I want to see you."

"In the middle of the night?"

"Yes."

There was silence for a moment or two. "I won't open the door until I know who you are."

He turned the knob and pushed gently at the door. He could feel her resistance.

"Don't you dare!" she cried.

He continued to push. Slowly the door opened inward.

She turned and ran, and as the door sprang open he saw her disappear into the dark hallway. Almost at once the scuffing footsteps returned down the hall. As she came into the kitchen she switched on the light. She was clutching an old green bathrobe around her. She walked straight up to him, her head up, her back stiff.

"Now, sir. If you can explain yourself." For the first time, then, she looked directly at him. She breathed in sharply. "Jared."

"That's me."

"What . . . I don't . . . Come in. My, you gave me a start."

"I'm sorry. I was trying to surprise you, I guess. It was a silly thing to do."

"It's so late."

"I'm looking for John."

"John? Your tiny John?"

"He ran away. The way he talked about wanting to visit his grandma in Lone Rock, I wondered if he may have tried to find his way here."

She groped her way toward a kitchen chair and sat on the edge of it. "I haven't seen him. Nobody's said anything. What could have happened?"

"He must have just wandered away. I'm sure he's home by now."

"I hope so." She sighed. "Anyway, I'm glad you're here. I've wanted to talk to you."

"What about?"

"I guess it's this memorial that reminded me. I wanted to tell you I'm sorry."

"Sorry?"

She seemed to flinch. "It wasn't right—what Lyman did. What we all did. I know it wasn't right."

He took a chair across from her. "You mean the farm?"

"I don't know what happened. I was angry at you, but that's no excuse." She gnawed at her lip. "When you were boys I treated you the same. I loved you as my own." Her eyes had wandered. "Are you happy?"

"I wouldn't trade places with anybody."

"You forgive me?"

"There's nothing to forgive."

She moved on her chair, to rest her back against it.

"And Lyman? You forgive Lyman, too?"

Jared hesitated.

"You have to forgive Lyman. He was no more to blame than me."

"I can't. Not unless he asks for it, too."

"You still blame Lyman for everything that happens," she said. "I think you even blamed him when your father disappeared."

"Why should I do that?"

"You said it. Don't you remember?"

There was an uncomfortable silence.

Her eyes widened. "You're just in time. It's your father's memorial service tomorrow."

"Yes, I know."

"You'll stay, of course."

"If I find John."

She sighed. "That's strange, isn't it? Your father and son both disappear."

On the wall above her head there hung a photograph of Alma, bigger than life-size, in a heavy oval frame. Somehow it brought home to Jared the full impact of the passing years—perhaps because the photograph was the only thing that had not changed. Bessie, the town, even he himself had aged. But like a weight standard set in a bell jar, the picture remained the same, a constant against which he could measure life's progression. He could even hear his father's words:

"Jared, You don't have to die to take a look at hell—or heaven either, for that matter. They're both right here on earth. Some people live lives as much a hell as any devil ever dreamed of. And there are others who live so close to the Lord that heaven for them will be no more than a move across town."

Jared stared at the photograph. He wondered at the simple faith of his father, where right and wrong were as clear as squares on a checkerboard. The squares on Jared's board had somehow faded and run together, the edges grown wavery or gone completely.

Bessie finally looked back over her shoulder, as if Jared's scrutiny of the picture made her wonder if she might have missed something in it. "He was a good man, Jared."

"Yes, he was."

"You've gotten away from the church, haven't you?"

"There isn't any church out our way."

"Your father had such plans for you." For a few minutes they sat without speaking. Then Bessie began to talk, softly, without looking at him. "After you left, I knew you were angry. I didn't think you were attending to your duties.

Somewhere I heard that you had been hurt—maybe even killed, and I thought—God help me—I thought, 'Better dead clean than alive unclean.' I've heard fathers say that—preach it from the pulpit. They'd rather see their son die than fall into sin, they said. I used to believe it, but it's a lie!" She reached in the front of her dress for her handkerchief.

Jared didn't know what to say.

"I know the gospel's true," she went on, "but sometimes they teach us nonsense. They say all we have to do is live the gospel and we'll be happy. Well, I've tried to live the gospel all my life."

"Haven't you been happy?"

"Sometimes."

"I thought . . . I don't understand."

"It's not easy, sharing your man with another woman."

"But you're the one that had him."

"It was your mother he loved . . ." She sniffed primly and put her handkerchief away. "That's enough of that."

Jared rose. "I have to go."

She caught him at the door. "Stay with me tonight. You can't find John in the dark."

"Maybe Lyman's heard something."

"He'd have told me."

"I can't just sit here, Aunt. I have to do something."

"Don't forget the memorial."

"I'll come if I can." He turned and started down the walk. Behind him the screen door screeched, and closed with a slap.

**6** As Jared rode up to Lyman's gate he scarcely recognized the farmstead which he and Alma had built. By now it sprawled across a couple of acres—house and barn, granaries, shops, trees, corrals, bunkhouses. Lyman had made a lot of improvements in seven years. The house especially had been enlarged and renovated.

There was no light anywhere. A large dog came off the

porch and barked at Jared as he dismounted. He ran his palm over the dog's head. At the door he raised his hand and stood for a moment, like a man taking an oath, but with his fist clenched. Then he knocked.

Presently the light in the house came on. A voice spoke from behind the door. "Ly, is that you? What are you doing?" It was a woman's voice, hard with impatience but spoken with the childish lilt of a little girl: Paula's voice. "Ly?"

Jared remembered that voice; he could still hear it whisper to him, "Don't go on a mission. I can't stand for you to go."

Now, speaking through the door, it took on a note of alarm. "Who's there?"

"I'm looking for Lyman."

"He isn't home."

"When do you expect him?"

"Two days ago I expected him."

"He hasn't been home since he went to Lethbridge?"

"Who are you? Do I know you? Your voice sounds familiar."

"You know me."

She took in a sudden breath. "Jared?" She opened the door. "Jared. It is you. Come in."

"No. I'll come back later."

"Come in. Do you know how long it's been?" She led the way into the living room and then turned to face him. She had kept herself surprisingly young; her face, like her voice, was still that of a young girl. Beneath the kimono the lines of her body seemed fuller, but firm and slender still. She sat down and arranged the kimono over her legs. "You really scared me. I won't have the hiccups for a hundred years."

"I'm looking for my boy, John. He ran away from home. I thought he might have come to Lone Rock."

"And I thought you came to see me." She laughed. "Why don't you sit down? You're not afraid of me, are you? Can't you see I'm getting old? But you look wonderful. You're more handsome than ever."

She rose and came toward him. He could smell her body, as faint as the scent of blossoms—the same soft, pungent air that he had first smelled when he was seventeen.

As he turned toward the door, she went swiftly past him and stood with her back against it. "You're a funny squirt, Jerry. You haven't changed a bit." She laughed again, but bitterly now. "And neither has Lyman, except he's gotten worse."

"He's the one you wanted."

"Oh, Jerry. You're such a fool. When I think of what we've missed, you and I . . ."

"I haven't missed anything."

She took his upper arm between her hands. "Believe me, honey, you've missed something."

Jared walked out onto the step.

Car lights appeared far down the street, their rays shining dimly among the trees. "That's Lyman coming now," Paula said. "Suppose we let him catch us kissing? Maybe that would get his heart started again. It hasn't beat for years; his blood just oozes up and down his body."

Jared pulled away from her and walked down off the step. "What's the matter with you?"

"Can't you take a joke? You don't think I'm serious, do you?"

The headlights swung past the porch. The car engine roared and stopped. In a moment or two Lyman hurried up the walk. He looked at Paula, then at Jared. "I wondered whose horse that was."

"Horse?" Paula asked.

"Tied at the front gate."

"It's Jared," Paula told him. "Aren't you surprised?"

"Why would I be surprised? I invited him. Besides, where the carcass is, there the vultures will be gathered."

"Meaning what?" Jared asked.

"I'm glad you came for the memorial. But I should warn you that as far as the estate's concerned, there's very little property to divide."

"There's nothing here I want."

"Too bad you didn't stay around. We could have done great things together, you and I."

Jared was surprised. "You really don't remember, do you?"

"Remember?" Lyman brushed by them and continued into the house.

Jared followed. "Why I didn't hang around." Lyman breezed through life with elbows flying, unaware of the lives he bumped as he passed.

Behind them Paula said, "I'll bet you thought I had a lover."

Lyman scowled at her. "What?"

"When you saw the horse tied at the gate."

"What are you talking about?"

"You can't imagine a man being interested in me, can you?"

"Why can't you be serious? If the house was on fire, you'd want to roast marshmallows." Lyman gestured with his arm. "Speaking of houses, how do you like what I've done with it, Jared?"

Jared looked around the room, at the mohair and walnut and Persian carpets. "It's nice."

"Nice? It's the finest home in the country."

Paula said, "This isn't a home. It's a museum for Lyman's money, all the things that Lyman can buy."

"Paula'd feel more comfortable living behind the blacksmith shop," Lyman said. He ran a hand across his stomach. "I haven't had anything to eat for hours. Come on, Jared. Let's see what we can find." He led the way into the kitchen and stood at the open cupboard door. "Just sit at the table there."

Paula took a chair and sat with her elbows on the table, staring at her reflection in the black windowpane.

"What are you so antsy about, Jared?" Lyman asked. "Sit down. Relax."

Jared sat at the end of the table.

"How about scrambled eggs? No. I'd have to build a fire."

"Never mind, for me," Jared said. "I'm not hungry. I have to go, anyway."

Lyman lifted the lid of a pan that sat on the cupboard. "Well, look at that. Doughnuts. I'll say that much for the old girl. She can make doughnuts. How about some doughnuts and milk?"

Lyman was like a little girl playing with her toys, sitting this doll here and that one there, fixing tea for the party. "You might as well stay the night, Jared. We've got plenty of room." He set a glass of milk and a couple of doughnuts on the table in front of Jared. "You want something?" he asked Paula.

She shook her head.

Lyman sat down and bit into his doughnut twice, filling his cheeks, and began to chew. "You into cattle at all out there, Jared? I was looking at some Aberdeen Angus here a week or so ago. Think I'll get a few head and . . ."

Jared held up his hand to signal "stop." "There's something I want to ask you, Trash."

"Ask on, little brother."

"Where did you go that night that Father disappeared?"

"Are we back on that again?"

"We never left it."

"You think I killed Father?"

"Just answer my question."

Lyman glanced at Paula. "You can forget it. I even have a witness."

Paula continued to stare at her reflection in the window.

"Aren't you ever going to learn, little brother? We have fought about a lot of things, you and I, but I always won. Didn't you notice that? I used to feel sorry for you, you were so easy to beat. You still are."

"What happened, Trash? Where is he?"

Lyman looked at Jared with hard, steady eyes. "'I told you I was going home early to do the chores. I was really going home early because I had a date with Paula. I was with her the whole time, wasn't I, Paula?"

Jared felt as if his insides were painted black.

"That was when you still thought Paula was your girl. I couldn't tell you where I had been, could I?"

Paula stared into the windowpane and patted her hair with her fingers.

"Go ahead and eat," Lyman said.

Jared pushed back his chair. "You haven't changed."

"Why would I want to change?"

Paula rose from her chair and went around the table toward the window. It seemed to Jared that she must be peering out at something, but as she leaned near the pane he saw that she was only checking her complexion in that imperfect mirror. She did not see anything that lay beyond the dark glass, only her own features dimly reflected against a Stygian world.

Close behind her image Lyman's face could be seen as round as a moon, yet strangely distant, like Jupiter himself slowly turning through the firmament, untouched, untouchable.

A line of Scripture came to Jared's mind, and he spoke it. " 'Vengeance is mine, saith the Lord.' "

"What?" Lyman asked.

No wonder God reserved to Himself the right of vengeance —nobody else could do the job so well.

Jared shrugged. "I forgive you."

"You forgive me!" Lyman said. "What do you forgive me for?"

"Aunt Bessie hoped I would forgive you. Well, I forgive you."

"Forgive? Forgive what?"

"Everything. Anything." Jared shook his head. "I can't explain it to you. You swim through life like an otter—he never wets his fur. How can I explain the ways you have hurt me, when you don't even recognize your own hurt?"

"I'm not hurting."

"I hurt," Paula whispered.

"We all hurt," Jared said.

"What do you know?" Lyman asked him.

"I know more than you realize, Trash. And I still forgive you."

"You forgive! You forgive! You sanctimonious son-of-a-bitch. What have you to forgive?" He waggled a large finger at Jared. "Well, I'm warning you. I don't forgive. And I never forget."

"I'm sure you don't."

Lyman was like an elephant, or an eagle, with eyes so large there was no room left in his skull for a brain big enough to comprehend what he saw.

"I knew you'd be back here hanging around sometime," Lyman went on. "It stuck in your craw that Paula chose me instead of you, didn't it? You had to find out how it worked. That's the real reason you came back—to spy on us."

"No, Trash. I came back to look for John."

"John?" The big man flinched, the attitude of his body softened. His red face paled, blood and anger seemed to recede together. "Your son? I almost forgot. He's in the car."

"What?"

"He's asleep out there. When I saw the horse I forgot . . ."

Jared rushed through the door and down the steps. On the back seat of Lyman's car he found the boy wrapped in a blanket, fast asleep. Jared leaned forward, bracing his arms against the car with his head bent between them, looking through the window. A shudder passed through his body.

Behind him, Lyman spoke. "He's all right. Tired, that's all."

"Where'd you find him?"

"At the ranch. I rode back out to the Arrowhead last night to pick up my car."

"Well, what happened? Kelly and I were gone."

"So I found out. The ground had dried a lot, so I was able to get out of the mudhole. But while I was in the stable unsaddling the horse I heard this noise. At first I thought it was a kitten. It didn't sound right though, and when I tracked it down I found John hiding in a manger."

"Hiding?"

"I didn't know you'd left him alone with Hickory Jack."

"Hick dotes on that boy."

"After John stopped crying, I left him at the stable and went up to the house and knocked on the door. 'Get out!' Hickory Jack shouts. 'Leave me alone!' So I knocked again. 'Who is it? Get out! Go away!' I pushed the door open. He was sitting there in front of the fireplace. He had the fire going, and sat looking at it, so his back was toward me. His arms were hanging over the sides of the chair. In one hand he held a bottle. I couldn't see what was in the other one. When he saw me he started to curse, 'Damn Mormons!' He raised his other hand and I saw he had a pistol in it. He fired a shot through the ceiling. Then he aimed the gun at me."

Jared said, "I didn't know Hick had a pistol."

"It wasn't a figment. That barrel looked ninety feet deep."

"He wouldn't shoot you."

"He started to laugh. 'You want to see the Cee-lestial Kingdom?' he asks me. 'I can send you there, right quick.' And he fired another shot through the roof, and laughed again. He tipped back his head to drink from his bottle a couple of times. So once when he was looking at the ceiling, I jumped him. Turned out I made a mistake—he was not so far gone as I figured. I swear when that bullet went by I felt the wind. But I nailed him, and him and me and the chair went end over teakettle across the floor. When we came up against the wall I was on top, and holding the gun. Man, I got out of there. I fetched John from the stable and tossed him in the back seat of the car, and I started to crank, and by now old Hickory Jack had stumbled out onto the porch, cursing."

"I've seen Hick drunk all right," Jared said. "But never like that."

"Falling-down drunk, he was. Crazy. As quick as that Model T started, I was in it, and we were gone."

Jared shook his head.

"I didn't know what to do," Lyman went on. "Had no idea where you were. It was getting late. Finally we just went and got a room at the hotel in Lethbridge."

Jared lifted John out of the car, still wrapped in the blanket, and followed Paula to the bedroom where she had turned down the covers. The boy lay like a rag doll, unwaking, as Jared took off his shoes and socks and overalls, then he turned on his side and curled into a ball against the cool sheet. Paula drew the covers up over him. The three of them returned to the living room.

Jared said, "Kelly'll be in a state."

"She's still with the cattle?" Lyman asked.

"No. She went back to the Arrowhead to look for him there."

"Then she knows he's all right. In the morning John and I drove out to the ranch again. I thought maybe you'd be home by then, or that Hickory Jack would have sobered up, at least. But he had gone."

"He came to the mountains to tell us that John had run away."

"I couldn't leave the boy there alone, so we waited around until afternoon. But nobody came. I had to get back home for the memorial tomorrow. Finally I decided the only thing to do was bring John home with me. I left a note tacked to the door to say he was all right. Your wife will see it."

Jared sank into a chair.

"The roads were terrible," Lyman went on. "Mostly dry, of course, but mudholes every mile or so. We got stuck a half a dozen times—took us all day getting home." Lyman, too, sat down and rubbed his big meaty hands up and down his face.

For a moment Paula looked at Lyman, half affectionately, half fearfully, then her groping hand reached the banister and she slowly climbed the stair.

Jared said, "I had begun to wonder if I'd never see John again—if he'd vanished, like Father."

"Are you still looking for Father?" Lyman asked.

"In a way, I guess I am."

"I might have something that will help you." Lyman opened a drawer of the desk and took out an envelope. "This was among Father's things." He handed it to Jared.

On the front of the envelope Jared read, "To be opened by the family following my death," and beneath it the familiar signature, "Alma Roseman." The handwriting was the same as in the journal he had read so long ago—perhaps a little more crabbed—but the paper was newer, the ink darker. The envelope had been opened. He took out the thin sheaf of pages and glanced at the top of the first one: "Lone Rock, Alberta. August, 1912. My dear family: It is hard for me to write this—I fear that it will be hard for you to read." He looked up at Lyman.

"Take it," Lyman said.

"Has Aunt Bessie seen it? The rest of the family?"

"No. Luckily I was able to cover it up when we went through his papers. They don't know there is any 'confession.'"

"Does it explain what happened to Father?"

"It explains more than you want to know." Lyman yawned. "Well, I've got to get some sleep. Goodnight, little brother."

"Goodnight." Dumbly Jared went into the room where John lay sleeping, and switched on the light.

7 The little room was comfortable, but a cover seemed to close over Jared's heart. He sat on the bed and slowly unfolded the paper.

My dear family: It is hard for me to write this—I fear that it will be hard for you to read. But I know that sometime, here or hereafter, we will meet again. I dare not face you in that hour when all our secret evil is shouted from the housetops, and hear you say why didn't you tell us?

How can I explain? If I cannot understand, why should I expect you to? And yet I must explain, and you must understand.

Oh, black day. But all we saw was red—the red of anger, of war, of retribution. The red of fear. Fifty years have passed, and more, and still I can feel the dread, like a fever that swept our town.

Johnston's army was marching on Utah, sent to destroy us. News came on horseback, a week late and at odds with itself. The army at Fort Bridger, at Salt Lake City, nowhere near. Brigham ready to fight, determined to flee, bent on appeasement. Another army in California on its way, and we, caught in the middle without any escape. Reports, conjecture, rumor, supposition. We slept lightly those nights, with loaded guns beside us.

Then came the Fancher party down through Utah, spitting and hissing all the way, shouting insults, cursing at oxen they called Brigham and Heber, brandishing the very gun "that shot old Joe Smith."

They expected us to sell them supplies, but we were in a state of war and had nothing to spare. So they broke our fences, scattered cattle, trampled crops, poisoned wells. We were happy to see the last of them, and the whole town seemed to sigh when they were gone.

Two or three Indians died from the meat of poisoned cattle, and the Indians went on the warpath. They attacked the wagon train about two or three days out of Cedar.

One day the bell in the town square began to ring—the call to battle! My father and I took our guns and rode to the square. When the militia was assembled, it was announced that the emigrants had been killed by the Indians. Were there any volunteers willing to go and bury the dead?

Somehow, in spite of our dread of annihilation, this peaceful mission angered us. We would rather have fought. Why should we bury our enemies? Let the dead bury the dead.

We returned to our homes for shovels, reassembled, and rode

as a cavalry brigade to Mountain Meadows. As we approached the emigrant camp we could see figures moving around inside the rude enclosure of wagons. It seemed apparent that the Indian attack was not yet over, though for the moment at least the firing had ceased. This was not what we had been led to expect, but no explanation was given to me.

Three of our men approached the wagons under a white flag. When they returned, they said the emigrants had accepted the terms of their deliverance, and the rescue operation would proceed according to plan. Leaving our horses, we marched toward the wagons.

The emigrants greeted us with a cheer. They were horribly dirty, some of them wounded, some shaking, many women and children with tear-stained faces. They had been under heavy attack by the Indians for four days.

Two wagons were hitched up, and moved into line. In the first the emigrants came and placed their guns, along with a number of small children. Several badly wounded men were lifted into the second wagon. With one of our men driving each outfit, and one walking between them, the wagons moved off, followed by the women of the company and their older children, walking. When they had gone some distance, the men started, walking two by two, one of our men beside each emigrant.

I looked at the man beside me—an unkempt ruffian, tall and powerful: ragged beard, torn clothing, covered with dirt.

Suddenly there was a rifle shot.

A voice cried, "Do your duty!"

My father raised his rifle and shot the emigrant beside him. Suddenly the air was thundering with rifle fire. Looking back down the line, I saw first one emigrant fall, and then another.

"Kill him!" someone shouted.

I looked at the man beside me again, his face contorted now with rage and horror. He gave a strangled cry and drew a six-gun he had concealed in his clothing.

With a desperate thrust of the rifle butt, I knocked the pistol out of his hand. As he bent to pick it up I lunged forward, grasped the gun, and tried to wrench it away. We wrestled, each with both hands grappling for the pistol, and my rifle beneath our feet.

It seemed that all around me the world was a place of confusion—screams mingled with gunfire and galloping Indian ponies. I expected to be shot or ridden down at any moment. As we struggled I caught the stench of the man, and felt his sweat drop on my face.

He stumbled, and we both went down, rolling over and over in the dust. At one point he pinned me from above, though his hands, like mine, still contested for the gun. He managed to get a thumb on the hammer and pull it back, and I saw the barrel slowly lowering, though shaking somewhat from the strain of our efforts.

A shrill voice beside us screamed, "Papa!" The emigrant glanced up, only for an instant, but in that shred of time I twisted the gun and fired. He slowly rose to his feet, his mouth slack, his face gone suddenly grey, his empty hands curled in front of him. "Papa!" the boy cried again, even more desperately.

A red flower bloomed on the front of the emigrant's shirt. He stumbled away, clutching his body with his hands. The boy, who must have run back from the wagon when the first shot was fired, was half dragging his wounded father.

Rising, I ran close behind the emigrant and discharged the pistol into his body. He plunged forward against the ground. I shall never forget the face of that lad. For an instant he looked at me, his eyes like wells of hatred and despair. Then with a cry he flung himself across his father's body.

I turned away and stumbled back to the wagons, mounted my horse and rode west into the desert. I found that in my delirium I had forgotten my rifle but had unconsciously thrust the pistol of the murdered man into my belt.

I returned to the camp the next morning. After breakfast we stood in a circle with right arms raised to the square, and swore an oath that we would never speak of what had happened, either among ourselves or to any living mortal. Then we went to bury the dead.

It took me years to realize that my crime was not my father's fault. At the time I thought I had no choice but to act as I did, but I know differently now. I was fully accountable for my actions; I did not have to shoot that man.

I can understand how it was for Father. He had seen the murdered prophet and helped to bury him. We talked of it long afterward. He told me, "It was the Missouri Wildcats who killed Joseph—the same men you saw at Mountain Meadows. They murdered the prophet in cold blood. It was the Lord's will that they should die."

Maybe my father was right; perhaps it was the Lord's will. I have prayed to know, but he has never answered me—has never given me peace of spirit. Should it happen that we never meet again—if my place is beyond that awful gulf—remember that once you had a father, weak though he was, who loved you, and loved the Lord . . .

**8** Jared could not have said if he slept that night or not. He lay in the darkness beside his son and stared up at the dim ceiling of the room. His mind felt impervious, or encased in a shell which protected it from the horror in which it lay. But gradually, as the hours passed, the encasement failed, eaten away by truth as strong as quicklime: his father had killed a man at Mountain Meadows. He lay on his bed and stared into the darkness with dry, burning eyes.

Baloo, my boy . . .

It seemed odd that his mother's lullaby should return to him now.

> Baloo, my boy, lie still and sleep,
> It grieves me sair to hear thee weep.
> If thou'lt be silent I'll be glad,
> Thy mourning makes my heart full sad.

The song that had both comforted and puzzled him when he was a boy seemed foreign now, strangely threatening. He tried to put it out of his mind, but the words came back, drawn into his consciousness by the irresistible melody.

> Baloo, my boy, thy mother's joy,
> Thy father gave me great annoy.
>> Baloo, my boy, lie still and sleep,
>> It grieves me sair to hear thee weep . . .

> Baloo, my boy, weep not for me,
> Whose greatest grief's for wronging thee,
> Nor pity her deserved smart,
> Who can blame none but her fond heart:
> For too soon trusting latest finds
> With fairest tongues are falsest minds.
>> Baloo, my boy, lie still and sleep,
>> It grieves me sair to hear thee weep.

Every day the Lord works his purposes through the labor of mankind. Wasn't it possible that sometimes a man might be appointed as the arm of the Lord's vengeance? Look at Nephi. Couldn't God have killed Laban with a bolt of lightning, rather than send an angel to tell Nephi to do it? He tried to remember the angel's words to Nephi: "It is better that one man should perish than that a nation should dwindle and perish in unbelief." Then even God sometimes justifies a man in killing another.

Daylight brought no relief to Jared. He rose and dressed, and joined Lyman and Paula for breakfast. Though he could hear them speaking, he seemed unable to understand what they said. Afterward Lyman went out in the yard to wash his car. Jared tended his horse, which had been left standing at the gate all night. Then he joined his brother.

"Did you read the letter?" Lyman asked him.

"Yes."

"I decided you can never tell about people. Every man is like an iceberg—only the tip of him shows." Lyman took his broom and swept out the inside of the car, raising a cloud of dust and sending clumps of dried mud flying onto the ground. "I almost forgot," he said as he took a pistol from under the seat and handed it to Jared. "This is the gun Hickory Jack was waving the other night."

Jared flinched as he took it—a long-barreled Colt Paterson, with a wildcat carved on the wooden handle. He had seen this gun before. On his father's birthday seven years ago, it had surfaced from somewhere out of Alma's past, and promptly disappeared with him. Now here it was again, mysterious and sinister.

Hickory Jack!

Jared's flesh moved.

"Is anything wrong?" Lyman asked.

"No." Jared turned away, the gun in his hand. "No." Inwardly he reeled. Could there be a mistake? He held the evidence in his hand. Gradually his mind became calm, as cool and hard as a pond in winter.

He slipped the gun inside his boot and went to the house. "Is John awake?" he asked Paula.

"He hasn't made a sound."

"I have to leave."

"Aren't you going to the service?"

He had forgotten about the service. "Ah . . . Yes. Of course. I'll leave after the service." He went into the bedroom and sat on the edge of the bed. When the springs settled under Jared's weight, John opened his eyes. For a moment he looked about him uncertainly. Then he saw Jared and sat up.

"Daddy!" He scrambled out of the covers and threw his arms around Jared's neck. "I found you."

"Yes. You're all right now."

Later when they drove over to Bessie's house, they found that the family had begun to gather. Grace and Orville and their children were there, scrubbed and wearing their Sunday clothes. Rachel and Tom arrived from Cardston with their family, and Stanley from Edmonton with his wife, whom Jared had never met. Stanley's children all seemed to have inherited their father's long frame and dour countenance. They stood about awkwardly, watching their more lively cousins test the limits of acceptable behavior on their grandfather's memorial day. Jane came, with her handsome young husband and two small children. Norma lived in British Columbia and Belle in California; neither of them had been able to come.

At a little before one o'clock the family formed itself in a sort of marching order, with Bessie between Lyman and Paula at the front, and walked across the street to the meeting house.

The congregation rose when the mourners entered at the rear of the chapel. To the uneven sound of the old pedal organ the little battalion moved slowly up the aisle and took places reserved for them on the front benches. With a massive creak and shuffle, the congregation sat down. The organ stopped. On the stand the bishop stood up behind the table which served as a podium, and looked down at Bessie.

"Today is a melancholy day," he said, "as we gather to remember our brother, Alma Roseman. We will no longer carry the hope of meeting him again in mortality, but will rather look forward to a day when we shall meet him in that place which the Lord has prepared for His righteous children —those who love Him and keep His commandments."

That would not be Alma. He was beyond the claim of mercy. But was it fair that a single act, committed when he was scarcely more than a boy, should overshadow sixty years of righteousness?

The service progressed. A prayer was offered, the choir sang. Arthur Hays gave the eulogy.

"No man knew Alma Roseman who didn't love him. He moved through his mortality with a quiet dignity that strengthened all he met, saying little but doing much. It is estimated that in a period of seventy-seven years he spoke exactly a hundred and fifty-four words"—there was a relaxing chuckle from the congregation—"which, if they had been recorded, we each might profitably take for our personal credo.

"If salvation depends on our readiness to forgive, I would that all mankind were as easy to forgive as Alma Roseman."

Hickory Jack had not forgiven. But what had been Alma's offense? What sort of hurt required that you kill a man?

Jared could feel the gun rubbing against his ankle. It made a slight bulge in his trouser leg, but nothing that anybody would notice. As he sat there listening to the service his foot seemed to grow unbearably heavy: heavy with blood and vengeance, as if it might crash through the boards of the floor and drag him into the cellar.

John sat quietly beside his father, his eyes wide; perhaps he was overwhelmed by the strange surroundings and so many people perched in rows like chickens at sunset. The boy leaned his arms on Jared's thigh, and whispered, "What are they talking about?"

"My father," Jared softly replied. "Your Grandpa Roseman."

"Because now he died?"

"We don't know. Ssh. You mustn't talk in church."

"Is this church?"

"Kind of the same as church."

John turned to face the front again. "I don't like church."

After a discourse on the resurrection, and the closing hymn and prayer, Jared stood to file out with the other mourners. John clung to his hand. "Can we go home now?"

"We have to take a little ride first," Jared said. "Then we'll go home."

"Where are we going?"

"Up to the mountains. To the summer pasture."

Old friends gathered around to greet Jared and other members of the family, but Jared excused himself and hurried with John up the street to Lyman's house. He saddled his horse, mounted, reached down, and taking the boy's hand, lifted him scrambling to the horse's back. John sat behind him, his arms tight around Jared's body.

As they rode down the street they met the others just returning from the meeting house. "Don't go yet," Bessie said. "The Relief Society's serving lunch. Folks will want to visit."

"I have to go," Jared said.

Lyman said, "Hang around, Jared. I thought maybe we could settle the estate today, now everybody's here."

"I can't stop," Jared replied. "Whatever the rest of you decide is fine with me." He turned his horse and rode toward the river.

**9** Jared rode south across the empty land of the Indian Reserve, his small son clinging behind the saddle. He felt as if he could not rest until his work was done. Then there would be time enough to rest—years of it; eons, perhaps.

Today's sun was almost gone. Riding through the trees as they approached the pasture, they passed through intermittent light and shadow. Jared rested his hand on the pommel of the saddle as if that pressure were enough to mute the sound of the horse walking through the grass. He seemed to start inwardly each time her hoof clicked against a branch or stone—why, he couldn't say. He wasn't trying to sneak up on Hickory Jack, at least not in a physical sense.

As they approached the camp Jared saw the old man bent above the fire, stirring his supper with a wooden spoon. He looked back across his shoulder when he heard them, then raised himself, turning. "Praise the Lord," he breathed, looking at John.

Jared stopped his horse. His senses all rushed to the surface; coolness came, control, power—and a keenness of vision that enabled him to look into the depths of Hickory Jack's soul. The pond of guilt had laid there putrefying all these years, and he had never seen it before—never even sensed it.

"Supper's ready," Hickory Jack said. Leaving the spoon in the kettle, he came over beside them and raised his hands to lift John down. Jared turned his horse so her rump shoved Hickory Jack away, then swung down and lifted John to the ground.

Jared couldn't eat. Despair and misery clogged his throat, his whole body felt distended with hate. Hickory Jack was silent. He didn't even ask about John—where he'd been or where they'd found him. When the boy had finished his supper Jared made a bed on the ground and tucked him in. For a while, then, he and Hickory Jack sat on opposite sides of the fire.

"Sunset," said Hickory Jack, looking at the sky. "Best time of day. Work all finished. Chores done. Nothin' ahead but sleep." He looked at Jared. "I know what you're thinkin'. And I guess you're right. I'm the wust grandfather in creation. I can't even remember what I done." He looked at his grandson's face turned toward the fire. "Look at him—asleep already. Rosie, I'd dig out my good eye 'fore I'd hurt that boy, you know that. I had a thousand devils in me that night."

Jared didn't reply.

"I been drunk before, but never like that. That liquor had nails in it." He waggled his head. "I ain't never gonna touch the stuff again."

Jared said, "I know what happened to my father."

"Well, I'm glad that's settled."

"I didn't say it was settled."

"No, you didn't." Hickory Jack took out his pocket knife and began to dig into the bowl of his pipe, shaking the ashes out onto the ground. "What happened to your pa, anyway?"

"You ought to know."

"How would I know?"

"You killed him, didn't you?"

Hickory Jack stoked his pipe, lit it, and sucked until the bowl glowed red. "Why would I do a thing like that?"

"You don't deny it?"

"That means I'm guilty? Rosie, if I could kill a man, do you suppose I'd gag on a little fib?"

"No." His spirit seemed to descend through his rage into a cool, merciless plateau. "Just tell me one thing: where did you bury him?"

"Why would I want to kill your pa?"

Sitting on the log, Jared took the six-gun from his boot, and as he straightened he pointed it at Hickory Jack. "Remember this gun?"

The old man whistled.

"Where did you put my father's body?"

Hickory Jack hitched at his belt and drew his shoulders back. "You gonna shoot me, Rosie? I don't think you got the mustard."

"Don't count on it."

"Takes a special breed to be able to kill a man."

"A breed like you, Hick?"

"It's hard. You'll find out. You think you're all worked up to it, but when the time comes, it's hard."

"Then you admit it?"

"There's only one thing. Bein' as how it is hard, a feller has to be sure of his facts. Dead certain. If he ain't, he could never do it."

"I'm certain enough."

"What do you know? That your daddy and me were in the same township when he took off? Fish, you might as well hang the mayor."

"You're forgetting the gun. Father had it with him when he disappeared. And then one night you get drunk and haul it out from under your bed, and start shooting."

"Maybe I traded your pa—a cow for a gun. Kid, you don't

even know if he's alive or dead. You couldn't send a blind nigger to the workhouse on evidence like that."

"That's the advantage I have," Jared told him. "I don't have to prove a thing."

"You're not listening, kid. You've got to be sure, or you'll never go through with it."

The gun was heavy. Jared noticed its muzzle beginning to droop. He raised it with fresh resolution.

Hickory Jack went on. "I hope you don't make a career of this, Rosie. You wouldn't last a week." The smoke puffed from his lips like silent cannon fire. "Would you like some good advice?"

"Not from you."

"Never start somethin' you can't finish. Ain't nothin' harder on your self-respect. You're not some green kid any more, you know. You're a man, or supposed to be."

Jared stared into the darkness. He seemed to be part of it, made from the same substance, a heavier lump that had settled to the bottom of the night. Perhaps if he sat there long enough, he would dissolve and his particles slowly drift upward among the stars.

"Forget the whole thing," Hickory Jack said. "You take my advice, you'll forget it. What chance have you got, after seven years? Whatever happened to you pa, you can't help him now."

"Did you kill him, Hick?"

Hickory Jack sighed. "Kid." For a long time he didn't say any more. They sat across from each other in the light from the fire. The old man shrugged. "Go ahead. Shoot me."

"Then it really was you?"

"You see. You don't know. And there is no way for you to ever find out. Give it up, Rosie." He smiled, but sadly, without humor, and slowly shook his head from side to side. "You'll never know. That's what I keep telling you. You've got to forget it."

"I can't forget it."

"Not your father—I don't mean that. Forget what happened to him. Forget this mystery."

"Am I getting too warm for you, Hick?"

"You still don't understand, do you? Even if you kill me, you won't know. You think you can bull your way ahead and find out what you want by plain strength and orneriness. It doesn't happen that way. You have to draw back and watch. Don't touch anything. Watch."

"Watch what?"

"Everybody. Everything. I had a father too, you know."

"You're not making any sense, Hick."

"Before we left Missouri, he said to me . . ." Hickory Jack stopped.

It was as if a sudden gust hit Jared's memory, and his mind turned like a weather vane. "You never told me you lived in Missouri."

"Yah. I was a kid in Missouri."

"What did your father tell you?"

"It doesn't matter. I can't remember what I was talking about." Hickory Jack stood up and started to break up a board.

Jared looked at the six-gun, turning it so he could see the handle in the firelight. The crude image scratched into the walnut handle was of a long-legged, short-necked cat.

"Missouri Wildcat," Jared muttered.

Hickory Jack was making a lot of noise, stomping on the board and twisting it. "Eh?" he said.

"Where did this gun come from, Hick?"

"How would I know? It's your pa's gun, you said."

"But before that?"

"Why ask me?"

"You killed him with it, didn't you?" Jared pulled back the hammer. He felt the trigger emerge from its recess in the handle, hard and cold against his finger. Killing was such a simple thing. Just squeeze his finger—how far? Less than half an inch.

Hickory Jack swung the board and knocked the gun from Jared's hand. It glinted with firelight as it tumbled through the air, hit the ground and bounced into the grass. Both men dived for it, but met halfway and tumbled over and over, each trying to hold the other back. Hickory Jack was surprisingly quick and strong for an old man with a wounded arm.

238

"I've got it!" he huffed suddenly, and pulled away. Jared saw the shine of metal in his hand.

Hickory Jack rose and backed toward the fire, the gun barrel as steady as a bridge, pointed at Jared. "Now the shoe's on the other foot, kid. I told you to forget it, but you wouldn't listen."

Jared sat up on the grass.

"I like you, Rosie. You're the father of my grandchild."

"You did do it," Jared breathed.

"You see that spot yonder, back under the trees where the grass is a little longer? That's your pa."

Jared stumbled over and knelt beside the hump of grass. A shudder passed through his body. He felt hollow. Until now, nothing had struck him with the sense of loss that this lonely grave did. He tried to remember his father. It was amazing how quickly life's ashes cool, once the fire is out. He could remember times, events, even conversations shared with his father, but he could not regain the living pulse of that companionship. Worse, he discovered that in his mind's eye he could not remember his father's face. He felt a sense of guilt and shame. He whispered, "He was just a harmless old man. How could you kill him?"

"I was like you."

"What do you mean?"

"Watch, I told you. Watch everybody. Everything. That's what I did, for nigh on sixty years. Every day watching, watching . . ."

"Watching what?"

"Everybody. Everything. Watchin'. Listenin'. One day in Salt Lake City, I heard a man call your daddy 'Alma.' Ain't too many Almas in the world. I followed him to Canada, watchin' all the while, see if he was the right one." Hickory Jack had slowly lowered his hand, until his arm hung straight, stretched at his side by the weight of the gun. He turned away from Jared and looked at the flames.

Jared said, "I don't understand what you're talking about."

"I was at Mountain Meadows," Hickory Jack said. "You've heard of Mountain Meadows?" There was a long silence. "See, I was just a little kid. Not much older'n John there. I couldn't remember your pappy's face, but I knowed his name—Alma. I'd never forget that. But how could I tell he was the right one? I didn't know. I got me a ranch, and I watched." Like a man in a dream, he took his seat on the log. "I had to be sure—if I wasn't sure, the right one would get away." He turned toward Jared. "Cold, kid? Come on. Set a little closer to the fire."

Jared didn't move.

After a minute Hickory Jack looked back into the flames. "I was just a little kid. How did I know what was happening? These men seemed so friendly, comin' to save us. When they started to take us out of there, I near fell to blubberin' I was so happy. You ever been in an Indian fight?"

"No," Jared said.

"I got in the wagon with the other kids, and I even prayed to God—I thanked Him we was safe at last." Hickory Jack pressed one palm against his face and lifted it, as if blotting up the heat from the flames. "Suddenly they started to shoot. First they shot the wounded men in the wagon. Then the Indians came and started to kill the women and the older kids. I got out of the wagon and ran back to my pa. He was fighting with one of the men. I tried to help him, but the other man got the gun and shot him—shot him with his own gun. Then he turned and ran, carrying the gun in his hand. I heard somebody call him—'Alma!' "

Jared didn't say anything.

"They loaded us kids in a wagon and took us to a ranch somewhere. Some of the kids went to live with Mormons. I never did. I ended up in an orphanage in St. Louis. As soon as I was old enough, I came back to Utah and started to look."

After a long while Jared said, "How did you find out it was him?"

"When I saw the gun." Hickory Jack held the pistol on his open palm. "It was my pa's gun."

"Your father was one of the Missouri Wildcats?"

"That day at the birthday party, when I saw the gun, I knew your pappy was the one. I knew, at last."

Jared sighed, a sort of spasm that worked its way up his throat.

"Sixty years!" Hickory Jack shook his head. "Sixty years with my gut full of bile and my eyes dry, watchin'."

Jared stood up. His rage seemed to create a new sense in him compounded of all the others, as though sight and sound and feeling had melted down into a single nerve end that moved ahead of him, searching out its victim. "What happened to the horse, Saratoga?"

"I took him across the line and sold him."

With a roar Jared leaped straight through the flames at Hickory Jack. The old man raised his arm as if to shield himself. When the gun went off, its flash was pointed upward. The force of Jared's charge knocked the gun from Hickory Jack's hand, and the young man dived for it, grasped it, rolled, and pointed it at the other. He pulled back the hammer.

Hickory Jack stood over him, motionless, looking down. A thrill ran through Jared, a strange, exultant wave. Across the sight of the gun—only a nick of bright metal in the firelight—he could see Hickory Jack's face, see the pores inside the pockmarks on his cheeks. He fixed his sights on the middle of that face.

His hand wavered slightly. His body throbbed with dread. Still he was determined; he was capable. He drew down on the gun with both hands, steadying it.

A voice said, "Daddy."

It was John, wakened by the shot and sitting up in his bed on the ground. "Daddy. What are you doing?"

**10** An hour passed. A minute—Jared couldn't tell. Time was not linear, but spherical, encompassing, as if the hate and vengeance of so many years could be distilled to a single drop. It had all been done before—murder tripping over itself, and rising again with each new generation; boys' lives determined in an instant, molded to the shape of vengeance and placed to dry, waiting their day. Could it never end? He looked

at the gun curled in his hand, its barrel pointed at Hickory
Jack. Men grew old and died, flesh returned to dust, but the
gun lived on, ageless, its venom still potent. He tossed it on the
grass, where it slid with a tiny hiss, and stopped.

Softly Hickory said, "It's all right. I doubt you could have
done it, anyway."

"*You* did."

"That's how I know. It ain't easy."

"But you did it."

The old man talked almost in a whisper, as if he were speaking to himself. "When the time come, the anger's missing, the
rage. It ain't there any more, like it's all wore out. Sixty years I
dragged it up and down the country, and now when I need it,
there's nothin' left but tatters. A hundred times in my life I
could have done it, and laughed, and painted my face with his
blood, and gone on a drunk. But when the time finally come, it
was too late.

"After I leave Tom Baxter's place that day I catch up to my
cattle, round 'em up and get 'em started down the road again.
Soon I hear Al comin' up behind me. I can't believe what I'm
seein'. Here he is, all alone, barely half an hour after I find out
he's my man. It's fate, that's what it is, handin' him over to
me.

"Well, I ride ahead of the cattle and wait there on the
bridge for Al to catch up to me. He rides up close, and stops.
He can't get past, 'cause my horse is crossways on the bridge.
'What do you want?' he says. 'You,' I says, and I ride up and
yank the reins out of his hand. 'Just a minute,' he says, but I
start my horse off at the trot, leadin' his behind me. At the
fork I know he wants to head over the hill to Fielding's Corner, but I keep the creek road toward the mountains. Al don't
say anything. I look back, and he's just settin' there with a
kind of surprised look on his face, one hand holding the pommel, and the other his hat.

"When we hit the next ford I stop in the middle of the
stream. I guess the water is about eighteen inches deep, but
slow-movin'. It's nigh dark, with a little light still showin' in
the sky and on the water in crescents around the horse's legs.

"Al's settin' there, watchin' me get down into the water. He looks tired. I walk back close beside him, on the right-hand side of his horse.

" 'Who are you?' he says.

" 'Jack Haggedorn,' I says.

" 'I know your name,' he says. 'There's more to it than that.' "

Hickory Jack rose and began to break up another stick, throwing the pieces into the fire. The wood was dry and splintery; it burned like straw. He sat down on the log again.

Jared looked uneasily toward his son, but the boy had returned to his bed, and to sleep.

"He knew something was wrong," Hickory Jack continued. " 'Who are you?' he says. 'What you bringin' me way out here for?'

"I says, 'You killed my pa at Mountain Meadows.'

'He kind of sucks in his breath, and his hand drops, but I grab the gun out of his belt before he can touch it. I don't need to draw him no pictures—he knows what's goin' on. For a long time he just sets there starin' at me. 'You was that little tyke?' he says. 'That little kid, a-beatin' me over the back?'

" 'That was me,' I says.

"Well, he looks at me for a while. 'I been waitin' for you,' he says.

" 'I had to know for sure,' I says. 'I didn't know for sure until I saw the gun.'

" 'That's the same one killed your daddy,' he says.

" 'I know,' I says.

"Well, he straightens up sort of, and tries to set still. 'Don't shoot too close to the heart at first,' he says. 'Let me see the blood.' He kind of strikes a pose, settin' his hat just so, like he's havin' his picture took. 'This all right?' he says. 'If it's jake with you, I'd just as leave set here in the saddle.'

"Well, sixty years I follered his trail, follered them footsteps smokin' with murder, and here he is at last. I've got him."

Hickory Jack stared into the fire. "But all my rage is gone. And he just sits there waitin', as stiff as a monk."

The fire sent off wavering tendrils of light. Between the men the gun lay, faintly winking. Jared reached and picked it up. Its polished grip felt cool and hard against his palm. It had no blurred edges.

"Your pappy says to me, 'Why don't you do it? What you waitin' for?' " And I says, 'I want to see you suffer.'

"He says, 'Mister, any pain you got ain't a patch on what I can tell you about.' "

" 'Ever step I follered you was over hot coals,' I said.

"He says, 'Sixty years I never close my eyes but what I see your daddy's face, I hear the women scream, and the shots, and the children cryin'. Ain't sixty years enough?' He gets down out of the saddle, pretty slow of course, with the current pushin' him. He's older than I think. He starts toward me, but he turns back to steady himself with his hand on the saddle. He's standin' there in the water with his head down, his face turned away.

"This ain't the way I seen it all these years. 'Why ain't you scared?' I says. 'Let's see you beg me to forgive you.'

" 'Forgive,' he says. 'Forgive? No. Don't forgive me. I can't stand your forgiveness.' He still don't look at me. 'Spill my blood,' he says. 'Wash me . . .' And he rubs his hand against his coat."

"And you shot him!"

" 'Don't wait no more,' he says. 'It's the pain of livin' I can't bear.' My heart comes up somehow. My eyes begin to burn. I go over and put my arm around that old man's shoulders. 'You mean it,' I says.

"All he does is nod his head. And I put my gun against his body and shoot. I forget he wanted to see the blood . . ." Hickory Jack stared into the fire. "I tie Al over the back of his horse and lead him upstream, all the way to the campground. I still kept a few tools here in those days—in that old shed. I dig that grave and put Al in it and brush it down and cover it with leaves and chaff—you fellows could have walked right by it when you were lookin' for him."

"We weren't looking for a grave."

"Ol' Saratoga stands in the water while I bury your pappy. Then I lead him further upstream, stow the saddle and bridle under a tree, and leave him in a rope corral. Later, after I bring my cattle on in, and pass you and Siwash on the road so you'd think I was home to the Arrowhead, I double back through the hills, pick up Saratoga and head south across the border with him."

After a long time Jared asked, "Why didn't you tell me this before?"

"I couldn't chance it, could I? You know when you come to the Arrowhead, I did my best to run you off. But before you mended enough to leave, Kelly was in love with you." Hickory Jack paused. "And so was I. I never had a son."

Jared took the shovel from the pack and dug a shallow hole in the ground above Alma's grave. Kneeling, he laid the gun in the hole and covered it over with earth. It looked like a second grave, much smaller, half hidden by the rustling grass of the first. He remained there, kneeling, for a long time.

Hickory Jack had hitched up the team. "Ready?" he said.

Jared rose to his feet, but still stood for several minutes looking down at the twin graves. The earth was heavy with the bodies of men: some lying alone, some side by side with others; some clustered, as were those emigrants in their mass grave in Utah; some unmarked, like the prophet's grave in Illinois.

They lifted John into the democrat, bed and all. Jared loaded their other things. He tied his saddle horse behind the outfit and climbed in beside Hickory Jack. The old man snapped the lines; the team sprang forward through the darkness, back toward the Arrowhead. Before they reached the ranch the sky was beginning to burn, its fire hidden behind the distant black hills. Then as the sun came up they could feel its warmth on their faces. The prairie colors brightened. Jared glanced back and watched the hurrying shadows of the horses and rig emerge from the morning grey.